DISCRIMINATING LAWYERS

Professor Philip Thomas
Cardiff Law School, Cardiff University

Cavendish
Publishing
Limited

London • Sydney

First published in Great Britain 2000 by Cavendish Publishing Limited,
The Glass House, Wharton Street, London WC1X 9PX, United Kingdom
Telephone: +44 (0)20 7278 8000   Facsimile: +44 (0)20 7278 8080
Email: info@cavendishpublishing.com
Website: www.cavendishpublishing.com

© Thomas, Philip   2000

British Library Cataloguing in Publication Data

Discriminating Lawyers
1 Lawyers – Great Britain   2 Procedure (law) – Great Britain
I Thomas, Philip A (Philip Aneurin), 1940–
340'.023'41

ISBN 1 85941 603 9

Printed and bound in Great Britain

FOREWORD

The familiar stereotype of the practising legal profession (in both its branches) is of a white, middle class, middle aged, Oxbridge-educated elite. Like most stereotypes, this one is misleading. Among newly admitted solicitors there are more women than men, and among newly called barristers nearly as many. The ethnic minorities are better represented in the legal profession than in the population as a whole. Sharp increases in the number of those recruited as solicitors and barristers have led to a preponderance of younger practitioners. It has always been possible for those lacking any privileged background to qualify as lawyers and achieve success in their profession. But, again like many stereotypes, this one does not lack all foundation in fact. It is not easy for anyone, whether as a solicitor or a barrister, to qualify, secure a training contract or a pupillage, obtain employment in a leading firm or a tenancy in flourishing chambers and rise through the ranks of the profession; but, despite the best efforts of the Law Society and the Bar Council, the difficulties which face a female member of an ethnic minority, with a modest family background and a degree from an unfashionable university, are even more formidable than those which face the young, privately educated white man with a comfortable family background and a reasonable Oxbridge degree. The contributors to this book do not raise this conclusion as a conjecture; they demonstrate it as a fact.

It is a worrying conclusion for all who regard the goal of equal access to, and opportunity in, the legal profession as an important one to achieve, and even more worrying for any who thought it had been achieved. But we cannot escape from the facts, even if we would; and an accurate diagnosis is the first step towards an effective cure. Some of the opinions expressed in the book will no doubt provoke dissent. But the underlying problem to which the book is addressed is a real and important one. All those seeking a remedy should profit from this rational and informed discussion.

The Right Honourable Lord Bingham of Cornhill
Senior Law Lord
August 2000

CONTRIBUTORS

Luke Clements was educated at Newcastle and Leeds Universities. He entered private practice in 1981. He is currently a Senior Research Fellow at Cardiff Law School, Cardiff University. He has written widely in the areas of human rights and gypsies.

Fiona Cownie is Senior Lecturer in Law at the University of Leicester. She has published in the area of legal education and is a member of the Socio-Legal Studies Association. She is currently researching the effect of gender on the law school.

Andrew Francis has both LLB and LLM degrees and is currently Lecturer in Law at Keele University. His research interests lie within the fields of the legal profession, legal education and access to justice.

Jerry Garvey is co-founder of, and is the Law Society's Officer to, the African Caribbean and Asian Lawyers Group, as well as Equal Opportunities Officer to the Law Society. His formal training was in careers counselling and he previously comes from the Civil Service.

Robert Lee is Professor of Law at Cardiff Law School and the Director of its Centre for Professional Legal Studies. He is a consultant to Hammond Suddards Edge. He is also a member of the Training Committee of the Law Society and a reporting assessor for the Legal Practice Course.

Kate Malleson is a solicitor and Lecturer in Law at London School of Economics. Her main research interest is the judiciary. Her most recent work is an empirical study of the silk and judicial appointments processes in England and Wales.

Iain McDonald was educated at Glasgow (LLB) and Bristol (LLM). He is Lecturer in Law at the University of the West of England. His research interests include access to legal education and law and popular culture.

Alison Rees studied at Liverpool, Leicester and Cardiff. She is also a barrister. After joining Cardiff Law School as Research Assistant in 1994, she became Research Associate and law tutor in 1998. In 2000, she left to take up a research position in London.

Peter Sanderson has degrees from Cambridge and York University. He lectures at Huddersfield University in the School of Education and Professional Development. His research interests are centred on the sociology of professional development and change.

Sir Stephen Sedley was educated at Cambridge (BA) and was called to the Bar in 1964 and became a QC in 1983. He was appointed a Bencher of the Inner Temple in 1989 and a High Court Judge in 1992. In 1999, he was appointed Lord Justice of Appeal and a Judge, *ad hoc*, to the European Court of Human Rights in 2000. As of 1999, he is also President of the British Institute of Human Rights. He is an Honorary Professor at both Cardiff and Warwick. Public lectures delivered include the Morris of Borth-y-Gest, Sieghart, Laskin, Simons, Hamlyn and Radcliffe lectures.

Michael Shiner is employed by the Public Policy Research Unit in the Department of Social Policy and Politics, Goldsmiths College, University of London. His research has focused on ethnic relations, entry into the legal professions and access to higher education.

Hilary Sommerlad studied at Cambridge and obtained her PhD in Political Science at York University. A qualified solicitor, she now teaches at Leeds Metropolitan University. She has researched and written on women solicitors and the restructuring of the legal profession.

Philip A Thomas is Professor of Law at Cardiff Law School, Cardiff University. He was educated in Wales and the USA. He is the founding and current editor of the Journal of Law and Society. He is also a founding member of the Socio-Legal Studies Association. His research interests include the legal profession, legal education and civil liberties.

Sumitra Vignaendra manages and conducts research on legal education and training and equal opportunities at the Law Society's Research and Policy Planning Unit. Her formal training was in psychology and in education. She was formerly Senior Researcher at the Centre for Legal Education in Sydney, Australia.

Marcia Williams is the Law Society's Policy Adviser, specialising in equalities policy for the legal profession, and Secretary to the Law Society's Equal Opportunities Committee. Her formal training was in law, particularly in discrimination law issues in the UK and Europe. She was previously a lecturer in law in the further education sector.

CONTENTS

INTRODUCTION

This book owes its existence, in large measure, to the generous support of the Lord Morris of Borth-y-Gest Trust Fund. The fund was endowed by the former Law Lord of Appeal in Ordinary and each year becomes available to one of the constituent colleges of the University of Wales. In 1999, it was again the turn of Cardiff University, and in particular its law school, to access the funds. We were fortunate that Lord Justice Stephen Sedley was prepared to make space in his already overfilled diary. This was partly due to his ongoing interest in and public commitment to legal education. In addition, Sir Stephen is also the Honorary Professor at Cardiff Law School. Sir Stephen has things to say and issues to discuss on matters of legal education and the practice of law. The public lecture, delivered in Cardiff in September 1999, was an opportunity for him to present his challenging views on aspects of the future of the legal profession. The lecture is reproduced as the book's lead chapter.

Cardiff University's previous opportunity to host the Morris lecture was in 1995. At that time, Mr Justice Albie Sachs, of the Constitutional Court of South Africa, accepted the invitation to speak at Cardiff Law School. As a former legal academic based at Southampton University, he was anxious to speak about the activities of the new court of which he is a member. Fortunately, again by virtue of the Lord Morris Trust Fund, he was able to bring with him a small group of legal clerks who worked at the court. The public lecture was followed immediately by a weekend seminar out of which came the book entitled *Making Rights Work*, edited by Penny Smith, a colleague in Cardiff Law School.[1] It was this development that provided the opportunity for many more people to access the Morris lecture and the associated scholarship. It also provided me with the format for this book. As a result, I invited a number of academics, researchers, and (equalities) equal opportunities practitioners to take up issues addressed in Sir Stephen's lecture. The following chapters are the result of that invitation. I informed the contributors that it would be helpful for the purposes of continuity and cohesion if all of us attempted to sing from the same hymn sheet. I am pleased to note that all attempted to do so, nor did the deadlines I set prove to be totally meaningless. For the authors' commitment and time-keeping I am grateful. In addition, I also wish to recognise and thank Sue Campbell, Zafar Khan, Dennis Lee and Penny Smith for their time and support in helping prepare this text.

Researching lawyers is not easy. Researching the powerful brings with it special difficulties. Researching 'up' into professional groups is more complex than researching 'down' into the visible and less powerful sections of society. The powerful place a premium on their time, privacy and exclusivity. 'What's in it for us?' is the unspoken question. Is the research about the profession or for the profession?

Most of the contributors to this book faced and overcame these questions. For some, such as myself, the methodological issues were relatively simple, as

---

1   Smith, 1998.

was the power relationship which controls the issue of access. First year law students, when asked by a professor of law and the course leader, to fill in a questionnaire at their desks during the lecture period, are likely to comply. A response rate of 67% can be considered robust, especially since the shortfall can be accounted for by student absenteeism! To a lesser extent, a similar research profile is applicable to the work of Iain MacDonald and Andrew Francis, although they were dealing with mature, part time students who would be expected to display greater independence and possible caution than the 18 year old, first year, first semester law students whom I questioned. For Robert Lee, the issues were far more complex, because he was interviewing at senior levels of City of London global practices. The imprimatur of the Law Society and written presidential support undoubtedly opened doors, but his status and personal reputation as a former City lawyer and now [re]turned academic was also important. Senior partners of the large firms are not renowned for offering non-billable time to discuss the innermost workings of their firms. The promise of confidentiality is not of itself a sufficient incentive to win over such people. However, given that most people enjoy talking about themselves and subjects they know about, coupled with the previously indicated, non-invasive direction of the interviews, his research project received significant support from the City firms. Likewise, the research of Kate Malleson benefited from the public and formal support and financial backing of the Lord Chancellor's office. Her remit was to produce a report for the Lord Chancellor. Consequently, heavy doors swung open for her. Indeed, new researchers who think that interviewing powerful people will mean that they will be unapproachable, reticent, and unco-operative are likely to be pleasantly surprised by the interest shown in the work and the positive responses received. Getting through the door is invariably more difficult than the interview itself. Thereafter, it is often down to the individual social skills of the interviewer. For Sumitra Vignaendra, Marcia Williams and Jerry Garvey of the Law Society, the information for their chapter is based on a series of interviews with ethnic minority solicitors and barristers. Their different, but equally valid research processes are spelt out in detail as an annexure to their chapter. The authors make an open and honest statement about how they thought they had contributed to the research process. Therein lies much of the validity of their research. While Michael Shiner provides representative findings, statistics, and figures on minority ethnic groups (among others) through the Cohort Study, Vignaendra, Williams and Garvey take one step back, and explore some of the issues raised by the findings and statistics generated by the Law Society and other organisations on minority ethnic groups and asked some of these minority groups what they thought were the issues relevant to them (through an exploration of their identity within the profession). They gave these groups the opportunity to speak for and about themselves, rather than assuming that the researchers knew what were the relevant issues. Often, the researchers were surprised by what they were told. As such, there were no leading questions, only an agenda which is common to all research studies.

What their black/Asian status enabled them to do was probe and challenge their research participants in a way people outside black and Asian groups may find difficult to do. The motives of the latter group may be misunderstood by the research participants if they challenged and probed in a manner similar to that of Vignaendra, Williams and Garvey. The authors' proven track record further improved their ability to challenge and probe without fear of causing offence.

In methodological contrast, Sir Stephen Sedley was provided with a personal research assistant for the summer of 1999. Dennis Lee, an undergraduate at Cardiff Law School, acted as an academic 'beater' for his principal as he flushed out various articles, information and data to be considered and possibly used in the lecture and the chapter for the book. Thereafter, Dennis undertook a similar task for Luke Clements.

Some of the research participants are central players in the legal world, others are marginal to it, while the law students are yet to enter the profession. The authors of this book addressed the issues of discrimination circuitously rather than approaching it in a confrontational manner. Indeed, all the contributors – except one whose chapter involved field work – had finished their field work prior to being invited to become involved in this project. The exception was a project waiting to happen and the invitation accelerated, rather than initiated, the work. My invitations to contribute to this book allowed the other authors to review their existing data and extract that which is relevant to the issues addressed herein. Evidence is important, especially to lawyers, and with this in mind I make no excuse about the book being heavy with both primary and secondary data. Information comes in different forms, but the intention is to present a block of evidence about ways in which discrimination in its many forms and levels operates within the legal world.[2]

In terms of discrimination, the legal profession has made considerable progress since 1903 when Bertha Cave unsuccessfully applied to join Gray's Inn. A tribunal consisting of the Lord Chancellor, the Lord Chief Justice, and five other judges deliberated a full five minutes before declaring that there was no precedent for a woman to be called to the English Bar and that they were unwilling to set such a precedent. The Law Society, in 1913, refused to enrol a woman as an articled clerk because, as a woman, she would not be admitted to practise. In *Bebb v Law Society*, this position was upheld on appeal before the Master of the Rolls and two Chancery judges. Ultimately, it was the Sex Disqualification (Removal) Act 1919 that compelled both branches of the legal profession to admit women. The changing composition of the legal

2   Mungham and Thomas, 1981.

profession in terms of race, gender, class, and age was initially slow, but the acceleration towards inclusivity is marked.[3]

In 1998–99, the number of men called to the Bar totalled 769, compared with 624 women. This reflects the almost equal numbers of males and females who enter the Bar Vocational Course. Currently, 8.8% of barristers in private practice are of ethnic minority origin. The latest, but preliminary, figures show that, in 1998, 21% of all first six months pupils, 19% of all second six months pupils, and 16% of all new tenants were of ethnic minority origin. The figures from the Law Society indicate a similar changing composition of the profession. Women account for 35.1% of solicitors with practising certificates. Whereas, since 1989, the total of solicitors holding practising certificates has grown by 49.5%, the number of women holding practising certificates increased by 153.6%. In 1998–99, solicitors from ethnic minorities accounted for 7.3% of solicitors on the Roll, 5.5% of solicitors with practising certificates and 5.3% of solicitors in private practice. Of the new admissions in that year , 52.6% were women, and admissions from the ethnic minorities represented 16.6% of all admissions with known ethnicity. This trend is likely to be maintained. In the year ending 31 July 1999, women constituted 59.9% of new enrolments and 19.4% were from ethnic minorities. Fifty-two per cent of women graduated with first class or upper second degrees as opposed to 46.2% of men. Of the new trainees registered, 56.4% were women and 15.4% of trainees with known ethnicity were drawn from the ethnic minorities. The composition of the legal profession has changed and continues to change.[4]

Nevertheless, discrimination in its many forms continues to affect the legal world. Both the Bar Council and the Law Society of England and Wales have taken strong and positive steps to ensure that the term 'equal opportunities' has real, rather than symbolic, meaning and effect. The Equal Opportunities Committee of the Bar Council was awarded the status of a main Bar Council committee in 1999 with a commitment to build in rather than bolt on policies to ensure appropriate behaviour and standards. The Race Relations committee, established in 1984, is currently chaired by Linda Dobbs, and undertakes an active role supporting ethnic minority lawyers. There is also a Sex Discrimination Committee, set up in 1992, as well as a Disability Committee which arose out of the Disability Panel, created in 1991. BLAGG, the Barristers' Lesbian and Gay Group, was formed in 1994 and is represented on the Sex Discrimination Committee. A version of the Equality Code for the Bar was first placed before the Bar by the equal opportunities officers, Pamela Bhalla and Kathryn Hamylton, in 1993. It was noted, but not adopted. In 1995, a second version was circulated and was adopted by the General Council in September 1995. A comprehensive review of the Code is about to occur. The Code of Conduct, at para 204:

---

3   This process is documented in detail in Abel, 1988.
4   See Law Society's Research and Policy Unit, 2000.

Prohibits a practising barrister from discriminating directly or indirectly against or victimising anyone on the grounds of their race, colour, ethnic or national origin, nationality, citizenship, sex, sexual orientation, marital status, disability, religion or political persuasion.

The Law Society of England and Wales has its own solicitors' anti-discrimination rules and code. These are laid out in the *Guide to the Professional Conduct of Solicitors*.[5] In addition, there is a model anti-discrimination policy issued under para 3 of the Solicitors' Anti-Discrimination Rules, 1995. In 1980, a Race Relations Committee was established, followed by an Equal Opportunities Committee in 1995.

Complaints procedures are in place at both the Bar Council and the Law Society of England and Wales. In addition, the Bar Council recommends that there should be a written grievance procedure as part of general chambers management and that this should include procedures for handling complaints of discrimination and harassment. However, laying a formal complaint against another barrister has proved to be a most challenging process. For example, the last formal complaint of sexual harassment, made to the Professional Conduct and Complaints Committee (PCC) and referred to a disciplinary tribunal, was in 1997 by a pupil, Claire Kavanagh, against Christopher Sutton-Mattocks. When details of the case were made public, Ms Kavanagh was doorstepped and the the media interest was so intense that she went into hiding. Her complaint was upheld by the PCC. The chairman of the Bar helped her move chambers to complete her pupillage. She is currently listed as a non-practising barrister. After being fined £500, Mr Sutton-Mattocks remained in his original chambers although he did resign from his recordership.

The Law Society of England and Wales has gone a step further by laying down mandatory requirements. Since the implementation of a Practice Rule of July 1995, firms are required to operate an anti-discrimination policy. The Law Society's Research and Policy Planning Unit's Panel Study of Solicitors' Firms revealed that only two-fifths of firms reported that they had a written equal opportunities policy. The larger the firm, the more likely it was to have such a policy. While less than a fifth of sole practices had such a policy, half the two to four partner firms, three-quarters of the five to 10 partner firms and most firms with 11 or more partners did so. Of those firms with a written policy, 43% were using the Law Society's model anti-discrimination policy; 20% a modified version of it; and 35% had written their own policy. The larger firms, with 11 or more partners, were likely to have written their own policy. In the majority of firms with a written policy, either an equity partner or personnel manager was responsible for implementing the policy, but in a 10th of firms, there was no particular person responsible for it. Almost all firms with a

---

5   *Guide to the Professional Conduct of Solicitors*, 1999.

written policy stated that it applied to each grade of fee-earner and to all non-earners in the practice.[6]

The issue of discrimination, both direct and, particularly, indirect, is complex and some activities are not covered by legislation. For example, in my chapter with Alison Rees, we discuss the difficulties arising out of poverty, access to schools and, thereby, access to the law school most appropriate for the ability and achievements of applicants. Given that many chambers and law firms 'discriminate' in their selection process by looking first, or exclusively, at a limited number of institutions, the result is that able students are not afforded the opportunity to work in the most prestigious or financially rewarding firms or chambers. Such actions are not discriminatory in law and, indeed, could be promoted as sound recruitment practice. Few lawyers are principally motivated by altruism or social engineering. Income and profit margins are more compelling. The informal 'clubability' factor that Kate Malleson and Fiona Cownie describe as helpful for promotion is yet another illustration of unchallengeable discrimination. There is nothing improper in making oneself known in the appropriate circles to powerful people. Patronage is as old as society. Another concern is that highlighted by Luke Clements where he points out the class distinctions between magistrates and defendants and the ability of would-be magistrates to nominate themselves for consideration to the Bench, via the secret selection procedure. The 'glass ceiling' in legal education that Fiona Cownie describes may be easy to identify, but is difficult to break with legal tools. Robert Lee's description of solicitor retention in the City firms being based on spiralling salaries with a concomitant expectation in the increase in billable hours squeezes out the single parent, the mother of children and those determined to enjoy a private life outside the work environment. Unpublished work I undertook with Alan Bradshaw, on behalf of the Association of Women Solicitors, demonstrated in the clearest of terms why some women leave the profession. One woman in a busy London practice stated she left because what she needed to stay in legal practice was a wife and what she had was a husband! Others talked about the sharply increased domestic demands associated with the birth of a second child; the unsatisfactory nature of part time practice; returning to practice after maternity leave and feeling isolated; or following the husband who moved job and relocated. The working environment is a culture created by men who, in turn, are usually supported by women. Therefore, it suits most men, but women must behave like men to be equally successful. Once again, the possibility of challengeable discrimination is limited. Sanderson and Sommerlad spell out in detail the many levels on which discrimination, both direct and indirect, currently operates. Their analysis of discrimination against women in the legal workplace and the redress limitations that they experience presents a disturbing pattern, but their chapter also offers strategies for

6   Law Society, 1997.

positive change: for example, through the process titled 'gender mainstreaming' and stronger self-regulation by professional bodies.

Within the two professional bodies, internal tensions exist and questions remain unanswered. The Law Society faces the issue of its own survival as the large City firms continue to express their concerns over its activities and seek to give it direction through membership of Council and subordinate committees. On the other hand, members of smaller firms demand that their professional body protect their interests. Issues such as franchising, legal aid, civil justice reforms, indemnity insurance, and conveyancing take a higher priority with the majority of members than do issues of equal opportunities. This somewhat problematic area for some members was formerly treated as a public relations issue before being given its own equal opportunities committee and staff.

The Law Society staff runs to some 1,000 people, of whom 829 are white, with 50 staff 'not returned'. The experience of the Bar Council is somewhat different, given both its much smaller membership and administrative staff of 75. The public perception of the Bar is of a profession dominated by white, middle aged men educated at public schools and elite universities. The Bar Council is seeking dispell this image and sees addressing equal opportunities issues as one positive and important step to reconstructing both the image and the reality of the Bar.

As bodies such as the Equal Opportunities Commission have experienced, enforcing legislation through tribunals and the courts is not without its problems. The professional bodies have similar experiences. Scrutinising office and chambers practice is difficult and time consuming. Effective equal opportunities policies cost money and, in practice terms, these are perceived to constitute on-costs in that they are non-productive activities. Some practices, especially the smaller practices, are reluctant to build these costs into their business overheads.

Making a formal complaint is a decision that has significant implications for a solicitor or barrister. Equal opportunity officers in both branches of the profession told me that they receive many telephone calls from lawyers who seek advice, but do not wish to proceed to laying a complaint. The person seeks support, information, feedback, and may ask how many other people have laid complaints. They question the safety and possible benefits and repercussions of such an action. They are wise to do so. Whistle-blowers, trouble-makers and boat-rockers would be seen as disturbing the settled harmony of some practices. Currently, the Office for the Supervision of Solicitors, which deals with external complaints, is seeking to reduce its backlog of complaints to 6,000 by December 2000. On the other hand, the internal picture is different: there is no backlog of complaints arising out of equal opportunities claims and there are no complaints lodged with the Bar Council's Professional Conduct Committee.

The privacy aspect is such that when the Bar Council included a question on the Pupillage Applications Clearing House (PACH) form asking applicants to state whether they had a disability requiring a special adjustment on the part of the BVC provider, some applicants were reluctant to provide information which they thought might have a negative impact on their chances of being offered a place on a course. Within the Law Society 'cohort study' on which Michael Shiner's chapter is based, questions on sexuality and disability were mooted in the draft questionnaire, but ultimately excluded for similar reasons.

The term 'discrimination' is both equivocal and ambiguous, and may also be seen as such within the professional bodies. For equal opportunity officers, titled in the Law Society as equalities officers, it means work on the ground: seeking to inform on best practice which, hopefully, impacts positively on both perceptions and attitudes; it involves advising and supporting those who are unwilling to proceed to a public review of improper practices. In that sense, life on the street is different from life in the council chamber. Policy and practice may be strange companions. The chapter by Sumitra Vignaendra, Marcia Williams and Jerry Garvey raises the idea that the profession views its membership by slotting them into categories, including ethnic ones. While this is limiting, some black people feel that they have no choice but to communicate with the profession within the parameters set by the profession. Nevertheless, given the choice, their interviews suggest that black people would not want to be seen as Black lawyers but simply as lawyers. They do not seek an ethnic role within the profession. This process of 'labelling' may also be true for other groups.

This book seeks to address the wider understanding of the term 'discrimination'. It takes in the legislation dealing with race, sex and disability, but recognises there is much more that requires attention. The good work in tackling the ugly side of discrimination undertaken by the professional bodies, pressure groups, judges, senior partners, heads of chambers, equal opportunity officers, university admission tutors, researchers and academics is commended: much more remains to be done.

Philip A Thomas
Cardiff Law School
Cardiff University
July 2000

ABBREVIATIONS

ACA	African, Caribbean and Asian Lawyers Group
ACLEC	Advisory Committee on Legal Education and Conduct
ADR	alternative dispute resolution
ALT	Association of Law Teachers
Berkeley Women's LJ	Berkeley Women's Law Journal
Br J Crim	British Journal of Criminology
BVC	Bar Vocational Course
Chicago UL Rev	University of Chicago Law Review
CIHE	Council for Industry and Higher Education
Cincinnati UL Rev	University of Cincinnati Law Review
CLJ	Cambridge Law Journal
CNAA	Council for National Academic Awards
CPE	Common Professional Examination
CPS	Crown Prosecution Service
Crim LR	Criminal Law Review
European LJ	European Law Journal
GLS	Government Legal Service
Harv L Rev	Harvard Law Review
Hastings LJ	Hastings Law Journal
HEFCE	Higher Education Funding Council for England
IJLP	International Journal of the Legal Profession
IJSL	International Journal of the Sociology of Law
Indiana LJ	Indiana Law Journal
JLS	Journal of Law and Society
JP	Justice of the Peace
Kobe L Rev	Kobe University Law Review

LA	Legal Action
LPC	Legal Practice Course
LS	Legal Studies
LSF	Law Society Finals
Med Sci Law	Medicine, Science and the Law
MLA	Muslim Lawyers Association
MLR	Modern Law Review
NLJ	New Law Journal
PACH	Pupillage Applications Clearing House
PCs	practising certificates
Pennsylvania UL Rev	University of Pennsylvania Law Review
PL	Public Law
QAA	Quality Assurance Association for Higher Education
QC	Queen's Counsel
RAE	Research Assessment Exercise
RPPU	Research and Policy Planning Unit
SBL	Society of Black Lawyers
SLSA	Socio-Legal Studies Association
SPTL	Society of Public Teachers of Law
Stanford L Rev	Stanford Law Review
UCAS	Universities and Admissions Service for the UK
UFC	Universities Funding Council
Vermont L Rev	Vermont Law Review
Wisconsin LR	Wisconsin Law Review
Yale LJ	Yale Law Journal

CHAPTER 1

THE FUTURE OF ADVOCACY*

Sir Stephen Sedley

Although I have not framed my topic as a question – 'Has advocacy a future?', or something like that – I don't want it to be thought that I am taking advocacy for granted. For many people, especially those who have had a bad experience of the law, advocates are a menace: they complicate and prolong things which ought to be short and simple; they obscure rather than clarify the issues; they bully and perplex witnesses who are doing their best to tell the truth. To their clients the same advocates, equally often, are heroes who run rings round the opposition and expose its witnesses as fools or frauds; though the litigant's desire to win can sometimes obscure the reality remarked on by a celebrated Italian advocate: 'Often the client doesn't realise when he wins his case that rather than embracing his own lawyer it's his opponent's lawyer he should be thanking.'[1]

Whether a system of true justice requires advocates has been questioned for centuries. Three hundred and fifty years ago, the radical pamphleteer John Warr wrote:

> If there be such a thing as right in the world, let us have it [unvarnished]. Why is it delayed or denied or varnished over with guily words? Why comes it not forth in its own dress? Why doth it not put off law and put on reason, the mother of all just laws? Why is it not ashamed of its long and mercenary train? Why can we not ask it and receive it ourselves, but must have it handed to us by others? In a word, why may a man not plead his own case, or his friends and acquaintances, as formerly, plead for him?[2]

But as Warr and others since have had to recognise, courts and professional advocates are here to stay, and it is to professional advocacy in the courts that I want to devote this lecture. This means that I will not be looking at some important aspects of advocacy, among them the growing availability of advocacy services provided by non-lawyers for mental patients and others whose needs and desires often go unarticulated and therefore unaddressed, and the use of lawyers and non-lawyers in a great range of tribunals less

---

*   The Lord Morris Memorial Lecture, Cardiff University, 28 September 1999. The author records his gratitude to Lord Morris' bequest, which provided him with a most able research assistant, Dennis Lee.

1   Calamandrei, 1989, p 88.

2   Warr, 1649. Warr cites the statute 28 Edward I c 11 as showing that, at one time, litigants' 'parents and next friends', as well as professional advocates, could speak for them. The word quoted in square brackets is in Latin (*sine suco*) in the original.

formal than courts of law, but just as important in the functions they carry out; though it may be that some of what I have to say – for example, about the ethics of advocacy – will also have a bearing on these larger fields.

Nor am I going to have time to discuss the role of advocates in mediation and other forms of alternative dispute resolution, an important issue in the light of the emphasis placed by the new Civil Procedure Rules – the Woolf reforms – on non-confrontational forms of recourse. Perhaps surprisingly, there is a recognised role for advocates in mediation; but perhaps unsurprisingly, given the culture of aggression at which I shall be looking, experience so far suggests that they sometimes impede a negotiated outcome.[3]

So let me begin at what, for someone who has decided to make a career of advocacy, is the beginning. To have to put the starting point here itself begs a large question: why should a trainee lawyer have to opt for advocacy before he or she or anyone else knows whether they will be any good at it? In New Zealand, for example, you qualify and embark upon practice as a member of a single profession. Within a law firm you may try your hand at advocacy, and if, in due course, your aptitude takes you that way, you may hang up your shingle as barrister sole and make advocacy your career. It has repeatedly struck me as wasteful of time and talent that law students in this country have to opt for or against advocacy as the mainstream of their future work before they or anyone else know whether it's the right choice for them. The result can be seen daily: some young barristers, often of great intellectual ability, for whom every hearing in court is an ordeal which eats holes in their lives, but who are now on a career treadmill which they cannot get off; and other lawyers who, lacking confidence at 21, chose to become solicitors and have since found that they have a talent for advocacy which is painfully frustrated every time they have to sit mutely behind counsel less able than themselves. The anomaly is enhanced by the fact that there are practising barristers – conveyancing counsel, for example – who barely ever go into court, and solicitors – magistrates' court advocates, for example – who rarely go anywhere else.

I will return to the spin-offs of this problem when I look later at rights of audience, but for the moment let me return to the new graduate who has decided to become an advocate and who needs, therefore, to be called to the Bar. She or he will have first to join an Inn of Court[4] – one of the four ancient collegiate institutions through whose doors all intending barristers must pass, but whose modern and future role is still undetermined. As disciplinary bodies, they have passed on their summary functions to the Bar Council – a necessity if consistent standards are to be applied – though they retain the

---

3 Genn, 1998, para 7.3.1: 'The settlement rate was, however, highest in mediations that took place in the absence of legal representation and lowest when only the plaintiff was accompanied by a legal representative at the mediation.'

4 Gray's Inn, Lincoln's Inn, the Inner Temple or the Middle Temple. It will be apparent that, from here on, I am dealing only with England and Wales.

ultimate powers delegated to them by the judges. As educational bodies, which for centuries they were in a haphazard but indispensable way, their core work has now been handed on to the professional providers of a modern Bar Vocational Course (BVC) which the Inns themselves could not have hoped to provide. The dinners at which trainee barristers for centuries somewhat casually absorbed the culture and some of the learning of the profession have correspondingly lost much of their point, and the Inns have accordingly, if at first reluctantly, substituted optional collegiate activities for the slightly ridiculous process of eating your way to the Bar. They are turning their attention to the provision of advocacy training and wider forms of legal education than the BVC needs to provide. They continue to provide major law libraries and are, in any event, established entities of very considerable wealth, principally through the land they own and occupy. Their future existence is, therefore, not in question: it is their role in an already complex professional structure, weighed down with its own history and culture, which – as I think they all accept – needs to be addressed and modernised.

Meanwhile, what matters for the intending Bar student is that the Inns hold and distribute considerable sums by way of scholarships to their student members – not nearly enough to fund them all through the Bar Vocational Course, but enough to help a proportion of them through a worrying and expensive period of their lives.[5] Even so, it is plain that the money distributed to their student members by the Inns of Court cannot meet anything like the full extent of need.

Joining an Inn is unproblematical, provided you have the fee and do not have a criminal record. Nor is it too difficult, if you can get on to it,[6] to complete the Bar Vocational Course and be called to the Bar in due course by your Inn of Court. The result, however, is a throughput of qualified students, many of whom are then unable to find a pupillage; without having done a pupillage, they cannot practise. These students find themselves in a situation in which, after years of study and the acquisition very often of a crippling burden of debt, they are denied the opportunity to seek work in a profession which welcomed them as newcomers, but is now turning its back on them. This is an unhappy situation which the Bar collectively, in spite of the real concern of its representative body, tolerates by inertia.

---

5   Last year, a sum approaching £2 m was distributed among 321 students, the majority of them on the Bar Vocational Course but about a fifth of them non-law graduates taking the Common Professional Examination to qualify them for professional training as lawyers. As a non-law graduate myself, I strongly favour this route into the profession: it enlarges and humanises a culture which can easily become dry and inward-looking.

6   The Bar Council's 1997–98 figures show that the uniform criteria used to select candidates for the BVC admitted a somewhat higher proportion of white applicants (62%) than of ethnic minority applicants (53%), suggesting some initial educational disparity. The failure rate in 1998 was 28%.

There has been a conscious, if modest, expansion of the number of students taking the Bar Vocational Course. To replace the monopoly of the Inns of Court School of Law, the Bar has since 1997 validated professional training courses in seven other academic institutions. Together, acting through a central clearing house, the providers now offer a total of 1,442 full time and 100 part time places on the BVC, all of them oversubscribed and permitting the better qualified candidates to be chosen.[7] The new syllabus is a much-needed departure from the old Bar Final Examinations: it recognises, for the first time, that interpersonal and advocacy skills are something barristers don't just possess and need to learn. But the result – allowing for failure and dropout – is an annual output of about 1,000 aspiring barristers, academically fully qualified after either four or five expensive years' study, called to the Bar by their respective Inns at a glittering ceremony, but still unable to practise until they have served out a full year's pupillage. Their numbers are swelled – currently almost doubled[8] – by the residue of previous years' students who are still trying to find a pupillage. They face a distressing and, in places, anarchic situation. We know that fewer than half of them will succeed in getting a pupillage.[9] Some – perhaps as many as half – will now give up and move on to desk jobs in the employed sector or leave the law altogether. Of those who do find a first pupillage, perhaps six out of 10 will eventually obtain tenancies.

In these circumstances it is necessary, first of all, to be clear about where the Bar's obligations begin and end. No profession can guarantee work to everyone who qualifies for it unless entrant numbers are limited, with legal underpinning, to those it knows it can absorb. In earlier years, this was done by the simple expedient of limiting to eight the number of students each Inn would call to the Bar in any one term: an annual total of 128 students.[10] But the Bar has proved a poor forecaster of its own prospects. Early in the decade which has now come to a close, the Bar Council, in its then customary mood of defensive pessimism, predicted that the profession would shrink by one-third by the end of the century. Instead it has grown by more than a half:

---

7   See Watson, 1997, p 82, for a description of the new system and its syllabus. The ICSL, before it diversified provision, offered up to 1,400 places, so the expansion has not been great. About 2,500 students apply each year for places. The Bar Council's brochure Steps to the Bar describes the qualification process well. Both it and the Inns' brochures warn intending applicants of the serious obstacles to success. It also lists some of the main attributes needed by a barrister: 'intellectual ability; presentation and advocacy skills – that is, the ability to put across a point of view convincingly in public; personal coping skills – that is, the ability to digest large volumes of information in a short time and to handle the stress of long hours, tight deadlines and great responsibility; motivation.' I would have liked to see integrity in the list.

8   In 1998–99, PACH had 1,967 applicants seeking pupillage placements.

9   In 1997, 840 out of 1,870 applicants obtained a pupillage; in 1998, 747 out of 1,826; in 1998–99 there were 1,967 applicants.

10 Odgers, 1901, p 31.

today, there are 10,847 barristers in practice.[11] To have allowed the Bar in this period formally to limit its intake to its self-predicted needs would have robbed advocacy of its seed-corn. But to accept this is not to reject the case for a limit on numbers: it is to point to the need for cautious and objective forecasting. Instead, trapped by the Office of Fair Trading's view that a limit on numbers would be unacceptably anti-competitive,[12] the Bar has left it to a process of natural selection – as cruel and arbitrary as anything observed by Darwin – to whittle down the numbers to those the Bar finally wants. I do not suggest that the Bar's numbers can be forcibly expanded: only individual chambers can decide what room they have for new tenants. But without a completed pupillage, the opportunity to seek a tenancy does not exist.

Even in the present situation there is no moral or practical reason why every student who requires a pupillage should not have one, and a welter of reasons why they should. The Bar, through its collegiate bodies and through the Bar Council, has invited them to invest a crucial year of their lives and money which most of them do not have in the first stage of vocational training. It does not, and cannot, promise them eventual work; but it has an inescapable moral obligation not to arbitrarily deny any of them the second stage of a barrister's vocational training, pupillage, without which none of them can ever seek work at the Bar. There are enough qualified junior counsel to take the BVC's annual throughput, yet probably fewer than 800 of them in this year will take on a pupil,[13] a large proportion of them unfunded or underfunded.

It was not always like this. In the days (which lasted into the 1970s) when pupils paid a hundred guineas for a pupillage, there was no shortage of juniors willing to take them.[14] Today, for good organisational reasons, the acceptance and allocation of pupils is a function of chambers rather than of individual practitioners; but, for economic reasons, chambers are now typically many times the size that they were, and some of them, including

---

11　Ie, from a 1990 base of 6,645 – a process which, curiously enough, after the postwar doldrums which, by 1960, had reduced the Bar's numbers to under 2,000, has restored the Bar to the size it had at the beginning of the 20th century. ('In 1800 there were only 598 men at the Bar; now there are no less than 9,457': Odgers, 1901, p 30.)

12　This was in response to the recommendation of the Taylor Report, 1991.

13　The Inns' registers of qualified juniors, now being pruned, till recently carried over 3,000 names. PACH statistics show that in 1997, 840 out of 1,870 qualified applicants obtained pupillages; in 1998, 747 out of 1,826 – 161 of them unfunded. I do not accept the argument that, since this is not far above the number of new tenants taken on in those years (viz 613 in 1996–97, 502 in 1997–98 and 446 in 1998–99), the Bar is giving the right number of pupillages. What it is doing in effect (I do not suggest that it is planned) is preserving a seller's market in advocacy, expanding the size of existing chambers where the surplus of work justifies it, but ensuring that there is no pool of qualified young non-tenant barristers such as in past years have set up their own new chambers and enlarged the market.

14　There are many accounts of juniors with small armies of pupils, some within living memory. Campbell, the future Chief Justice, was one of 12 pupils simultaneously under the aegis of Tidd (Odgers, 1901, pp 31–32).

many of the most prosperous, recruit pupils not with any sense of obligation to train the profession's next generation but simply in order to maintain their own establishment. The consequence is that a set of 60 barristers who in past years might have composed three separate sets of chambers with half a dozen pupils in each, may now take on a single pupil or at best a handful. This process of attrition, in different proportions, is widely replicated across the Bar.

As a consequence of the want of a fair and uniform system, the selection of pupils is in many instances arbitrary and possibly discriminatory. The Bar in this respect has shown a depressing nonconformity between what it says and what it does. What it says is exemplary. The Bar Council supported the extension to the legal profession of the race and sex discrimination legislation.[15] It has adopted an advanced Equality Code, setting out detailed practices and principles for ensuring that pupillages and tenancies go to the best applicants, not simply the best-connected ones, and has made observance of the Code a rule of professional conduct.[16] It has set up a clearing house for pupillage applications, PACH, which depends upon chambers observing common standards and which in return assumes the initial burden of sifting and ordering applications. And it has recommended that all pupils be paid a modest salary by their chambers, giving credit against it for anything they earn in their second six months,[17] when they are allowed to take briefs. The reality, by contrast, is a reproach to the profession. Some chambers – a creditable number – sift and interview the applicants forwarded by PACH who have indicated a preference for those chambers; they take on a number of them as pupils, warning them that there is unlikely to be room for many, or any, of them as tenants, but recognising the obligation to give all of them the chance they have worked so hard for; and they pay them, out of the chambers' income, a decent salary, often well above the Bar Council's recommended figure.[18] But these chambers, and the Bar as a whole, are let down by those who buck the system. These are the chambers which refuse to participate in PACH and, instead, go headhunting at universities of their choice among the second year students, looking for a star student who will be paid perhaps £25,000 as a prospective tenant; or chambers which participate in PACH but refuse to take any candidate but their own first choice (who, in the nature of

---

15 Courts and Legal Services Act 1990, s 64.

16 See the Bar's Equality Code and the brief account given by Anthony Thornton QC, 'The professional responsibility and ethics of the English Bar', in Cranston, 1995, pp 95–96.

17 The figure, £6,000 a year, was adopted in 1990 upon the recommendation of Sir Nicholas Phillips' Report, which envisaged 450 funded pupillages a year. The target has never been met and the figure has never been increased. See Bowley, 1999.

18 See the Bar Council's annual Pupillages and Awards handbook for the range and terms of pupillages on offer through or outside the Bar Council's Pupillage Applications Clearing House (PACH).

things, may well have been the first choice of other sets too); or chambers which take on pupils but pay them little or nothing.[19]

It is not simply that the end product is an inadequate and unfair allocation of pupillages, though it is both of those things. In some ways the most serious consequence of the present situation is that the Bar's intake risks reverting to what it was at the beginning of the century: a social, economic and racial elite. It does the Bar credit that its ethnic minority component at present exceeds that in the UK population generally.[20] Statistical evidence of racial disadvantage in the progression from BVC to pupillage to tenancy is worrying, but, at present, inconclusive.[21] What may matter more for now is the risk that some of the Bar's present practices may unwittingly be lending themselves to such a process.

Take, for example, the apparently innocuous question of the university where pupillage applicants took their degrees. It is right, of course, that individual chambers should set their own criteria of selection. But little attention seems to be given to the indirectly discriminatory effect of the preference which is in many cases accorded to particular universities, or to first class degrees. A student's chance, up to the age of 24, of being offered a pupillage ranges from nearly nine out of 10 for an 'Oxbridge' first to one out of 20 for a 2.2 from a former polytechnic; for older students, the disparity gets worse. But doesn't this reflect the class of degree, rather than the institution? Unfortunately not: even with a 2.2, an 'Oxbridge' graduate has almost a 38% chance of a pupillage – one percentage point higher than a student from a former polytechnic with a first.[22] The possible social, economic and racial implications of this can be glimpsed in the comparison, first of all, between the ethnic make-up of the law schools in the older universities and those in the former polytechnics. Leaving out overseas students, the Oxbridge law schools are 85% white; but some former polytechnics – Nottingham Trent, Glamorgan, and Derby, for example – are not far off that figure. Moreover, all these institutions have, for known and creditable reasons, a higher ethnic minority component than in the population as a whole. But if you compare the ethnic minority component in the law schools of a city's old university

---

19 Thus, in 1998, of 671 pupillages offered through PACH, only 586 were allocated; and, of these, not more than 226 were funded, in many cases at token figures of £1,500 or less.

20 Of the known ethnicity of the current membership of the practising Bar, pupils and squatters included, almost 10% is ethnic minority (Bar Council records).

21 The Bar has different recording systems for the successive career stages, making it impossible at present to track an ethnically or gender-differentiated cohort though the stages. The static picture available for 1996–97 shows overall about a quarter fewer candidates obtaining tenancies than obtained an initial pupillage. Broken down by gender and ethnicity, the proportionate drop is about 20% for men against 30% for women; but, importantly, there is no drop at all for white candidates against about 24% for ethnic minorities. If this turns out to be replicated over time for a single cohort, it will be serious cause for concern.

22 Figures published by PACH.

with that in its former polytechnic City neighbour – Oxford, Birmingham, Leicester, Leeds, Liverpool, Manchester, and Nottingham, for instance – in each of these cities there is a higher concentration of ethnic minority students in the former polytechnic than in the old university. Of the working sample of 25 universities which I have used, only Bristol's two universities invert the pattern.[23] Averaging the sample, rather more than a fifth of the UK law students in the established universities are from ethnic minorities – a creditable figure; but in the former polytechnics, this proportion is almost doubled.[24] It is possible, then, that chambers which give preference to graduates of the established universities are unwittingly making it harder for ethnic minority students, taken as a group, to obtain pupillages.[25]

Such skewing, if it exists, is troubling not only because all English and Welsh degrees are, and have for a long time, been validated to the same national standard, but because there seems also to be an element of localised grade inflation which may exaggerate the differentials I have mentioned. A law student at Cambridge has a chance of almost one in five of getting a first; at Oxford, of better than one in six; at Cardiff, however, less than one in 100; and on average outside Oxbridge, little better than one in 50. There are, no doubt, reasons for this: the tendency of many schools to steer the brightest of their students towards Oxbridge; the supervision system there, which offers personalised tuition; and, possibly, a more catholic approach to the syllabus. There is certainly no direct racial correlation: Cardiff Law School, 91% white, gave only two firsts last year. But when one observes the relatively low ethnic minority representation in the Oxbridge law schools, the potential racial implication of reliance on a combination of degree class and university begins to be seen.

Women now form almost half the annual intake to the Bar Vocational Course, and they succeed at a rate pretty close to that of male students.[26] If the Equality Code is taken seriously by chambers, the marked under-

---

23 Figures from a sample of 25 universities' 1998 returns, published in full by the Higher Education Statistics Agency. Ethnicity figures relate to UK-domiciled students; overseas students are excluded from these statistics.

24 Figures *ibid*: the law schools of the established universities in the sample average 77.7% white; those of the ex-polytechnics 61.4%.

25 If this is right, the recently proposed change to a sandwich-course system, slotting pupillage into the BVC, will make things worse: if students without a pupillage cannot get on to the BVC, any racial differential in access will be brought forward in time and perhaps seen more sharply. The proposal is set out in a Bar Council discussion paper, 'Restructuring vocational training for the Bar' (June 1999): in essence, it suggests 20 weeks' BVC; six months' pupillage; 10 more weeks' BVC; assessment and call to the Bar with a provisional practising certificate; and a full practising certificate after a second six month pupillage.

26 In 1998, 795 men and 728 women were called to the Bar. In 1922, the first year when women were admitted, 10 out of the 387 called were women. The steep climb in recent years is traced in *Without Prejudice?*, the report on sex equality at the Bar and in the judiciary, prepared in 1992 for the Lord Chancellor's Department and the Bar Council by TMS Consultants.

representation of women at the practising Bar (less than a quarter were women in 1995) will be redressed in the course of the next generation.[27] There is already encouraging evidence of a significant drop in sexual harassment at the Bar since it was first highlighted.[28] But there are also incipient grounds for concern. I have mentioned an apparent gender gap in obtaining tenancies. Added to these is another less-noticed problem: age discrimination. The Bar historically has benefited greatly from late entrants; but current figures show that, from the age of 25, candidates are finding it increasingly difficult to obtain a pupillage.[29] This may well now be aggravated – though for reasons which I am going to suggest are not respectable – by the High Court's ruling that pupils rank as apprentices for the purposes of the minimum wage legislation, since it is from the age of 26 that apprentices benefit from it.[29a]

I will not spend time on the knock-on effects of this situation. It is well known that, among other things, it constricts the flow of capable female and ethnic minority candidates for silk and for the bench. The Lord Chancellor's Department takes seriously the need for non-discriminatory criteria for appointments, to the extent that the complaint now most frequently heard – and equally mistaken – is that women and ethnic minorities do better than they deserve to. What does, I think, deserve mention is the odd way in which talent and discrimination interact. There are a number of women, and a smaller number of ethnic minority barristers, who have shone and prospered at the Bar and (mainly in the case of the former) on the bench. Most of these will tell you that they have encountered no discrimination in their careers; and their success confirms what they say. There is no doubt that the Bar is a profession in which a real star can shine regardless of gender or race – though we have no way of knowing that it is always so. The worry is not the outstanding but the average practitioner. A woman barrister, or a black barrister, who is no better than average may well find in the dismissiveness of some colleagues and the paucity of good work a handicap which the average – sometimes very average – white male barrister does not experience.[30] It is here that the potential for indirect discrimination begins; and it is why it is to

---

27 Bar Council figures – an excellent example of the value of ethnic and gender audits – for 1996–97 show fall-offs of 7% and then 20% for men, compared with 10% and then 30% for women. Choices in relation to child care are likely to account for some continuing disparity, however. For ethnic minority pupils, there was a rise (from 93 to 106) from first to second six month pupillages, but then a dramatic fall (to 71) for tenancies.

28 The Shapland and Sorsby Report on Work and Training at the Junior Bar, 1994, found that 40% of women had encountered sexual harassment, about one-eighth of it serious. The same authors' follow-up in 1997 found that the incidence had dropped by about a quarter, and by more for serious cases. This was almost certainly an example of an enforced and beneficial change in the Bar's sense of acceptable behaviour.

29 In 1998–99, the best chance of pupillage (31.2%) was for men aged under 25; for women under 25 it was 26%. Aged 35 or over, the chance for both fell to around 10%. See, generally, Bowley, 1998.

29a Since overset on appeal: *Edmonds v Lawson* (2000) unreported, 10 March, CA.

30 See *Without Prejudice?*, above, fn 26. In 1991, the proportion of women barristers in the bottom earnings bracket was twice that of men; in the top bracket, half that of men.

the Bar that the public ought principally to look when it asks – as it rightly and repeatedly does – why there are so few female and black QCs and even fewer judges.

I have spoken about racial, sexual and age differentials. There are also serious social and economic ones, which the present system may be tending to promote. It starts most obviously with the near-abolition of local authority grants and the introduction of student loans. It continues with the need for more borrowing during the BVC year. In spite of Inn scholarships[31] and favourable bank loans,[32] it is not uncommon for a student without private or family means to embark on pupillage with a burden of debt of £25,000 or more. It is not surprising that a substantial proportion of such students go from the BVC into employment because they cannot face the further risk and stress of seeking a pupillage and then, if they manage to get one, seeking a tenancy. Nor is it surprising that between a quarter and a third of students rely on parental support to see them through the BVC year.[33] But it is plain that any group which can fall back on parental means in sums running to many thousands of pounds is a socially and economically advantaged group, and where that group makes up over a quarter of the BVC intake it is equally plain that a privileged cohort is making its way through the system. We should not be surprised, if this pattern persists, if in the years to come the Bar returns towards the narrow stereotype from which, in the last two decades, it has been escaping.

But the means of escape are still there. They require, first and foremost, that the Bar acknowledge the straits it is in. While the leadership of the Bar Council has shown a far less defensive face to government in the drafting and passage of the Access to Justice Act 1999 than it has in the past shown to measures which threatened the Bar's prosperity, it still has to grasp the nettle of access to pupillage. This has two aspects: the first is equitable consideration of candidates, which I have now considered in some detail; the second is relief from economic hardship while pupillage is completed. Until pupillage is reached, students may have to continue to find funding where they can. After it is completed, they must expect to compete for work without cushioning. But the Bar has a clear moral obligation, once it has accepted them on its vocational course, to enable them at least to complete their vocational training. First, then, the Bar has to make it a breach of professional etiquette to refuse without good cause to take a pupil. Good cause may be as personal as a personality clash or as impersonal as the physical or organisational capacity of chambers; but the ground rule for chambers admission procedures has to be

---

31 About 27% of BVC students rely on Inn awards for their fees, but only 10% for their living expenses: Goldsmith Report, 1998.

32 See the Tuckey Report, 1999.

33 *Ibid*, Goldsmith Report. A further 29% depend on loans; 7% on LEA grants, but for fees only; 20% live on savings or earnings; and 11% on 'other' sources, including, presumably, private incomes.

that a qualified junior barrister has an obligation to help to train the next generation of the Bar, not merely the next tenant in his or her own chambers. In turn this means that PACH, at present in a parlous state for want of full support, may have to be restored by rule, so that every BVC student who wants a pupillage has an equal chance of getting one – indeed, is guaranteed one.

Then there is funding. At present, perhaps the greatest disincentive to taking on more pupils than is absolutely necessary is the expectation that chambers will pay them a salary. To abandon payment would simply exaggerate the privilege differentials.[34] The answer is not to withhold pupillages: it is to spread the cost of supporting pupils equally across the Bar. Until this year, any such proposal was a pipe-dream, because there was no way of making the Bar pay and every prospect of a legal challenge to a levy. But at a late stage of the passage of the Access to Justice Bill the government introduced what is now s 46(2)(b), authorising the Bar Council to raise funds, by way of fees for practising certificates, sufficient to pay for the training of pupils. The Bar's total gross income in the last complete financial year will probably be between £1.2 and £1.4 bn.[35] A levy of, say, 1% (deductible from taxable income, but spread, I would hope, unevenly so as to spare the often unacknowledged 'thin cats' at the Bar who work hard on unglamorous cases for very little reward)[36] would raise enough to guarantee 1,500 trainee barristers an income, when earnings are taken into account, of perhaps £10,000 in their pupillage year – a sum corresponding well with the national minimum wage for a 60 hour week.[37] It would be for the Bar to decide whether to means-test the grants. The important thing is that, in combination with an allocation policy which recognises every BVC student's moral entitlement to a pupillage, it will go some way to equalising opportunity in a profession which will eventually die if it fails both to attract and to accommodate the brightest students, whatever their means or their origins.[38]

---

34 The Bar Council has been advised by specialist leading and junior counsel that pupils are 'workers' for the purposes of the Working Time Regulations 1998.

35 BDO Stoy Hayward, 1999, para 5.1. This projection corresponds reasonably well with the total of just under £1 bn recorded by Bar Mutual Assurance for the year 1997–98.

36 See Carr, 1999.

37 At £3.60 an hour, a 60 hour week for 48 weeks a year carries a minimum wage of £10,368.

38 I have not touched on the case made in the report to the Bar Council of the committee under Sir John Collyear (*Blueprint for the Future*, May 1999) for the non-practising first part of a pupillage to be served in employment. The proposal may well be viable in certain areas of work – the Government Legal Service, for example – but any idea that it can bail out the Bar by absorbing all the hundreds who want a practising pupillage is to be treated with great caution, not least because employers, who do not necessarily share the interests of the practising Bar, may not want them.

It is fair treatment of pupils across the board, not trying to compete with the big solicitors' firms by expensively headhunting individuals, which will set and keep such a process in motion.

But there is one corollary which government, in its turn, must be prepared to accept. A well ordered but small profession cannot hold its door perpetually open. A point will have to come, indeed has probably been reached, at which the numbers admitted to the BVC have to correspond with what the Bar can realistically absorb. To pour unsustainable numbers into the Bar, once the obligation to provide all qualified applicants with a pupillage is recognised, would inexorably put the profession once again in breach of faith with its students.[39] Anti-competitive or not, sanction will need to be given to a negotiated[40] cut-off of numbers at the point of entry into – not, as at present, exit from – the BVC; not so as to regenerate a seller's market in advocacy, but so as to prevent continuing waste, disappointment and the eventual slide of standards.[41] So long, however, as the Bar recognises no general obligation to see trainees through their pupillage, it has no basis on which to seek authority to restrict student numbers: the answer will always be to go on relying on 'natural' wastage with all that that implies for the many who finally lose out.

I have devoted much of this paper so far to access to the profession because I believe it to be a key issue for the future of professional advocacy in England and Wales. If the Bar slips back into being a socially unrepresentative elite, the quality of its service may not be enough to save it from the competitors at its gates. Before I consider these, I must explain why I am going to pass over a welter of other issues – the QC system and the appointment of judges, for example – which also have a bearing on my topic. These are subjects of real and legitimate concern both inside and outside the Bar; but they are difficult subjects because, while valid criticisms are apparent, solutions which are both principled and workable are not; and time is not on my side.

The competitors at the gates are, at present, solicitors and employed barristers. Both have for a long time enjoyed rights of audience, but not in the

---

39 The Taylor Report, 1991, concluded that numbers should be limited at the point of entry to training, but the Director General of Fair Trading took the view that to do so would be anti-competitive. It is the throughput of the consequent validated courses which now determines the number seeking entry.

40 By 'negotiated', I mean agreed between the Bar and government, as well as other interested professions and bodies, such as the Consumers' Association. Much is going to depend in the immediate future on the effect of the radical reordering of legal aid under the Access to Justice Act 1999 on the volume of work available, in particular, to young barristers. Even more will depend on the uptake and impact of the extension of rights of audience under the Act to non-practising barristers, solicitors and, in due course, other professions.

41 For the reasons I have given, the superficially attractive expedient of limiting numbers on the BVC by requiring entrants to have obtained a pupillage first (see above, fn 25, on the proposed sandwich course) would accentuate any racial and other disadvantage in the present state of pupillage allocation. In a better-ordered system, no doubt, it would work well, though the accredited providers would have reason to feel let down as their student numbers fell.

higher courts until, under the Courts and Legal Services Act 1990, suitable solicitor advocates were enabled to acquire rights of audience there. The new Access to Justice Act 1999 is intended to open up the field dramatically, principally by removing the two main constraints on the Lord Chancellor's existing powers – the advice of the powerful Advisory Committee on Legal Education and Conduct (ACLEC) and the veto given in the 1990 Act to the four senior judges on any proposal to enlarge rights of audience in the higher courts. Both are to be abolished. Neither had, in itself, any decisive constitutional role, but there is a serious constitutional dimension to the consequent omnipotence with which the Lord Chancellor is now clothed. It means that the control of the right to practise advocacy in the higher courts is now taken entirely from the judges and the Bar and vested entirely (discipline apart) in an officer of State whose titular role as head of the judiciary is increasingly eclipsed by his working role as a minister and Cabinet member. The potent objections to this situation, with its implications for the independence of the Bar and, therefore, of the legal system as a whole,[42] are weakened by the history of restrictive practices by which the Bar has exploited its monopoly in the past and by the scepticism with which much of the public views the cab-rank rule which underpins the Bar's claims.[43] But however untenable the Bar's claim to a continuing monopoly might be – and the Bar itself no longer makes the claim – the collapsing of all power to license and control advocacy into the sole hands of a minister places in the hands of future governments a weapon for ill. In particular, it carries the risk that the advocate's duty independently to gauge the limits of what can fairly and honourably be done in the conduct of a case – a duty under constant pressure from clients, but potentially under the greatest pressure from the greatest client, the State – will be compromised if the State's advocates are also its employees. It is a risk, however, which has to be seen in context. Crown prosecutors are probably more criticised at present for abandoning cases or under-charging defendants than for going for the kill. And barristers in independent practice, it has to be said, have been known to succumb to the pressure to satisfy the client at the expense of fairness or propriety. Although

42 ACLEC's early opposition was crucially influenced by its then chairman, Lord Steyn, whose anxieties about State domination of advocates and advocacy, deriving largely from his experience under apartheid in South Africa, are strongly echoed by Sir Sydney Kentridge, 1998, p 24. See Lord Steyn, 1999.

43 The rule is described by Anthony Thornton QC (*op cit*, fn 16) in these terms: 'No brief or instructions may be refused, whether to act as an advocate or to advise, unless the barrister is professionally committed already, has not been offered a proper fee [which all legal aid briefs are deemed to carry], is professionally embarrassed by a prior conflict of interest or lacks sufficient experience or competence to handle the matter.' Its importance as a cornerstone of the advocate's role was written by amendment into s 17(3)(c) of the Courts and Legal Services Act 1990 as a requisite of the recognition of the members of any professional body as qualified to practise advocacy. But counsel have been known to be surprisingly unavailable for unpopular cases when sought by solicitors who, though possessing a right of refusal, had accepted instructions to act. I return briefly to the rule at the end of this paper.

not of the Bar's making, the introduction of conditional fees as part of the reconstruction of the legal aid system is going to place fresh ethical pressures on the independent Bar – and also, it should not be forgotten, on solicitors; pressures which employed barristers will not face. To bypass by legislation the roadblock which has prevented even qualified barristers who are employed by the Crown Prosecution Service from conducting jury trials is not going to aggravate the problem appreciably. We are, without doubt, taking a large risk with a constitutional principle, but it is not happening without reason and we are not going from light into darkness.

There is a real worry, however, about the eventual absorption by solicitors of all but the heaviest advocacy. If this happens – and there are signs that it may be beginning to happen[43a] – the incremental experience which finally makes a reliable barrister will dry up, and the Bar itself will finally die. To let this happen would not only be a tragedy for a skill in which this country has for generations been a world leader; it would ultimately defeat the ends of the very profession – the solicitors' profession – which had brought it about, by robbing clients of a specialised resource and the courts of a source of assistance on which they depend. Much the same would be true even if the professions were merged: advocacy would remain a specialised skill within the unified profession, needing concentration and nurture.[44]

I realise that the Bar's history has been littered with predictions of its demise every time law reform has interfered with its monopolies or restrictive practices. Brougham's introduction, in 1846, of the county court system was attacked both because it would create a second-rate local Bar[45] and because, by opening advocacy to attorneys (solicitors), it would starve the Bar of work and thus – Lord Lyndhurst predicted – 'involve judges, barristers and attorneys in one common poverty and ruin'.[46] The cry of 'wolf' has been heard at intervals ever since; but sceptics in turn need to remember that there are wolves out there. They need also to appreciate what a necessary and difficult art advocacy is.

It is necessary because in an imperfect world, as I began by saying, most people involved with the law need someone to speak for them who is both familiar with the law and able to marshal and present a case at its most persuasive. The experience which solicitors accumulate undoubtedly equips them, if they have the inclination for it, to do much advocacy and do it well.

43a BDO Stoy Hayward's figures show barristers in their first five years earning a median figure of £29,500 net in 1999, but only £25,000 in 2000. Higher overheads may play a part in this.

44 Among other things, the unit cost of barristers' services is significantly lower than that of solicitors. With the move to larger and more efficient chambers and the replacement of the last of the anachronistic percentage clerks by salaried managers, this differential is likely to be maintained and possibly increased. A unified profession, although there is a lot to be said for it, would forfeit these savings.

45 Lord Lyndhurst, 1833 – an indication of how long it took to get the reform through.

46 *Ibid*, cited by Turner, 1971, pp 193–94.

Equally, however, if they are functioning at all as solicitors, the nature of their work prevents them from honing the skills of advocacy to the level of the best; and I have to say that the showing of even the best of those solicitor advocates now authorised to practise in the higher courts is bearing this out: I have seen none who, however capable, bears comparison with the best specialist counsel. Of course, it may be said, they will not reach that level until they have acquired many more flying hours; but to do that they will have to become full time advocates – in other words barristers, by whatever name they are called. And there is good reason for this. At an elementary level advocacy is something almost anyone can do. At its higher and highest levels it involves unique skills of preparation, learning, sensitivity and, above all, presentation, which require as many years of single-minded practice as make, for example, a first class conveyancing solicitor or corporate contract negotiator. Increasingly, too, advocacy is coming to rely far less on bombast and rhetoric and far more on reasoned persuasion than in the past: indeed, it's probably only on the screen (Rumpole and Kavanagh honourably apart) that the ponderous public-school oaf in a wig still makes a living. The new Civil Procedure Rules – the Woolf reforms – will encourage this transition by putting a premium on co-operation in getting the real issues before the court and by penalising aggressive and confrontational tactics. We are, I hope, going to see an end of American-style litigation in which stage armies, complete with partisan experts, set out to leave each other dead on the field. In the process, advocates will have to play a pioneering role and advocacy itself will change. In particular, I hope that the demeaning, in-your-face cross-examination of even the most difficult witnesses will cease: in my view it is generally an abuse of the privilege and the power which an advocate's status brings.[47]

We are also entering a phase of information technology which is going to affect advocacy in several ways. In the search for an economic use of judicial time, pre-reading has become an important tool, and with it the use of skeleton arguments. These developments in turn have been propelled by an earlier piece of technology now taken for granted – the photocopier – which replaced the agonising process of retyping every document for use in court by the debauchery of throwing the entire file on to the sheet feeder and delivering the lot to the court in – if we are lucky – approximate chronological order. The result has been a proliferation of paper capable of bringing the courts to a standstill, given that, on average, only about a twentieth of the documents, if that, turns out to have any worthwhile bearing on the decision.

---

47 This is a change which needs to be accelerated and reinforced both by the Bar's professional education and by the continuing education, which, if the Collyear Committee's advice is taken, is going to become a feature of all barristers' careers, as it now is (through the Judicial Studies Board) of all judges' careers. It is also a function of the degree of control exercised by trial judges in court. As John Mortimer's father explained (*Clinging to the Wreckage*), cross-examination does not mean examining crossly!

It is oral advocacy which has provided a solution by displacing on to counsel the task of sifting out the documents that matter and basing the presentation of the case on them. For counsel, the incentive is the well known inverse ratio between the complexity of a presentation and the likelihood of its succeeding. The judicial workload in systems in which oral advocacy is marginal – the French administrative law system, for example[48] – groans under a burden of copy documents which the judge has to read from end to end, with serious consequences for the time taken to decide cases. On the other hand, the constriction of advocates' time, both in leading evidence and in addressing the court, to what the court judges reasonable, works well in other common law jurisdictions and is showing signs of working well here as the Woolf reforms come into effect. Never again, I hope, will our legal system put itself passively at the service of powerful litigants for however long it suits them to fight their cases out.

But the real case for the preservation of orality in advocacy is, it has to be said, as much an aesthetic as a practical one. For counsel, the experience of arguing a difficult case well, perhaps before a difficult court, offers an unparalleled sense of achievement, whatever the outcome. Outcomes, in truth, are false friends: most cases win or lose themselves; it is only every so often – probably more in jury trials than in other cases – that advocacy makes the difference. But when it does, there is nothing to touch it. For the court, by contrast, fine advocacy presents a dilemma, for justice may lie with the weaker presentation. Part of the judge's role, and the jury's too,[49] is to distinguish between what the advocate has usefully highlighted and what has been pure advocacy – not an easy task with a compelling advocate, but one which no judge I know would want to be relieved of. Written submissions may replace, but cannot replicate, the intensive and organic character of debate in open in court. It is this which enables our courts in turn to get to the heart of a case – if necessary, with some input from the bench – and reach a conclusion which, if not right, is at least rational.

The Bar of England and Wales has a tradition and a standard of oral advocacy which, at its best, contributes something irreplaceable to the English language and to the culture of both countries. Most of it goes by on the wind, unrecorded but not unappreciated. How much of it reaches the superb level of Erskine's apparently impromptu speeches, recorded by assiduous shorthand writers, is impossible to say; but as a benchmark of oral prose, as well of

---

48 A senior French judge, the president of a regional Tribunal administratif, described his first impression of English oral advocacy to me as 'un luxe que vous vous permettez'. Subsequent comparison of his lead times (three to eight years) with that of the Crown Office list (five months on average from leave to hearing) suggested to both of us that using counsel to focus the case on what mattered might be less a luxury than a necessity.

49 As a trial judge I made a practice of reminding juries that their verdict was not a prize for the best advocacy.

professional standards, we have in perpetuity Erskine's speech to the jury which in 1792 convicted Tom Paine of sedition. Erskine had been publicly and privately criticised for accepting the brief:

> Little indeed did they know me [he said to the jury], who thought that such calumnies would influence my conduct. I will for ever, at all hazards, assert the dignity, independence and integrity of the English Bar, without which impartial justice, the most valuable part of the English constitution, can have no existence. From the moment that any advocate can be permitted to say that he will or will not stand between the Crown and the subject arraigned in the court where he daily sits to practise, from that moment the liberties of England are at an end.[50]

Tempting as it is to end on this high note, there is a coda. A few years after his defence of Paine, Erskine – consonantly with the principle he had described to Paine's jury – accepted the brief to prosecute Paine's printer, Thomas Williams, for blasphemy in publishing *The Age of Reason*. The conviction which Erskine secured not only reduced Williams to destitution; it had the intended chilling effect, so that Paine had to go to France to find a printer for the open letter he addressed to his former counsel, Erskine. In its introduction, Paine wrote this:

> It is a matter of surprise to some people to see Mr Erskine act as counsel for a Crown prosecution commenced against the right of opinion, I confess it is none to me, notwithstanding all that Mr Erskine has said before; for it is difficult to know when a lawyer is to be believed: I have always observed that Mr Erskine, when contending as counsel for the right of political opinion, frequently took occasions, and those often dragged in head and shoulders, to lard, what he called the British Constitution, with a great deal of praise. Yet the same Mr Erskine said to me in conversation, were government to begin *de novo* in England, they would never establish such a damned absurdity (it was exactly his expression) as this is, ought I then to be surprised at Mr Erskine for inconsistency.[51]

Some things don't change; others do. In more ways than one, a keynote for our era was struck in 1963 when Abe Fortas rose in the United States Supreme Court to open the appeal which established the right of every poor person charged with felony to the services of an advocate – *Gideon's* case:[52] 'Mr Chief Justice', he said, 'If you will look at this transcript of the record, perhaps you will share my feeling of despondency'.

Erskine must have turned in his grave at the bathos of it – but Fortas carried the day where Erskine's rhetoric might have failed. The manner changes with time, but the skill is the same, and so is the ethical obligation. It's

---

50 Erskine, *Speeches*, Ridgway (ed), 1810, Vol II, pp 90–91.
51 Paine, 1979. Punctuation *sic*.
52 *Gideon v Wainwright*, 372 US 335 (1963). Transcript from Irons and Guiton, 1993.

the rare advocate who can always appear in shining armour. For most advocates, even the greatest, the readier metaphor will be the hired gun – perhaps most precisely the superannuated gunfighter played unforgettably by Lee Marvin in *Cat Ballou*, who can only shoot straight when he is laced into his sequinned gunfighter's catsuit. It is the best argument I know for the retention of wigs and gowns. But it is going to take more than wigs and gowns, more than the tradition and glamour of what may well be the third oldest profession,[53] to see it safely through the reefs of competition and the shoals of its own bad habits in the coming decades.

---

53 Espionage has already laid claim to being the second.

CHAPTER 2

LAW STUDENTS – GETTING IN AND GETTING ON

Philip A Thomas and Alison Rees

Change is a feature and a goal of scholarship. British universities are in the process of change, though not necessarily for the better. Increasingly, universities are perceived and operated as competitive medium sized enterprises where accountants and balance sheets challenge staff and students for defining roles within the institutions.[1] Achievement is measured by winning, rather than by improvement, and league tables and associations have been constructed to promote the interests of these self-selecting clubs. Inside these convoluted university structures, students are both the subjects of, and contributors to, change. Increasingly, students identify themselves and act as consumers, with the staff functioning as service providers. Students, meanwhile, are seen by the government and, indeed, by the universities, as units of financial resource allocated to monitored cost centres. It is on the student body and, in particular, law students, that this chapter focuses.

There has been a political commitment from both Conservative and Labour governments to expand student numbers while maintaining academic standards. The financial provision, out of public taxes, necessary for such a programme has proved unacceptable to successive governments. Rising student numbers have occurred alongside declining Treasury subventions both to the universities and to the individual students and have resulted in the search for alternative sources of funding in order to maintain acceptable standards of scholarship. One increasingly important source of finance introduced by the State is the tuition fee levied on students, which was introduced in 1998. This chapter examines how students and, in particular, 550 first-year law students, currently studying at the five Welsh law schools, are preparing to meet these financial challenges. It also examines the likely impact of the challenges raised by the current financial constraints on students' educational experiences. Finally, it examines employment opportunities within the legal profession for the increasingly debt ridden student community.

---

1   'Nowadays Vice Chancellors talk about nothing but money, their performance ratings in research and occasionally in teaching, both of which determine their incomes.' Hills, 1999, p 6.

THE WELFARE STATE AND EDUCATION

The student grants system was introduced in 1962 as a result of the recommendations made by a government committee chaired by Sir Colin Anderson. The response, which did not incorporate all the recommendations, was the introduction of a means-tested system based upon parental income. This financial commitment in the 1960s covered an elite educational provision for the 5% of school leavers who entered universities. However, by the mid 1990s, over 30% were entering higher education and the Treasury bill was deemed to be unacceptably high. Until 1990, UK university students paid no tuition fees and received a tax-funded maintenance grant to cover living costs. The 1990s heralded serious inroads into the State's financial contribution to higher education with a move away from the system of maintenance grants in favour of a student loan scheme. This steady move away from the central funding of students was completed by the Labour government in the academic year 1998–99 when it introduced the payment of scaled tuition fees by students coupled with the abolition of maintenance grants a year later. Today, students are reliant upon the student loan, coupled with a range of private support facilities including paid employment. Whilst the problem of student debt is not novel,[2] its privatisation, placing the responsibilities essentially on the individual, has produced new challenges for current law students.

ENTERING HIGHER EDUCATION

Government policy is both clear and unequivocal in its commitment to mass higher education. The commitment is to widen, as well as increase, higher education opportunities. Tony Blair announced that his government's plan is that half of all young people will enter higher education.[3] Further, in the Queen's Speech of 1999, it was declared that 'Education remains my government's number one priority.'[4]

The history of higher education demonstrates why education in the 21st century needs to retain the premier position in governmental priorities. Despite increased participation, university entry remains socially exclusive, with the two highest socio-economic groups accounting for over 50% of all

---

2   See, eg, McCarthy and Humphrey, 1995, pp 78–86. For evidence relating to law students, see Thomas, 1993, pp 152–63.

3   DfEE Press Release, 581/98, 16 December 1998; Prime Minister's speech to the Labour Party Conference, October 1998.

4   (1999) *The Times*, 19 November. See, also, *The Learning Age: A Renaissance for a New Britain*, Cm 3790, 1998, London: Stationery Office and *Learning to Succeed: A New Framework for Post-16 Learning*, Cm 4392, 1999, London: Stationery Office.

entrants in 1998. The two lowest accounted for less than 10%. The social mix has barely altered over the last 20 years. In addition, public funding per student has declined by nearly 50% in real terms since 1980.

Between 1928 and 1947, some 8.9% of all boys from non-manual backgrounds entered university, compared with 1.4% from manual backgrounds. By 1963, the year when the Robbins Report was published,[5] the figures had altered accordingly: 16.8% of boys from the first group entered university, compared with 2.6% from the second group. Currently, 80% of children from social class one backgrounds attend university, while less than one in eight children from an unskilled manual family enters higher education.[6]

Looking at the gross figures, the overall picture is less gloomy, though ultimately misleading. In 1963, higher education figures stood at 216,000, including an undergraduate enrolment of 4,000 women. According to a newspaper report commenting on the General Household Studies Report of 1993:

> Men and women whose fathers belong to non-manual socio-economic groups have consistently formed a higher proportion of those gaining higher qualifications than would be expected ... while those from a manual background are over-represented among the unqualified.[7]

Currently, year on year, greater numbers of students are entering higher education. In 1999, there were some 1.4 million UK students in higher education in England.[8] Full time student numbers increased by 71% between 1989–90 and 1996–97. One in three young people now enters higher education, compared with one in six in 1989–90. This reflects, at a faster rate, a continuing growth trend. However, these figures fail to reflect the under-performance of students of working class background in the scramble for entry into UK institutions of higher education. In 1999, the UCAS breakdown of 413,000 university applications by neighbourhood demonstrated a further fall in applications from the country's poorest areas. For example, the 1.6 million households living in council flats form nearly 7% of the UK total, but 3% of UCAS applications originate there. There were 22,700 applicants from three million 'low rise' council households in 1999. Three times this number, 68,800 applications, were received from the UK's 2.5 million best-off families, making up a fifth of all new students for the new academic year.[9] In addition, students

---

5   Cmnd 2154.

6   (2000) *The Guardian*, 6 May.

7   (1993) *The Times*, 29 April.

8   DfEE Departmental Report, 1999, Annex Q. The total full time equivalent number (including EU and overseas students) was 1.165 m. Figures are for 1997–98 (estimated outturn).

9   (1999) *The Guardian*, 9 August.

from lower social classes are also over-represented in the category of students who fail to complete their degrees.[10]

The facts are plain, as is the conclusion. A student at a private school is 25 times more likely to get into an elite university than a student from a poor neighbourhood or a student from a lower social class. The class gap has widened as the premier law schools recruit even more heavily from private schools.[11] Other evidence backs up this picture. For instance, research for the Council for Industry and Higher Education concluded:

> Those from lower social classes are scarcely better represented in the 1990s than they were 10 (and probably 20) years ago ... those from the two lower social classes (semi-skilled and unskilled backgrounds) are highly under-represented at university.[12]

The Coalition of Modern Universities, in evidence to the House of Commons Education and Employment Committee in 1999, noted 'the failure of the educational system to encourage and accept participants at higher levels of education from the lower socio-economic groups in the UK'.[13] In addition, the Committee of Vice Chancellors and Principals noted that the lower socio-economic groups are still much less likely to progress to higher education than those from more affluent groups.[14] The National Adult Learning Survey concluded that the chief characteristic predicting participation in both vocational learning and non-vocational learning was socio-economic group.[15] Thus, basing university entrance simply upon the achievement of certain 'A' level grades can be misleading:

> If you get three 'A's from fee-paying schools, you know that they are good schools, with a very stable and well qualified staff. You set that alongside three 'B's from a person in an inner city comprehensive where there are a lot of pupils to every member of staff, and those three 'B's are probably a better achievement.[16]

Within Wales, a similar pattern of educational disadvantage is found. The former Chief Executive of the Higher Education Funding Council for Wales, John Andrews, presented a formula to gauge regional patterns of student take-up of places in higher education. The equation divides the number of people of traditional student age living in one area by the number who are students, and then multiplying that figure by 100. Andrews stated:

10 (1999) *The Guardian*, 9 August.
11 (2000) *New Statesman*, 17 April.
12 Metcalf, 1997, p 1.
13 Eighth Report, HC 57-1, November 1999, p vii.
14 'From elitism to inclusion', 1998, CVCP/SCOP, p 1. See, also, the Dearing Report, which makes this position clear. Dearing Report, Report No 5, Table 1.1, p 40: Main Report, paras 3.14, 3.16.
15 National Adult Learning Survey, 1997; DfEE Research Report No 49, 1998.
16 (1997) *The Sunday Times*, 29 June.

In a normal situation we would expect the average figure to be between 95 and 105, yet in some areas of Wales we are finding that not only is it well below that, but in some cases it is three times less than in areas where there is more wealth. In areas such as the valleys of south Wales and the far north-east the figure is likely to be less than 60, but in Cardiff and Ceredigion the number goes up to three times that figure, which is stark.[17]

The meritocracy that was expected through mass education remains just that: an expectation.[18] Within our survey group of 550 first-year law students who had registered in one of the five law schools in Wales, similar patterns of social background were found.[19] The parental occupations were coded and assigned to social groups in accordance with the Standard Occupational Classification of the Office of Population and Censuses and Surveys. Students at Aberystwyth and Cardiff have the highest percentage of graduate mothers (27% and 26%) respectively. The same schools have the highest percentage of graduate fathers (38% and 35%). At Swansea Institute, the figures for graduate mothers and fathers are 16% and 8%. Parents in social class one at Aberystwyth constituted 33%, compared with 9% at Glamorgan and 7% at Swansea Institute. In terms of geographic mobility, 30% of students at Aberystwyth live in Wales, whereas the Welsh-based law students at Glamorgan and Swansea Institute represent 67% and 84% of the student cohort. Finally, the retention figures for students failing to register for their second year of study in 1999, for whatever reason, show that, in Swansea Institute, 32% failed to re-register. Swansea and Glamorgan's failure to re-register rates stood at 17% and 16%, compared with 5% at Cardiff and 2% at Aberystwyth.[20] The pattern indicates that, in the older and more prestigious law schools, there is a wider demographic selection base alongside a clear numerical domination in those schools of students coming from social class one. There appears to be a relationship between social class and retention rates, although, as we shall demonstrate, there are other factors which are likely to impact upon retention figures.[21]

---

17 (2000) *Western Mail*, 11 April.

18 (1999) *The Guardian*, 9 August.

19 Rees, Thomas and Todd, 2000.

20 There is tabulated evidence that the well qualified, well heeled students produce the best completion rates. For example, East London University students, 40% of whom are from working class homes, are least likely to complete their courses. (1999) *The Times*, 3 December.

21 The law schools in question are Aberystwyth, Cardiff, Glamorgan, Swansea and Swansea Institute. Aberystwyth, the oldest, Cardiff, the largest, and Swansea, the youngest, are constituent colleges of the federal University of Wales. Cardiff University is the only one of the five institutions which is a member of the Russell Group, the elite, research-led consortium of UK universities. Glamorgan is a former polytechnical college, which became a university with the removal of the binary line in 1992, and Swansea Institute is a College of Higher Education.

POVERTY IN THE UK

University entrance does not simply happen as part of the natural educational progression of teenagers. Not all able students will go onto attend institutions of higher education, nor will they necessarily enter those institutions for which they are intellectually qualified. Poverty impacts negatively on opportunity and development. It may defeat knowledge, ambition and achievement. Poor people are not the same as rich people, but with simply less money. In 1999, the Education and Employment Committee of the House of Commons concluded:

> We have demonstrated that there are persisting inequalities in participation despite great progress in recent years in expanding participation and encouraging the participation of under-represented groups. Factors influencing participation and subsequent success are, as we have seen, family background and academic achievement during compulsory education. But the latter is strongly linked to the former. In the words of the Kennedy report, 'if at first you don't succeed, you don't succeed'. The obverse of this is also true: if at first you succeed, you continue to succeed. There are incremental benefits to early success in learning.[22]

The UK is rich. The principal issue is that of distribution of the financial resources. Average income rose in the 1980s by 23% in real terms, but for the lowest tenth of the population it fell by 6%. The proportion of citizens living in poverty, defined as 60% of the average income, rose to twice the level of 30 years ago.[23] In 1992, government figures revealed that, in 1979, the poorest fifth of the population had just under 10% of post-tax income and the richest fifth had 37%. By 1989, the poorest fifth had 7%, whilst the richest fifth had moved up to 43%.[24]

On the turn of the millennium, poverty remains a serious issue within the UK. Today, nearly 20% of children are rated as living in relative poverty, with 29% living in families with incomes below the official poverty line. While the number of children in poverty has remained stable in other industrial nations over the past 20 years, it has tripled in the UK. Children in lone families are nearly three and a half times more likely to fall prey to poverty and a child living in a household where there is no working adult is four times more likely to experience poverty.[25]

More generally, the numbers of those classified as very poor has increased by one million since 1996, according to another recent study by the Joseph

---

22 Eighth Report, HC 57-1, November 1999, p xii.
23 (1992) *The Guardian*, 18 November.
24 (1992) *Economic Trends*, January.
25 UNICEF survey, 'Child poverty in rich nations' (2000) *The Times*, 17 March and 13 June.

Rowntree Foundation.[26] Between 1995 and 1998, the number of people living on 'very low incomes', defined as below 40% of the national average, rose by one million to eight million. In relation to education, the co-author of the study, Katherine Howarth, stated: '... 11 year olds in schools where 35% or more children were on free meals did significantly worse in tests than those in other schools.'[27] This disturbing picture was reinforced by another recent survey. It stated that the gap between the rich and the poor has widened since the Labour government was returned and, in 1999, the gap reached the same proportions as at the end of Mrs Thatcher's term in office.[28] In July 2000, data from the Department of Social Security revealed that the number of people living in households on less than half the average income rose from 16.9% to 17.7% during Labour's term of office. The DSS figures also show that child poverty rose from 3.3 m to 3.4 m during Labour's first 24 months in office. During this period, the richest 10% of the population saw their household income rise by 7.1%, compared with 4.3% during the last two years of Conservative government. The poorest 10% saw their incomes rise by 1.9% under the Labour government. The social security secretary, Alistair Darling, stated: '... the report confirms the scale of the problem we need to turn around.'[29]

Within the context of a society deeply divided on the grounds of income, and the various resources that become both available and accessible as a result of individual status, the government declared that it intended to remove the maintenance grant for higher education students and to introduce student tuition fees.

STUDENT POVERTY

It appears that poverty is considered by government to be an inevitable condition of student life. The National Union of Students calculated that between 1979 and 1992, the value of the grant declined by 31% in real terms. In addition, a survey by the NUS demonstrated that 60% of students whose parents were assessed to make a contribution received no financial support from them.[30] During the 1990s, the Conservative government disentitled students to social security benefits, income support, unemployment benefit and, particularly, housing benefit. Various other student benefits, such as the

---

26 Joseph Rowntree Foundation Study, 1999, London: New Policy Institute. (2000) *The Times*, 8 December.

27 *Ibid*.

28 Office of National Statistics, April 2000. (2000) *The Times*, 13 April.

29 (2000) *The Guardian*, 14 July.

30 (1992) *AUT Bulletin*, March.

right to reclaim travel expenses, the provision of special equipment grants, vacation hardship grants and, in certain cases, free prescriptions for dental and optical work were removed in the latter part of the 1980s.

The student loan scheme was introduced in 1990. Barclays Bank, involved in the student banking market, commissioned a survey in 1992 which concluded:

> Over the past seven years, the government changes to benefit regulations have steadily eroded a major source of student income. The recent recession has destroyed a high proportion of vacation jobs. Hence we would expect student debt to be on a sharp rise at present.[31]

Lancaster University commissioned a project in 1992 on mature students and poverty. The findings were that the plight of many students with families, but limited access to State benefits, is desperate. Unlike younger students, who are barred from benefits, students with children could claim housing benefit if they paid rent, but that amount would be reduced because the maintenance grant contained a housing element. Those with mortgages could claim no help. The report concluded that mature students suffered more, because they were unlikely to be able to go home to parents during vacations. One student said:

> Having to pay child care fees during the term leaves you with a huge deficit despite the fact that the university pays about two-thirds of child care costs. I still have to find the money to buy books and paper and food for my children and myself.[32]

Given that the personal is also political, then the experiences of a student brings a sense of individuality and personal appreciation to the 'facts argument' which so often dominates the important issues of responsibility, welfarism and human dignity. Lee Walker was a young, final year undergraduate in London. He expected to graduate with significant debts. His observations were:

> I think the student grant reduction is terrible. Coupled with the terrible state of graduate unemployment, how can Kenneth Clarke say that poorer families aren't going to be deterred? If I'd heard that, as an 18 year old, I would think twice about going to university ... I lived in a Sherpa high-top van last year ... I spend very little on drink, probably about one or two pints a week and that's about it unless I have a night out occasionally. But I don't go out much – I can't.[33]

Lord Addington summed up the Conservative government's higher education policy and its achievements by declaring: 'Government has

---

31 Barclays Bank, 'Marketing to students', August 1992 and (1992) *The Times*, 15 August.
32 (1992) *The Guardian*, 3 August.
33 (1993) *The Independent*, 1 December.

expanded the ways into university, but not the ways of eating once you get there.'[34]

Current data makes equally depressing reading as students juggle their financial commitments with inadequate income, often obliging them to seek increasingly long hours of paid employment in order to maintain viable living standards. Researchers have identified increasing mental health problems amongst the student population to be an inevitable consequence of such stress-related lives. Money worries, poor housing, inappropriate diet, overwork, and less study time are classic ingredients for psychosocial stress.[35] Dr Roberts of Westminster University surveyed two London universities, one old and one new. More than half those questioned worked 20 hours a week for money in addition to studying. He said that his research:

> ... found students' general health, notably on measures of physical vitality, psychological and social functioning, was substantially worse than that of young people of the equivalent age and sex in the general population. Poor mental health was related to longer working hours outside university and difficulty in paying bills, while those considering abandoning study because of financial difficulties were likely to have poorer mental and physical health. Using these measures, students were on average twice as likely to be in poor health when compared to non-students of the same sex and age. Being in debt was further associated with increased drug use, lowered vitality, considering abandoning study, and being more likely to know students who are involved in prostitution, drug dealing and other criminal activities in order to support themselves financially.[36]

In February 1999, the National Union of Students published a national student hardship survey which found 75% of students to be in debt. Nearly 20% of undergraduates estimated their debt would be £9,000 at the end of their course. Students were spending over half of their income on accommodation and 40% of students undertook part time paid employment during term time. Twenty-five percent could not meet study-related costs, such as field trips and lab fees, owing to hardship, and half of the employed students stated that debt detrimentally affected their studies. Half of the students had contemplated giving up their course, with financial problems rating highly as the reason.[37] An underclass of students has been created.

In 1999, the research group Income Data Services established that nearly 900,000 students in full time education hold down part time jobs, compared with 320,000 in 1984. In a structured economy that supports portfolio and part time employment, it is no surprise that students accounted for a quarter of the workforce at Sainsbury's; a third at Waitrose and 40% at Kwik Save. The

---

34   (1993) *The Times*, Higher Education Supplement, 19 February.

35   Roberts, Golding and Towell, *The Psychologist*, 1998, p 489.

36   (1999) *The Guardian*, 2 February.

37   (1999) *NUS News*, 25 February.

report continued: 'The employment of students is no longer casual but has become structural. They are sought after by leading firms in the retail sector, in pubs and hotels, in fast food and in call centres.'[38] Students cannot be in paid work and at university simultaneously. A National Union of Students' survey discovered that one in five students has failed to submit study assignments because of paid employment commitments and one in three is missing lectures because of part time employment. Over 78% of students working during term time believed that their study has been affected detrimentally.[39]

Personal and recent experiences as a law school teacher include a student fainting in class and later apologising on the grounds that she had not eaten that day through lack of money. Another student had been unable to attend an interview as he did not have appropriate clothing and, finally, as one of the authors was working this chapter, he was asked for a phone interview from a reporter for a national newspaper. The interview was on student debt. During the interview, the reporter declared she was a recent history graduate and she was seeking to repay her student debts which stood at £11,000.

LAW STUDENT POVERTY

For law students, the financial commitments are even greater, as they are obliged to finance a fourth year of university study without any possibility of State funding or State loans for either fees or maintenance. Indeed, Lord Donaldson, when Master of the Rolls, highlighted the predicament of debt-ridden law students when he referred to the *de facto* 'pre-qualification means test' that now operates.[40] This position has prevailed for some years, as illustrated by the survey conducted by the College of Law in 1993.[41] A random sample of 10% of the college's 4,200 students showed that 40% had an outstanding overdraft before commencing the course. Half the sample indicated that they had less than £25 a week after payment of fees, rent and travel expenses. Despite advice to the contrary from the college, one-sixth had taken part time employment,[42] while 10% were seriously considering abandoning the course. Over 90% had borrowed money from parents, relatives or friends. In 1993, final debts of £10,000 were not uncommon.

---

38 BBC News Online Network, 11 January 1999.

39 (1996) *NUS News Release*, 25 March.

40 (1992) *Law Society Gazette*, 13 May.

41 Survey of Students' Funding and Finance on the Law Society's Final Course 1992–93 at the College of Law, February 1993.

42 There is evidence that female students are increasingly working in the sex industry. (1993) *The Observer*, 11 April.

One of the authors of this chapter undertook a survey of undergraduates at the then four Welsh law schools in 1993.[43] Fifty-one percent of the students had either received, applied or anticipated applying for a student loan. Seventy-one percent had either received or applied for overdraft facilities.

Professor Bob Lee, currently director of the Centre for Legal Practice at Cardiff Law School, asked this question: 'Will you, the student, really be brave enough to pursue a career in the law with £10,000–£15,000 of debt?'[44] The answer continues to be 'yes', but for some, the course appears to be, or becomes, too demanding. The cost of the vocational course, which does not attract automatic funding, coupled with the cost of living expenses which are on top of the debts accumulated as an undergraduate, add up to a awesome debt package. For example, Nick Armstrong, former chairman of the Solicitors Trainee Group, stated: 'I have a friend in a bigger firm whose loans all kicked in at the same time. She is trying to live on a £100 a month.' It is not uncommon for newly qualified lawyers to have outstanding loans in the region of £20,000.[45]

LAW SCHOOLS IN WALES

Our first-year law student survey was completed in 2000, and covers the five Welsh law schools: Aberystwyth, Cardiff, Glamorgan, Swansea and Swansea Institute.[46] Aberystwyth is the oldest institution; Cardiff is the largest and most prestigious; Glamorgan, based in Pontypridd, is a former polytechnic; Swansea is the newest school, and Swansea Institute is a college of higher education which commenced law teaching by offering the London external law degree and currently offers a franchised law programme. Aberystwyth, Cardiff and Swansea are constituent colleges of the federal University of Wales. The research project involved the use of a questionnaire administered in class in each of the law schools very early in the first semester of the first year. The timing was deliberate, and attempted to minimise the effects of the culturalisation process experienced by new students.

A brief profile of each school's intake is offered. Interesting in itself, it is particularly relevant when we move on to the issue of recruitment into legal practice. The gender division of the students in the survey is 40% male and 60% female. This breakdown is reproduced across each of the institutions with only marginal deviations. The average age of first year law students is 20.

43 For an account of the findings see (1993) *Solicitors Journal*, 12 March, (1993) *The Independent*, 12 March and Thomas (1993) 27 Law Teacher 152, p 153.

44 (1998) *The Lawyer*, 20 October.

45 (1998) *Law Society Gazette*, 30 September.

46 Rees, Thomas and Todd, 2000.

Overall, 89% of the first year student population are aged between 18 and 21. Aberystwyth, Cardiff and Swansea universities report above-average numbers of students in this category. With 97% in this category, Aberystwyth appears almost exclusively populated by students aged between 18 and 21. Glamorgan and Swansea Institute have well above-average numbers of students aged over 21 years. Almost 50% of the first year students attending Swansea Institute are over 21, while in Glamorgan this age category accounts for almost one-third of first year students.

Of the total survey, 93% of the students describe their status as single. Of the five institutions, only Swansea Institute varies significantly from this average, with 64% describing their status as single. The students were also asked if they were supporting any other person either physically or economically whilst studying. Overall, 5% indicated that they had dependants. Again, Swansea Institute, with its older students, varied substantially from this figure, with 29% indicating that they had dependants.

Students who described their ethnic backgrounds as Welsh or English comprise the overwhelming majority of students in all five schools. Overall, 38% of students described themselves as Welsh and 47% as English. Aberystwyth had the highest number of English students, 63%, and Swansea Institute had 74% who classified themselves as Welsh. Other ethnicities, as 'home' students, were poorly represented.[47]

Forty-two percent of the students in the survey are from social class 2. This figure is reflected across the five institutions with little variation. A third of the Aberystwyth students are from social class 1 compared with 7% at Swansea Institute. Glamorgan and Swansea Institute have the largest number of students from social class 3, with 42% and 48% respectively.

Eighty-eight percent of the students went to law school directly from full time education. However, 32% of Swansea Institute's entry went from either secondary school or sixth form college, as compared with 76% from those sources in Aberystwyth. Further education colleges and non-educational entry accounted for 64% of Swansea Institute's students, compared with 8% at Aberystwyth.

The introduction of tuition fees was not well received by the students. They went further, and 91% declared that the new levy will put off some people from going to university. The average tuition payment, scaled to reflect personal financial circumstances, is £868. A female Aberystwyth student wrote: 'I personally know a fair number of people who have now chosen not to go to university, simply because they believe they cannot afford it.' Eighty-nine percent believed that the fee will lead to some students experiencing 'real

---

47 The project was aimed exclusively at 'home' students. For example, the figures and results would be very different if overseas, full fee-paying students were introduced to the survey. In Cardiff, some 20% of the first year class is composed of overseas students.

poverty'; 77% of the students anticipate being in debt at the end of their degree course. On average, the anticipated debt figure was £6,000. However, for those wishing to pursue a legal career, they will have to add on the fees for the vocational year, which currently stand at around £7,000.

It was also clear from the returns that these students are forging a new relationship with their university. No longer should they be seen as grateful recipients of knowledge, provided as, when and how the academic staff choose to deliver it. Instead, their payment of fees has transformed them into consumers, with expectations and contractual rights. Of course, the contractual relationship existed previously, but surfaced infrequently, because of the overriding, more powerful student-professor relationship. Now, 68% of the students believe that paying fees will lead students to expect value for money. Glamorgan and Cardiff students made the following observations:

> Unfortunately, paying tuition fees is going to become the norm. I do not like the fact, but if we are required to pay them I believe the money should go to help improve the quality of education and the facilities offered.

> I think it is ridiculous we have to pay £1,000 for tuition fees. Why do our parents pay their taxes? I think that for our £1,000 we should have our stationery and books provided, because what are we getting out of the £1,000? Surely the teaching this year is of the same standard as last year. Tuition fees will dissuade able students from coming to university, which is discrimination.

> The introduction of tuition fees alongside the abolition of grants will inevitably lead to an even bigger class divide and result in more people being unable to even contemplate university as an option.

The questionnaire focused on how students were responding to the increasing financial pressures. Fifty-four per cent expected to undertake paid employment during the semesters as well as study. Sixty-five per cent of Glamorgan students intended to work; Aberystwyth had a figure of 36%. A female student at Glamorgan stated:

> Money is very tight and is going to be more difficult next year. I'm finding it difficult to hold a part time job of 12 hours and trying to cope with the work of a degree. My time management is all over the place. Which is more important, time devoted to the degree or paying your rent by working?

A female student at Swansea reported: 'Due to the introduction of the £1,000 tuition fee I need a job in term time as my parents have not had enough time to save for this unexpected expense.'

What emerges are law schools with very different characteristics, student profiles and student expectations. For example, Swansea Institute and Glamorgan service local, residential communities. They attract significant numbers of mature students, many of whom have family and domestic commitments. Their expectations are high, as is their commitment. Nevertheless, the attrition rate from year one to year two is also high. Thirty-two per cent of the students at Swansea Institute failed to register for the second year, and in Glamorgan and Swansea, the figures stood at 16% and 17% respectively. The Cardiff and Aberystwyth figures were 5% and 2%. On the other hand, Cardiff attracts highly qualified, young, single students from throughout the UK, 90% of whom have selected the school as their first choice UCAS selection. Their expectations are equally high, but the survey demonstrates that their expectations are matched by their higher levels of confidence, partly based on personal contacts, about obtaining appropriate employment as a result of having studied at a premier law school. Indeed, there is a strong correlation between their stated reasons for law school selection and their anticipation of subsequently obtaining a suitable legal position. Eighty-nine percent of the Cardiff students stated that they selected the law school because potential employers will have heard of it. We return to this relationship between school selection and employment later in the chapter, but it is clear that this is a significant feature for those students who can afford the extra costs of studying anywhere in the country and have the appropriate grades to enter the university of their choice.

TUITION FEES

These fees were introduced through the Teaching and Higher Education Act 1998. The Act, which was described by the Education Secretary, David Blunkett, as 'putting in place new funding arrangements designed to address the funding crisis we inherited',[48] also abolished the maintenance grant.

Tuition fees were greeted by students with widespread hostility. For example, the president of the National Union of Students responded by saying that the arrangements were unfair and unlikely to work.[49] Currently, bad debts from student non-payers stand at £3.5 m, although some 97% of students had paid for the first year of the tuition fee programme.[50] Non-payment programmes have been activated and at Oxford University, 14 students were suspended for non-payment. Earlier, 50 students had occupied an administrative building as a protest. A High Court writ was required to obtain their removal.[51] The tuition fee, in England and Wales, for the academic year 2000–01 is £1,025 and this figure, along with the principle of tuition fees, has been received negatively by university staff. It has been reported in a national survey that nearly two-thirds of academics are against fees for first degrees. Only 26% agreed with the principle of fees and most of

---

48   BBC Online Network, 17 July 1998.
49   *Ibid*.
50   (2000) *The Guardian*, 4 February.
51   (2000) *The Guardian*, 12 January.

them preferred graduated fees depending on the prestige of the university attended.[52]

The current debate involves the move towards top-up fees applied by those universities that are research-led and in more demand for student places. An enhanced, self-regulated fee structure imposed by the elite universities is not a new proposal. In July 2000, a report commissioned by the 19-member Russell Group of universities reopened the issue.

EDUCATION AND ELITISM

The selection procedures at top UK universities have recently come under close scrutiny. Elitism and bias against students from State schools has been at the forefront of media and political debate. Arguably, politicians from all parties have jumped on eradicating elitism in higher education as a popular and winnable issue at the expense of other, more fundamental and challenging issues. Behind the headlines and political soundbites there lie serious inequalities in access to higher education in the UK.

For the overwhelming majority of students, the offer of a place at university is based on a student's actual or predicted performance at 'A' level. To get into the top universities, students need to get the top grades. Private schools educate only 8% of the nation's children, but students from private schools account for one-third of all students achieving three 'A' grades at 'A' level. In the furore surrounding the elitism debate, this anomaly has attracted little attention. Addressing the reasons why pupils from State schools are not performing as well as their counterparts in the private sector does not appear to be a popular and winnable issue.

Turning cases into causes is rare, but not unknown within the political context.[53] Laura Spence was an 18 year old student in North Tyneside's Monkseaton Community High School. She applied to Magdalen College, Oxford, to read medicine. She had already achieved 10 GCSEs with 'A' grades and her predicted 'A' level grades were equally strong. She was one of 22 applicants interviewed for five places. As a result of a college interview, her classification was number 11 and, therefore, was unsuccessful. The leaked report of the interviewer described her thus: '... as with other comprehensive school pupils, low in confidence and difficult to draw out of herself despite being able to manifestly think on her feet.'[54] However, with the support of her American headteacher, she subsequently received admission to Harvard

---

52 (2000) *The Guardian*, 14 March.
53 A recent illustration is the murder of Stephen Lawrence, a black London youth. See, for a general account, Bridges, 1999, p 298.
54 (2000) *The Guardian*, 27 May.

University, along with a handsome financial support package of £65,000, which was granted on the basis of a means test.

Magdalen College's rejection of Miss Spence became a public issue as a result of the critical speech made by the Chancellor of the Exchequer, Gordon Brown, to a TUC audience in London. He denounced the rejection as 'an absolute scandal' and that she had been a victim of:

> ... an interview system that is more reminiscent of the old boy network and old school tie than genuine justice in our society. It is about time we had an end to that old Britain when what matters to some people is the privileges you were born with rather than the potential you actually have. I say it is now time that these old universities open their doors to women and to people from all backgrounds. And we are determined that in the next 10 years the majority of young people will be able to get higher education.[55]

The speech had been personally sanctioned by the Prime Minister and subsequently was supported by the Deputy Prime Minister. The Education and Employment Secretary, David Blunkett, described her rejection as 'an absolute scandal'. At the time of these statements, the government was experiencing a mid-term dip in the polls and the Prime Minister had been buffeted by a number of personal attacks and gaffes. Consequently, the political attack could be explained away as a diversion tactic. Certainly, Brown's statement set the political hounds running, as opposition spokespeople followed his trail into this debate. Even Spence's interviewer at Magdalen entered the lists and roundly condemned the government for introducing tuition fees.

In July 2000, the Sutton Trust found that the top five universities admitted 50% more privately educated students than would be expected and 40% fewer from lower social classes. The bias continued when the top 13 universities were included in the review.[56] The survey found that 39% of places in all subjects at the top 13 universities were filled by students from independent schools. The report concluded that, if the selection had been purely according to grades, the figure should have been 28%. The Trust's report states that a student from a private school is nearly 30 times more likely to get into a top-13 university than one from a disadvantaged background. About 600,000 children pass through the education system each year, around 50% of whom come from less affluent families. Of them, 3,500, or 0.9%, were admitted to the top 13 universities. The Trust concludes: '... the field from which the country recruits its future elite turns out to be extraordinarily narrow.'[57]

As central government funding has diminished, universities have been obliged to seek alternative sources of support. The tuition fee is one such

---

55   (2000) *The Guardian*, 26 May.
56   (2000) *The Guardian*, 27 May.
57   (2000) *The Guardian,* 28 May.

controversial source. In addition, the Russell Group is also investigating the prospect of top-up tuition fees. This suggestion is not new, but has not gathered serious support until the present time. For example, in 1993, John Ashworth, then director of the London School of Economics, promoted an additional annual tuition fee payment of £500. This was rejected by his staff colleagues. In the same year, a report commissioned by the Committee of Vice Chancellors and Principals mooted repayable loan schemes similar to those operating in Australia and also a graduate tax scheme. Another illustration of the financial plight of higher education was the threat by 104 Vice Chancellors in 1996 to impose a £300 registration levy on all students as of September 1997. Again, top-up fees were discussed by the elite universities. Professor Harris, Vice Chancellor of Manchester University, stated: 'If no appropriate funding arrangement is put in place, a substantial number of universities will be driven to go to income sources derived from students.'[58] In response to the suggestion that students should pay part of their tuition fees, a Labour spokesman said his party did not propose asking students to contribute towards the cost of fees. 'Once you start doing that, where do you draw the line? The danger is that you would end up with students paying all their fees.'[59]

July 2000 saw the publication of yet another report which seeks to address and help resolve the ongoing university funding crisis. The Greenaway-Haynes Report, commissioned by the Russell Group, notes that, in real terms, government financial support is down nearly 50% since 1980. The paper is premised on the challengeable argument that the rich students should subsidise the poor students and that the beneficiaries of higher education, the students who will earn above-average salaries, should pay the true cost of their education. Alongside this move, there should be generous scholarship funds and subsidised loan funds. The report states that a new annual limit of £4,000 could raise £3 bn a year, thereby funding bursaries to support less well-off students, improve the pay of staff and support less popular courses. The report notes that about 23% of undergraduates come from independent schools where fees can cost between £4,800 and £15,000 a year. Thus, it is suggested that, for a significant number of students, there is hardly an ability-to-pay problem.

The case of Laura Spence is used to illustrate the attraction of the US educational programme. This is a clear move in the direction of US university education, where market forces decide the tuition fees at various universities. For example, in the State of Massachusetts, home of MIT and Harvard, some 41 universities charge tuition fees of more than £10,000. The State university charges in-State fees of £3,000. Indeed, one of the authors of the Greenaway-

---

58   (1996) *The Independent*, 2 February.
59   (1996) *The Independent*, 18 September.

Haynes Report, David Blanchflower, a professor at Dartmouth College, USA, suggests that the tuition fees could creep up to US levels. The findings have found favour with some Vice Chancellors within the Russell Group. However, within a week of publication, a conference organised by the Royal Economic Society heard economists counsel caution against a move to increase or deregulate fees. Robin Naylor stated: 'Top up fees are likely to deter students from less privileged backgrounds and differential fees are likely to deter them further from courses which lead to better paid careers.'[60] One concern is that professions with potentially high financial returns, such as law, will remain the preserve of the middle classes.

The Greenaway-Haynes Report claims that poor students will not be excluded from the appropriate universities by virtue of deregulation of tuition fees. But existing data unequivocally presents a student community already segregated, not on the basis of ability, but along class and financial lines. The Labour government's commitment to oppose top-up tuition fees at the elite universities also appears to be increasingly wobbly. David Blunkett has announced that another strategic review of higher education will occur five years after the Dearing Inquiry, which reported in July 1997. He further stated that he 'would not be Secretary of State forever' and the question of charging differential fees could not be ruled out. Indeed, a spokesman for Mr Blunkett stated that, whilst the government's position was unchanged, 'he recognised that there is a need for an intellectually rigorous debate on the subject'. A rigorous, pragmatic response was forthcoming from Sir Howard Newby, Vice Chancellor of Southampton University, when he commented: 'We know there's not going to be any change in fees until after the general election.'[61] In the meantime, several governmental and non-governmental initiatives have been set in place.

David Blunkett has pledged £4 m to identify, recruit and retain bright students in areas of low university take-up by offering 'opportunity bursaries' of up to £1,000. The government is also providing places for 5,000 sixth formers in university summer schools. The scheme, entitled 'Excellence in cities summer schools', involves year 11 and 12 students from 24 inner city boroughs and has taken place in 70 universities. The aim is to raise the aspirations and awareness of these students.[62] David Blunkett described the programme 'an exciting initiative which should really make a difference, giving young people a taste of what higher education has to offer.'[63]

In the Comprehensive Spending Review, presented to Parliament in July 2000, the Chancellor announced an extra £100 m for higher education in

---

60 (2000) *The Guardian*, 11 July.
61 (2000) *The Guardian*, 16 February.
62 An account of the programme is found in Watson and Bowden, 2000.
63 (2000) *The Guardian*, 25 July.

England in 2001–02. Of this money, £50 m is for targeted pay increases; £20 m is for student access and the remaining £30 m is for initiatives, such as the e-universities project and the two year foundation degree prototypes. This money is in addition to the extra £10 m announced by Blunkett in May 2000 for bursaries for potential students from non-traditional higher education backgrounds. The Association of University Teachers welcomed this major investment and announced that the money 'may one day be seen as the turning point in Britain's universities. Gordon Brown has made a start on reversing two decades of neglect and starvation suffered by Britain's universities'.[64]

Other schemes endorsed by government include twinning universities with inner-city schools, and also employing 'ambassadors' to encourage students in poorer areas to apply to university and develop a process of talent-spotting able school students at an early stage. One leading law school, Bristol University, implemented a programme in the academic year 1993–94 which is constructed to attract non-traditional entrants into the law school. In October 1997, the scheme was allocated 20 ring-fenced undergraduate places and more seats were requested:

> The objective of the programme is to achieve greater diversity in the profile of our students – partly through widening educational opportunity and partly to enhance the quality of the teaching and learning environment – whilst not dropping the high standards expected of successful students.[65]

The principles which drive the scheme are recruitment of students from poorly resourced schools; students from backgrounds which suggest other educational disadvantages; local schools; students identified as outstanding by their institution; and also, students who have shown some recognised characteristics of academic quality. The tutors have analysed the results over the years and their conclusions are that: '... the results of the alternative admissions students so far suggest that, despite their sometimes lower 'A' level grades, these students in general do not fair any better or worse than their mainstream counterparts.'

Finally, arising out of the Laura Spence case, the House of Commons Education Committee announced, in May 2000, an inquiry into the admissions procedures of the leading universities.

---

64   AUT Press Release, 18 July 2000.
65   Internal memorandum, Bibbings, L and Cowans, D, *Alternative Admissions Tutors*, October 1998. Information supplied by the tutors.

CONCLUSION

During the 19th century and for much of the 20th century, the economy of the UK was dependent upon capital financial investment. It was the age of the machine. Today, we live in the knowledge society, where human resources, heavily dependent upon educated and trained personnel, are dominant. Whereas there is political recognition and approval of this major shift of economic activity, the necessary level of training required to ensure the success of the new economy appears not to be 'joined up'. Legal education is one such example.

With full time students increasingly turning to part time employment to underwrite their degree programme, their *de facto* status raises the question: how should university staff differentiate between full and part time students? Legal studies are notoriously demanding, but how much academic work can be expected of this new hybrid student? How should law schools schedule their classes, seminars, reading and writing commitments, and library opening hours? We know that, increasingly, students have other, often inflexible commitments that may take priority over their studies. Shift work may make library usage difficult, whilst on the other hand, financially constrained librarians may declare it uneconomic to keep open law libraries in the evenings and at weekends. Should law lectures and seminars be offered at what have traditionally been considered anti-social hours? Should classes remain compulsory? Should lectures be on video and stocked in the library? How can the internet be employed for the benefit of full time as well as part time students? How quickly will the 'virtual' university and law school develop? When will the computer's 'school room' replace the 'chat room'?

Financial considerations will also impact upon the realistic choice of university for many students. The number of home-based students is likely to increase dramatically as the cost of rented accommodation is factored into the rapidly rising price of university study. Inner city universities and those with a large travel-to-study population will become more popular. Universities sited in economically active areas or with large populations offer greater opportunity of part time employment in the leisure and retail sectors. In contrast, the smaller, the more remote and also the 'green field' universities established in the 1960s and 1970s may find it increasingly difficult to recruit residential students. For example, Aberystwyth, an old and prestigious law school, recruits up to half of its intake through the clearing process. The UCAS figures for 1999–2000 indicate that one in six students will elect to live at home whilst engaged in full time university study. This figure is up 2.3% on the previous year. Tony Higgins, chief executive of UCAS, stated that, whilst mature student applications are down, the deferred entry numbers are up. This could, in part, be accounted for by the need to 'earn money to help towards their costs at university and college'.[66] Those students with money and appropriate entry qualifications will have the widest selection of law schools, but for those who lack the financial support, the choice will be limited. The broad social mix, much talked about during the debate arising out of the Laura Spence case, will be even more difficult to achieve.

The 'new' inner-city law schools whose recruitment profiles identify disproportionately high numbers of access and mature students, local school leavers and ethnic minorities, may discover a new entrant: the highly qualified, but financially poor, local student.

A consequence of this emerging undergraduate 'selection' process will become apparent when students seek to enter the legal profession. Entry into the global law firms based in the City of London will be impossible under current hiring criteria. These firms are not instruments of social engineering. They are profit-making organisations run for the benefit of the owners: the partners. Their recruitment policies and activities do not stretch to the new generation of law schools. Clifford Chance, a 'global' law firm with 1,996 fee earners, advised law students that, in order to obtain a City training contract, they should follow a 'simple' formula: 'Go to a good university, get a 2.1 and have a fantastic personality.'[67] There has always been an informal league table of universities and of law schools. However, this has now received semi-official recognition through the creation of the Russell Group, the publication of the Research Assessment Exercise findings, and the funding-by-results policy adopted by the government. The paradoxical policy ensures that the weaker law schools receive less funding than the law schools that are perceived as successful. Thus, ambitious staff seek appointments at the research-led law schools, where staff to student ratios are more favourable, law libraries are better stocked, superior information technology resources are provided, and better-qualified students are attracted. The consequence is an increasing differential between the top and bottom of this ever-widening league table. However, the 'good' law schools will not necessarily have all the quality students if the financial picture we present continues to develop. The best law schools will have 'good', but also relatively wealthy students. A challenge for law firms and chambers is to recognise and respond to this emerging pattern of university law graduates.

Students applying to law school need to be aware of the training, career, and financial implications of where they study. For example, in 1998–99, some 66% of male graduates from Oxbridge obtained pupillage as compared with 10% from the 'new' universities. Solicitors' recruitment policies differ, but it is not unusual for some to reject applicants simply because they are from new universities. City of London firms offer 30% of all training contracts. The

---

66 (2000) *The Times*, Higher Education Supplement, 21 July.
67 (2000) *The Trainee*, May.

average salary for a City firm trainee is £20,000. The average salary for a trainee in Wales is £11,500. In London, as a whole, 5% of trainees are paid at or below the Law Society's recommended minimum salary. In Wales, that figure rises to 54%.

Students not destined to join 'the magic circle' of elite City law firms look to medium sized, provincial firms and small, high street practices. Law Society statistics indicate that the number of these firms is decreasing. For many of those law graduates, of whom many will have also completed their legal practice course, their initiation into the legal work place will be as paralegals. Paid below the recommended level for trainee solicitors, they will undertake similar work in the hope that their contracts will be subsequently converted to that of trainee solicitor.

On average, newly qualified solicitors in high street practices in Cardiff earn £17,000, dropping to £14,000 in legal aid practices in the economically depressed areas of South Wales. Base salaries for their counterparts in leading City law firms commence at over £40,000, with some US law firms, based in London, offering newly qualified solicitors salaries of £100,000. These are rich rewards, but only for very few graduates. The institutional discrimination of some leading firms and chambers in turn reflects the choices and non-choices that law graduates have experienced. Whilst the Law Society of England and Wales and the Bar Council seek to broaden access to the profession, senior practitioners appear reluctant to act in similar fashion. However, it is the government and its move towards free market economics, incorporating the relentless growth of self-financing by university students, which needs to review its position. Generally, if universities are to have principal reliance on current levels of public funding, then the political ambitions of increased participation, improved access, enhancements of the skills base, innovation, and world class research will be frustrated. Specifically, in terms of the legal profession, the government's educational policy will also frustrate widening recruitment into the profession. Thus, the role of gatekeeper into the legal profession has become a political function.

CHAPTER 3

ALL DRESSED UP AND NOWHERE TO GO? PART TIME LAW STUDENTS AND THE LEGAL PROFESSION[1]

Andrew M Francis and Iain W McDonald

I think this is the sort of thing that dreams are made of. (B5)

[Student commenting on the part time LLB.]

INTRODUCTION

The success of a profession's project has traditionally been linked to its ability to maintain homogeneity[2] through the preservation of the power to control entry to the profession. Although the solicitors' profession is facing increasing fragmentation over a variety of issues,[3] there is evidence that it maintains a strong homogeneity in terms of the social composition of the profession. Concerns over the profession's continued homogeneity in terms of class, gender and race have been acknowledged by the Law Society.[4] One of the strategies that emerged from the Dearing Report on higher education was a clear endorsement that opportunities for distance learning and part time study should be increased, specifically to encourage mature students and other under-represented societal groups to participate in higher education. In order to assess the effectiveness of this project in respect of legal education, this chapter draws upon qualitative research conducted by the authors, based on a sample group of students on the part time LLB programme at the Rutland Metropolitan University.[5] Their views and opinions on the part time law degree will underpin our discussion of the increase in part time legal educational opportunities and its potential to impact upon the homogeneity of the profession. Integral to this discussion is a consideration of the barriers to practice these students perceive themselves as facing, as well as a preliminary

---

1   The authors wish to thank the Research Committee of Cardiff Law School for its financial support in funding this project. We would also like to thank the staff and students who participated in this study.

2   Larson, 1977; Abel, 1988.

3   Hanlon, 1997, 1999; Glasser, 1990.

4   The Law Society, 1999, and elsewhere in this book.

5   Rutland Metropolitan University is a fictitious name for the real institution where the research was carried out, which remains anonymous to preserve confidentiality. We owe a debt to Twining (1994 and 1998) for the creation of the fictitious University of Rutland and hence the name we have chosen for the university that is the subject of this chapter.

assessment of part time students' likelihood of overcoming impediments to entry into the legal profession.

In a period of difficult financial choices, the provision of part time routes of study provides law schools with the advantage of embracing the new culture of access for life long learners[6] while increasing their sources of overall revenue. In particular, the new universities created since the expansion of the polytechnic sector in the 1960s and in the wake of the Further and Higher Education Act 1992 in England and Wales have embraced, or continue to embrace, their long standing and distinctive tradition of access and innovation in teaching delivery through the provision of part time LLB programmes.[7] Abel[8] noted the loss of the legal profession's traditional 'gatekeeper'[9] role following the increasing importance of undergraduate education as an entry requirement. However, following the rapid expansion of the higher education system in the 1980s and 1990s, we consider that our understanding of who controls entry into the legal profession must be re-assessed.

THE EDUCATIONAL CONTEXT: THE PROVISION OF PART TIME AND DISTANCE LEARNING ROUTES TO LAW DEGREES

Since its inception, the part time route to an LLB has remained firmly the preserve of the polytechnic and new university sectors. Of the 79 universities in England and Wales currently entitled to award the LLB, a relatively healthy 29 offer a part time route to graduation.[10] Also, in a number of institutions such as Nottingham Trent, Wolverhampton and, since 1999, the Open University, there has been provision for the LLB to be taught through distance learning programmes. However, of those 29 institutions offering a part time LLB programme in England and Wales, only two are 'old' universities (Birkbeck and Hull).

The entry requirements of all institutions offering part time courses are designed with the need to encourage access to higher education explicitly in mind. As a result, non-academic criteria, such as informal interviews and employer references, are frequently emphasised over a requirement for formal educational qualifications in assessing an applicant's suitability for entry.

---

6   The centrality of life long learning within the government's broader education strategies has seen the appointment of Malcolm Wicks as Parliamentary Under-Secretary of State for Life Long Learning.

7   Leighton, 1998; Partington, 1992.

8   Abel, 1989, p 286.

9   Twining, in Dhavan, Kibble and Twining, 1989, Chapter 1.

10 This information was drawn from the website of the National Centre for Legal Education, based at Warwick University.

The opening quote of this chapter emphasises our finding that, for many of those students we talked with, the ability to do a law degree in itself is a dream already fulfilled. A choice to embark upon a course of part time study rarely represents an easy choice. For the majority of students, they have existing work or family commitments to balance with the time and financial costs that go hand in hand with higher education today. To this extent, the thirst for higher education would serendipitously appear to correspond with the need identified in the Dearing Report[11] for increased opportunity for higher education. It is within the context of our admiration for these students' endeavours that this research was conducted.

The study of part time law students at Rutland Metropolitan University

We approached this research with few explicit expectations of what we would find. From reviewing recent literature on legal education, we were left with the impression that the exploration and analysis of the part time route to a degree in law was most significant in its absence.[12] While much research notes its existence and confirms that it is indeed an innovative form of widening access to previously under-represented groups in society, the main focus of concern has remained on the full time degree route, its composition and future.[13] Therefore, with an ambit to find out more about how part time law students might stand in relation to a legal profession facing considerable upheaval, many of the ideas contained in this chapter are based on and inspired by the study we conducted in Spring 2000 of a sample of students currently enrolled on the Rutland Metropolitan University part time LLB programme.

The decision was taken to focus on Rutland Metropolitan University to explore the concerns and expectations of students who, over the next few years, will emerge as the first graduates of this particular scheme of study. All students enrolled on the part time LLB programme were invited to attend our research event to discuss their needs, expectations and views of the part time programme. The students were divided into small mixed year groups. To help overcome any initial reluctance to participate in the discussion, we showed each group a selection of clips from film and television that presented a range

---

11 1997, Report No 1, Chapter 1.

12 Kibble, in Dhavan, Kibble and Twining, 1989, does briefly note statistical aspects of part time legal education, eg, the growth rate of the provision of this mode of study throughout the 1980s (p 141) and Marsh, 1983, discusses part time degrees in his review of the provision of CNAA programmes. However, it is the paucity of in-depth material exploring the position of part timers that we hope to address in this and future studies.

13 McDonald, 1982; Sherr and Webb, 1989; Partington, 1992; Leighton, 1998 and, generally, Bradney and Cownie, 1998.

of different representations of the legal profession,[14] on which we asked them to comment. Following this, we conducted a series of semi-structured discussions encouraging the students to reflect upon their educational experience at Rutland Metropolitan University, as well as their aspirations and concerns for their future careers. These sessions were videotaped and transcribed *verbatim* for later analysis. The students are identified in this chapter by a code assigned by the research team following the focus groups. The comments are, therefore, entirely unattributable. For the most part, the statements of the participants are reproduced in full within the chapter. However, owing to considerations of space, some irrelevant information within particular sentences has been omitted.

The qualitative data derived from the focus groups is supported by quantitative material gathered from a questionnaire completed by the attending students and, subsequently, by over another quarter of the students registered on Rutland's part time LLB programme. Through these strategies it has been possible to gain a better understanding of a significant proportion of the part time cohort at Rutland. Moreover, while we make no claims to represent the views of all part time students, we do believe that the major themes that have emerged from these students' views can legitimately form the basis of an initial inquiry into part time students' needs, concerns and expectations – both for their degrees and beyond.

Before turning to an account and analysis of some of our findings, it is important to clarify some points about the data we have gathered and the composition of the groups spoken to in depth. We spoke to 20 students in depth at our research day and collated 19 corresponding quantitative questionnaires (one questionnaire was not returned). It is from these discussions that much of our illustrative data has been derived. However, as mentioned above, an additional 22 students completed the study's questionnaire. In addition to providing us with a clearer picture of the part time law degree cohort and their concerns and expectations for the future, this information also supplied a basis for comparison when assessing the significance of the themes that emerged more fully on the research day itself. While these figures may seem of limited value as a foundation for findings, there are several balancing factors that must be noted. The scale of part time schemes of study is almost inevitably smaller than for full time degree and CPE routes, whether by design or demand. As such, the students involved in this study represent over half of the entire Rutland cohort and span all years presently enrolled. In addition, our research day was held on a Saturday, which was, therefore, an additional commitment for interested students to accommodate, in particular for those in full time employment and/or with

---

14 These clips were from *The Devil's Advocate* (dir: Taylor Hackford, 1997), *The Sweet Hereafter* (dir: Atom Egoyan, 1997), *The Client* (dir: Joel Schumacher, 1994) and 'Marge in Chains', *The Simpsons* (9F20, 1993).

children's care to consider. As such, that the final turnout was less than the number of students who had registered their intention to attend the research day amply demonstrates the difficulties that part time students can face in undertaking even this more flexible route to a law degree.

The diversity of the students we encountered in our research suggests that Rutland Metropolitan University is going some way to meeting its mission statement to 'widen participation in higher education in [Rutland]'. Across the research sample, a significantly greater number of women (68%) than men (32%) participated in the study. However, both groups spanned a wide age range, from 21 to 71 years of age. The greatest concentration in ages was between 30 and 39, with 54% of the entire sample falling within this category. The other significant age groupings fell on either side of this category, but in the ranges 20–29 and 40–49, they totalled only 15 and 22% of the entire sample respectively. (However, it should be noted that there were no male participants in the 20–29 age group.) Finally, there was a small number of participants 50 years of age or over (7%) and one male participant over 70. However, one important dimension is absent from the sample covered by this study and, to our knowledge, from the present part time cohort, in that the entire part time law student body is white.[15]

However, within the sample there was also a broad diversity of occupational backgrounds. These ranged from a number of unemployed students to those employed in local government or social services, to the head of creative services in a local advertising agency. Despite this, it is interesting to note that 12% of the sample were already working in some capacity within solicitors' firms.

Nearly 60% of the sample expressed a desire to enter the legal profession. A further 27% of the sample indicated that they are undertaking the part time law degree to enhance their current career and a further [24%] indicated some other future plans. These other plans ranged from entering the teaching profession, to the continued enjoyment of a retirement brightened by a law degree undertaken purely for interest. It should be noted that the overlap in terms of percentages results from some students entering two or three possible future career plans, thereby perhaps demonstrating some awareness of the uncertainty that their post-graduation careers may hold. Despite this uncertainty, there was a clear intention from this sample that they did intend to enter the legal profession. The potential barriers that they may face in joining the legal profession will be explored in the following section.

---

15 The absence of ethnic minorities from the Rutland Metropolitan sample obviously limits the potential generality of our findings. However, we would hope that any further research would be able to take account of a broader ethnic background.

OBSTACLES TO PRACTICE

Before part time students can hope to join the ranks of the legal profession, there are a number of significant barriers to overcome before they commence study, during their legal education and following the successful completion of the LLB. As the higher education sector continues to grow at a dramatic rate, there is an increased expectation both by and of many 18 year olds that they will enter into tertiary education.[16] However, many from the sample group in our study did not appear to have had the same expectation that they would be able, at any time, to enter higher education. Exploring this lack of expectation goes some way in helping to develop our understanding of the specific barriers that part time students can face at the earliest stages of pursuing their ambitions/careers.

PRE-DEGREE BARRIERS

It is perhaps ironic that, given the openness of part time routes of study to those without many formal qualifications, it is not just a perceived lack of ability that emerges as an important impediment to the pursuit of a degree education, but the lack of awareness of the available opportunities.

The initial – and, to some extent, intractable – problem, that many potential takers of a part time course of study do not even cast themselves in the role of prospective students, makes increasing awareness and participation problematic. As noted above, the entry requirements to the part time law degree at Rutland Metropolitan University and, generally, of most other providers of part time law degrees, reflect the aim of broadening participation in higher education. However, we found that, in line with an earlier and wider study of part time students conducted by Bourner *et al*,[17] many of our sample believed that their lack of formal educational qualifications would bar them from enrolling on a degree programme. The opportunity with which the Rutland sample felt that they had been presented by the degree course and the surprise that they felt in being allowed to enrol is clear from the following statement from one student: 'People are going to look at a law degree and think "oh my God" ... I would never have thought in a million years that I would have gone back into education, never mind a law degree.' (B4)

However, this initial reluctance to perceive oneself as a potential participant in higher education was, in the sample's view, compounded by the

---

16   Dearing Report, 1997, Report No 2, p 14.

17   Bourner *et al*, 1991, p 56

absence of any effective marketing strategy by the law department to suggest the contrary. That many of the sample attested amazement or luck to their entry onto the scheme is demonstrated by the following comments: 'I just went along to a general open day at Rutland and was interested in a humanities degree. I just came out of the humanities section and saw that there was a law stall. So I just sat down because I'd done an 'A' level in law and I got signed up. But otherwise I probably would have done humanities.' (A3) 'I'm only from [the next town] and I didn't know there was a [Rutland Metropolitan] University.'(B4)

While the essentially *ad hoc* marketing of the part time law degree at Rutland is acknowledged by its scheme leader, there is other evidence that a failure to market learning opportunities effectively may encompass a significant proportion of the whole part time sector.[18] Moreover, it must be of real concern that, as the traditionally new university providers face increasing demands upon already stretched resources, their ability to commit the funds necessary to reach potential part time students may be severely limited. Although it is difficult to draw firm conclusions from any study of those students who, by definition, have overcome the initial barriers to higher education, it is likely that many people who may be interested in undertaking a law degree through part time study are unaware of the existing opportunities. The new universities' historically recorded closer connections with the local communities in which they are situated may continue to provide a source of recruitment.[19] However, unless providers of part time law degrees pursue a more consistent approach to marketing these opportunities, the extent to which these schemes will be able to compete with the emergence of a strongly marketed new LLB scheme from the internationally recognised Open University must be seriously questioned.

DURING THE DEGREE

Halpern identifies the importance of achieving a degree classification of 2.1 or above for those wishing to enter the legal profession.[20] It is our belief that there are a number of personal and structural difficulties that may affect the part time law students' ability to achieve these higher classifications.

---

18   Bourner *et al*, 1991, p 59, found that roughly 75% of students were unaware of the existence of their course for more than two years before they enrolled and of the other 25%, 38% of these students stated that they had not enrolled earlier because they felt that they lacked the necessary educational qualifications. However, as with the present Rutland Metropolitan study, the principal flaw of Bourner *et al*'s findings is that it only accounts for the experience of those students currently in higher education. There is a strong likelihood that the lack of awareness is even more acute amongst those who never enrol for a degree.
19   Leighton, 1998.
20   Halpern, 1994, pp 76–81.

It is perhaps the educational demands of a degree level programme that present the greatest obstacle for part time students. The students enrolled on the part time law degree are required to have few formal further educational qualifications. Those that did possess some form of recent educational qualification had perhaps completed an access course or an HND with a very different emphasis on skills to the traditional law degree. The Bourner study found that, among those students for whom the ability to join the course despite a 'lack of qualification' was an important factor in the choice of course/institution, non-completion levels ran to 39%. Furthermore, that study also found that, among those students whose highest educational qualification was below GCE and 'A' level, 45% of those surveyed did not complete their degrees.[21]

The students we encountered in the Rutland Metropolitan study had not succumbed to these pressures, but they did find the rigours of degree study (with a focus on examinations) a particular obstacle to their success on the degree. In particular, it was not the subject matter in itself that they found difficult, but rather the woeful lack of preparation that they felt they had received from their previous experiences in their lives, jobs or education. Alarmingly, many from the sample also expressed concern that their previous educational difficulties were perpetuated within the law school:

> I'd done an HNC in Legal Studies before I did this degree and the only thing is that the HNC is more vocational, and then I've come to the degree and it's more academic ... It's very, very different, because I didn't realise what I was letting myself in for and I just had one big total shock ... it's still difficult to work out what's expected from you. I just didn't have a clue ... (A5)

> The exam was completely different to what we'd expected it to be ... I researched it in the wrong way and in the wrong area and now I've seen a paper I'll know better for next time ... I wasn't helped by the Law School in any way in preparing for the exams ... (B4)

> If you asked what would be a typical essay – you would be told, 'There isn't one'. And that was the answer that we got in our first year. I mean the last time I wrote an essay before beginning the course, it began 'Once upon a time ...' and ended 'and they all lived happily ever after'. (B6)

In this context, it is perhaps one of the saddest dichotomies about the part time law degree at Rutland Metropolitan that, although its structure allows people the opportunity to work full time while studying for a law degree, it is this very structure which also creates some of the most serious barriers to a student's success on the degree (and, therefore, entry into the legal profession). The opportunity that the degree presents to the students, in terms of the flexibility of study, is clear from the following observations:

> For me, the best aspect for me was that I can carry on working at the same time and have family commitments, that was the sole benefit. And I suppose the

---

21 Bourner *et al*, 1991, p 119.

fact that you could do it in four years as well, which wasn't that much longer than the normal degree. (A4)

You've opened up an opportunity [with the part time law degree]. If there wasn't a course in the evening, I wouldn't be able to do it. I think this is the sort of thing that dreams are made of, because we've been working, some of us, for quite a few years and never thought that we could attain our absolute goal. And this has given me and lots of other people the chance of absolutely going for it. (B5)

For most students, there is no other way that they would be able to study for a law degree. Many of the students had to work, both to support themselves and, in many cases, their families. However, while many of the sample reported the flexibility of the course as being one its strongest features, many also reported problems of time management as being one of the biggest obstacles they faced in their studies.

There are problems of time management for students who have to balance full time work, full time family responsibilities and two evenings of four hours of class contact per week, in addition to the preparation and 'wider reading' required for the part time LLB. What was striking from the students' perceptions of these difficulties was that, although some of the issues were clearly structural, the university itself could mitigate many more.

It is a feature of many options and core subjects on both the full time and part time law degrees at Rutland Metropolitan that there has been a conscious desire on the part of the staff to introduce a more 'student-centred' learning environment. One of the central strategies in achieving this is the introduction of group work for both assessment and non-assessment purposes. While most full time students can accommodate attendance at such groups, this issue can cause particular difficulties for (and, in some cases, resentment by) the part time students and their ability to balance competing commitments:

The group that I've been in, two members of the group work shifts, so the group was never altogether. You get difficulties when you are working and you are part time. As someone said, the full time students can arrange their time around their other things. With part time students it's difficult. (A2)

The only problems I find are time management. That's very difficult. I have a family, I work full time. I travel back and forth to work two hours a day. And I find the time element ... I really have to think about what's coming up, what I have to do. (B5)

The students also felt that their success on the part time law degree was being compromised by structural factors. The sample voiced strong concerns over the issue of library resources. Beyond universal problems of coverage and stock levels, part time students felt that they had particular problems to contend with in seeking to access library resources. They felt that, once more, this placed them at a disadvantage when compared with full time students:

> The problem with the library is the opening hours, so you can't take out books
> ... When you want to take out a book you find that it's not there because the
> full time students have been there before you, so you've got to be looking at
> the stocks that you have and whether they are adequate for the students that
> you have. (A2)

> The old bugbear is library resources. Not just in terms of the stock of the
> library, but also in terms of the opening hours and the accessibility of the
> library to people who have professional responsibilities during the day. The
> evening opening hours are very limited ... It's open but we can't get to it
> because we're in lectures, it's very limited. (B2)

However, these are perhaps not the most unexpected problems. Unfortunately, what is seemingly exacerbating these issues is the students' perception that the teaching team are not fully appreciating the differences between part time and full time students. This perception of a failure in staff to appreciate the difficulties of part time study has also been reflected as an important factor for those who left after their first year:[22]

> I think teaching part timers is entirely different to teaching full timers. I think
> some of the lecturers ... have really adapted to teaching part timers and really
> make things easy for us. However, others will say 'You read for a law degree, I
> don't care whether you're part time or full time, you go away and read for
> your law degree' – if only there was something to read ... (A4)

> I think we need lecturers to be understanding and to see things from our point
> of view. We just can't access everything that they want us to access. We're
> lucky with some lecturers that they do actually go out and photocopy
> particular parts of what we need. (A5)

> Feedback is very important in workshops and we don't always get that in
> workshops. Not with all lecturers ... I think there should be standards. (A2)

To teach all degree routes in the same way is to ignore the many problems and difficulties that particularly affect part time law students.[23] If law schools are not going to set great store by formal qualifications (and this is clearly an important aspect of widening access to higher education), then law schools must be aware of the problems that follow. One suggestion that many students favoured (both in the focus groups and in 'five point action plans' they developed) was for the law school to develop a more comprehensive introductory booklet detailing what was to be expected of them in higher education.[24] They felt that this, combined with an induction week, would go some way to answering a number of their concerns. An increased

---

22 Bourner *et al*, 1991, p 118.

23 At this point, the authors are keen to highlight the Rutland students' praise of the scheme leader, stating that they felt he understood the problems of part timers.

24 *How to Win as a Part time Student* (Bourner and Race, 1990) sets out a number of strategies to assist the students during their period of study. The students had not been specifically alerted to existence of this useful book.

involvement of part time students in forming strategies for learning can only assist in overcoming the potential obstacles that these students can face.

These personal and structural problems can create marked difficulties for part time law students and the cumulative effect of these factors raises two serious problems: the higher drop-out rate for part time as opposed to full time students and the threshold barrier to entry into the legal profession facing today's graduates who lack the higher degree classifications.[25]

Student non-completion is a problem throughout higher education. However, it has always been a particularly acute problem for part time students.[26] Various studies[27] suggest that the most likely explanation was reasons unconnected with the college, citing domestic or financial reasons as the most significant. However, Woodley and Partlett[28] argue that colleges and universities do, in fact, bear a greater responsibility for the non-retention of students, with evidence that the more interesting and better-organised courses are more likely to retain students.[29]

The Bourner study[30] found that far more students will leave during their first year of study than at any other time. This correlates with the experiences shared by the students and the scheme leader at Rutland Metropolitan, who acknowledged that it is a greater problem for part time students than it is for the full time LLB cohort. However, what emerged as a key concern was that they, as a collective student body, had often been involved in counselling and encouraging their peers to stay on. They reported a strong belief that the Law School as a whole was not doing enough to provide a safety net for those students who were considering leaving the part time LLB. The interviewed sample overwhelmingly agreed that students' difficulties in accessing staff outside teaching contact hours was a major obstacle in the way of tackling this problem. It is also interesting to note the correlation between the factors identified by the Rutland students as adversely affecting their studies and by the Bourner study[31] as likely to increase the drop-out rate – for example, poor

---

25 Halpern, 1994; Lee, 1999.

26 Kibble, in Dhavan, Kibble and Twining, 1989, p 141; Marsh, 1983, p 103.

27 Woodley and McIntosh, 1980; Phythian and Clements, 1982, all cited and discussed by Bourner *et al*, 1991, p 103.

28 Woodley and Partlett, 1983.

29 *Ibid*, Bourner *et al*, p 104, argue that the position is, in fact, far more complicated, with a variety of reasons for students leaving courses. Furthermore, they also suggest that there may in fact be some positive reasons for a student leaving a part time course, such as a switch to full time study, or the knowledge gained on the course leading to a promotion at work leaving less time for study.

30 *Ibid*, p 104.

31 *Ibid*, pp 118–25.

facilities and a lack of previous educational experience. It must be a matter of great concern that barriers to part time students' success identified 10 years ago persist today.[32]

While the authors do not seek to suggest that all participants in any type of legal education seek automatically to enter the legal profession, nearly 60% of the Rutland Metropolitan sample expressed just such a preference. In this respect, the less immediately apparent, but equally serious problem of being prevented from achieving one's full potential through a part time course of study may seriously impact upon the realisation of many of these students' clear desire to pursue a career in legal practice. Recent empirical research conducted by Halpern[33] and Goriely and Williams[34] suggest that a failure to secure a degree classification of 2.1 or above in today's market for legal trainees may create a serious barrier to a career in the legal profession. Even if only a proportion of the findings we suggest in this initial study of the part time experience can translate to the wider sector as a whole, the detrimental effect on students' legal education may present the final and, perhaps, most insurmountable barrier to the legal profession.

At this point, it is necessary to emphasise an important conclusion to be drawn from this Rutland Metropolitan study: part time legal education is *different* from full time legal education. Many providers in this sector seek to emphasise the equivalence of the part time LLB to its full time counterpart. However, even allowing for a more diverse national picture, there is a need for institutions to take a greater account of the distinctiveness of the needs and problems faced by part time law students. As study on a part time LLB programme is rarely solely undertaken by all students with the aim of entry into the legal profession, such courses face the same demands as full time LLBs in matching the vocational intentions of many of its students to an educational content that should reflect more broadly transferable skills.[35] However, in light of the 60% of students of our sample whom we found to express a strong preference for a career in law, it is necessary to ask what law schools are doing to meet the needs of their part time students.

This research does not seek coldly to condemn the new university sector for continuing its commitment to broadening access to higher education. However, in unpacking some of the implications of the project 'access to education', Dhavan merits quoting:

> [T]here is public embarrassment that the system of education and professional selection consolidates the social reproduction of class privileges. 'Access' does

---

32 However, that Rutland Metropolitan's programme has only been in operation since the mid-1990s may present at least a partial explanation of the persistence of these problems.

33 Halpern, 1994.

34 Goriely and Williams, 1997.

35 ACLEC, 1996, pp 22–25; Hepple, 1996.

not attack that process (unless demonstrably discriminatory) but holds out a promise of fairness. It does not guarantee – or, even, argue for – an assault on privilege, only asserts a willingness to affirm the need for due process ... Better access to educational advantages and the profession is designed to give the system a face lift without foreshadowing any radical changes – an invitation to join the 'rat race' with a gentle reassurance that fairer criteria may afford a better chance.[36]

When Dhavan's critique of increased access is considered in the light of the significant proportion of our sample who expressed a strong preference for a career in practice, we would argue that providers must be aware of this desire and enhance their efforts to ensure that these students receive a degree that will assist them in their aim. In general terms, given the financial and personal sacrifices that part time law students are required to make in order to re-enter higher education, part time LLBs should be repositioned as not *equivalent* to full time LLB programmes, but as *value-added* LLBs. For the many students currently enrolled or considering enrolment on part time LLBs, entry into the legal profession will be a difficult task. They will face further obstacles to continuing into the profession's vocational stages of education and, afterwards, in successfully procuring training contracts or pupillages (see below). Structural time constraints within part time degrees do impose certain immovable limits upon what can be achieved. However, without a further focus on how law schools can make their graduates more attractive to a prospective legal employer, there is a risk that the continuing provision of such schemes could be interpreted by outsiders as more financially useful to the providers than they will be to the majority of students whom we found were keen to break into the legal profession.[37]

Lest this argument be interpreted as judgmental of part time LLB providers, it should be reiterated that the increased access facilitated by these institutions is invaluable, and the acquisition of an LLB would, in the normal course of events, enhance a student's self-esteem and ability to find better employment. However, in a time when recent research confirms the difficulties faced by even full time LLB graduates in breaking into the profession, the specific barriers that stand in the way of part time students' success must be explicitly recognised and tackled. Moreover, as the following sections will argue, the challenge set down here to help satisfy part time law students' expectations also rests squarely on the shoulders of the legal profession itself.

---

36 Dhavan, Kibble and Twining, 1989, pp 275–76.

37 However, even within these constraints, increasing part time law students' exposure to the legal profession and taking simple and effective action along the lines suggested by Goriely and Williams, 1997, pp 123–24) might immediately help improve these graduates' likelihood of securing employment within the profession.

POST-GRADUATION AND BEYOND

What does the future hold for graduates of part time law degrees? From the data collected, it was clear that a desire to practise law was the primary motivation for almost 60% of the sample. Of this group, 75% wanted to qualify as a solicitor, and 23% wished to pursue a career at the Bar. One respondent, whose primary motivation for enrolling on the LLB lay in enhancing her present career, showed an interest in work as a paralegal. Of the remainder of the sample, 27% were hoping to enhance their existing careers through the acquisition of an LLB, while 24% expressed career interests in new or non-legal areas of employment. The diversity of options entertained by the Rutland Metropolitan sample might suggest an awareness of limited opportunities within the legal profession. However, the strong preference for entry into the profession may suggest that a high proportion of those students will be exposed to the 'idiosyncratic recruitment policies' ascribed to many law firms.[38]

If we return to the quotation at the beginning of this chapter, the student concerned expressed a belief that, for many, the part time LLB was a dream come true. However, we would suggest that from the responses we received from students, this dream is not limited to success in higher education, but, in fact, presumes an entry into the legal profession. Most students saw no insurmountable barrier to their eventual entry into the legal profession; however, they did identify significant obstacles along the path to an eventual career in law. The most common of these revolved round the themes of funding and their age as mature students.

Thirty percent of all the part time students in the sample felt that funding their professional training would present a particularly significant hurdle to their entry into legal practice.[39] Even following completion of the LPC/BVC, the students still expressed concern about the salary that would initially be available to them and their dependants. The financial difficulties that they expected to face as part time students are well illustrated by the following statement:

> The problem as a part timer, is to get the money together to do the LPC. If you can afford to get the £5,000 together, or your firm will allow you to take a year out, then that's excellent, but most of us haven't got deep pockets so it's a question of finance. We can just about manage to do the four years, but then

---

38 See, generally, Goriely and Williams, 1997, pp 23–35; and further, Halpern, 1994, pp 68–81.

39 This may be compounded by the likely need to transfer to full time study for the LPC. While part time LPC programmes do exist, their availability is more restricted than the provision of the part time LLB.

after that it's on hold, we just can't go on any further. That was a major disincentive for me, the cost of the LPC … In the four years it takes us to get a degree, they [full time students] can get a degree and an LPC, so they might have a big bill, but they can work it off in five/eight years. Some of us haven't got five/eight years to pay it off. (A3)

Most of the students recognised that they were entering a competitive marketplace. However, they remained adamant that they were would be able to succeed in that marketplace. This, despite the number of students (roughly one quarter of the sample) who felt that their age could be a significant hurdle when attempting to enter the legal profession (see biographical details above):

I spoke to a senior partner at [a major law firm in the local region] and he said that I would have no chance … He said we don't want people coming into the firm who are nine to five merchants, they've got to be committed to X number of hours per week and that if you don't fit that profile, a young person does … He said that if you do get an interview, you're unlikely to get into the firm … I can understand it. We'd be looking for more money and you'd have to pay youngsters less. (A2)

I also think that my age is against me. I'm 48 and I've got another three and a half years to go and I do sometimes wonder if I would be employable. So I've also been thinking about freelance advisory, for say, personnel or civil service or something like that. And it's economics as well, because it costs so much to go to the Bar. Years added on to the existing time at law school. It isn't on. I'm going to be retiring before I qualify! … That's what *The Trainee* said [that older entrants would struggle]. [The younger students] They're more ambitious. (A6)

The law degree itself is certainly creating opportunities. Whether the opportunities are there, thereafter in the professional circles of law, is probably a different point. (B2)

Perhaps, more importantly, it must be noted that, although students did see difficulties ahead, this did not sway them from their belief that they were building towards a career in the legal profession. Interestingly, 63% of those who saw their age as a potential problem in their career also believed that their life experience and maturity would be factors that would assist them in securing a place within the legal profession. Thirty-four percent of the entire sample felt that these factors would count in their favour in attempting to enter the legal profession:[40]

I actually went on to a firm of solicitors, just to sound them out, and they actually said to come back when I was in need of a training contract, because they'll snap mature students, such as myself, up. They want people with life experience … I deal with solicitors on a daily basis and all of them have been very encouraging to me … I'm working at the moment with two new girls

---

40 We were careful, in the discussion groups, not to ask whether they intended to enter the legal profession, but rather what they intended to do after graduation. Most answered unequivocally that they would enter the legal profession.

[who are 22] who have qualified at the Bar and can't get pupillages. They've been told to come back when they're 30 and have got some life experience. (A4)

There's no question [that this law degree is meeting my employment aspirations]. This is a law degree course, and it does open doors to many, many places. I'm clear about what I want to do, if I can achieve it ... I would like a qualifying law degree. So I'm settled in what I want to do and this is definitely the biggest stepping-stone in that direction ... I just see it as a huge challenge. I think it's something that's really gripped me for a very long time. And I never thought that I would be able to achieve it. And it's this course for a start. I have to work full time and I didn't think that I ever could have got on a degree course. So I never thought that I could attain this, so this is what's so exciting for me at the moment. And the fact that there is a goal. And maybe if I work hard enough and I'm lucky enough to get funding as well, I can achieve what I want. And I'm very interested in criminal law. (B5)

Cos I'm doing part time, and I'm already in a profession I want to be a barrister, because I think, when you're doing it at this age you've got to have aspiration, and barrister seems, sort of, a better job for me at the end of it. And that's what keeps me coming two nights a week because I've got an aim. (C1)

The majority of the sample still saw themselves practising in the future as either a barrister or a solicitor. This despite the fact that research appears to suggest that graduates (both full and part time) of new universities may struggle to secure training contracts.[41] We will next consider in more detail the profession's rekindled role as gatekeeper to the career and the implications this has for part time law students.

PART TIMERS IN PRACTICE?

Before the expansion of higher education in the wake of the Robbins Report,[42] lawyers had always successfully controlled entry into the profession.[43] In order to gain entry, it had often appeared necessary to have either a family or professional relationship with the solicitor who provided articles, or an ability to prove one's gentlemanly status.[44]

However, as Leighton describes, the rapid growth of polytechnic provision of legal qualifications (such as the CNAA degrees) played a role in the expansion of undergraduate legal education.[45] This explosion of legal

---

41   See, eg, Goriely and Williams, 1997, pp 23–36.
42   Robbins Report, 1963.
43   Abel, 1988, pp 141–68.
44   See, eg, Sugarman, 1996, pp 108–09.
45   Leighton, 1998, pp 87–92.

education shifted the entry barriers from the profession to the academy and significantly undermined the profession's control over entry.[46] However, as legal higher education has continued to expand and increase the supply of law graduates that already exceeds the profession's demands,[47] control of entry into a legal career has once more come to rest in the hands of the profession.

Suggestions from members of the profession in the past that an ability to translate Virgil and Homer were essential prerequisites of entry into the solicitors' profession were clearly unrelated to standards of professional competence.[48] However, the selection process and criteria now exercised by the firms employing the next generation of lawyers have also been criticised for their subjectivity.[49] Although Goriely and Williams[50] and Halpern[51] study the selection criteria across a range of law firms, it is worth reiterating that it is predominately the largest city firms who recruit trainee solicitors: 55.9% of trainees were located in the 11 plus partner firms and just 8.4% with sole practitioners.[52] Hanlon underlined still further the importance of the largest firms particularly in the commercial law fields, in which they overwhelmingly practise.[53] He found that 6% of all firms of his sample trained 59% of all trainees.[54] At the other end of the scale, 60% of those firms with fewer than 10 partners had no trainees, while the remaining 40% had fewer than 10 trainees each. Furthermore Hanlon found that firms with 55 or more partners, while accounting for only 0.7% of his sample, employed 35% of all trainees and 45% of all assistants within the commercial law field.[55] It is clear that the training of the profession is overwhelmingly falling to the largest commercial law firms.[56]

The selection criteria employed by these firms is perhaps best highlighted by the statement from Clifford Chance, in response to a query put to them by *The Trainee* about how best to secure a training contract: 'Simple ... Go to a good university, get a 2.1 and have a fantastic personality.'[57]

---

46 Abel, 1988, p 286.
47 See Cole, 1998.
48 Sugarman, 1996, p 108.
49 Goriely and Williams, 1997, pp 23–35.
50 *Ibid*.
51 Halpern, 1994.
52 *Ibid*, Cole, p 71.
53 Hanlon, 1999, p 127.
54 Hanlon, 1997, p 805.
55 *Ibid*.
56 It should be noted that the present concentration of training opportunities in the larger firms of the south east of England and Wales may serve as a further barrier to entry into the profession as the personal circumstances of many part time law students may discourage them from even applying.
57 (2000) *The Trainee*, May, p 28.

Empirical research also suggests further factors impacting upon the likelihood of a candidate successfully securing a traineeship. Halpern (1994, pp 77–81) identified that a graduate's chances of obtaining a training contract was significantly related to:

- their 'A' level score;
- the type of institution at which they studied their degree;
- their degree class mark;
- the type of school that they attended at age 14;
- their ethnic background;
- their work experience; and
- whether they had relatives in the profession.[58]

These are factors that have, in general, been confirmed in other research, such as Goriely and Williams.[59] Lee notes that the elite law firms place additional emphasis on vacation employment schemes, as a process of recruitment.[60] With many part time students entering study with few formal educational achievements, but with many pressures on their time and finances, it is apparent that these students' chances are significantly compromised by the operation of such criteria.

We would suggest that many part time law students will find it difficult to satisfy the basic threshold criteria that many law firms apply in their recruitment processes. Another issue that must be highlighted, however, is the fragmentation in the legal profession's definition of what comprises 'legal professionalism'.

In the past, the legal profession's explicit use of entry controls was an effective method of maintaining its social composition and hegemonic power, while advancing its claims to status in society.[61] These attempts to advance the collective mobility project for the legal profession were historically driven by the Law Society.[62] Today, it is perhaps increasingly debatable whether it could be said that the profession's interests are synonymous with its official professional association.[63] Furthermore, the significance of the Law Society has been increasingly challenged by the initiative and leadership shown by the elite firms on a number of issues affecting modern legal practice, not least their success in the global legal marketplace.[64]

---

58 Halpern, 1994, pp 77–81.
59 Goriely and Williams, 1997, pp 23–35.
60 Lee, 1999.
61 Burrage, 1996; Sugarman, 1996.
62 For the centrality of the Law Society in this project, see *ibid*, Sugarman.
63 Hanlon, 1997, p 822; *ibid*, Lee, pp 29–30; see, also, the City law firms' reported moves towards a break from the Law Society ((2000) *The Lawyer*, 29 May, p 1).
64 See Lee, 1992; Flood, 1996.

The fragmentation of the legal profession has been well documented across all areas of practice.[65] A consequence of this has been the increased fragmentation of conceptions of legal professionalism. Hanlon charts the emergence of 'commercialised professionalism' within the powerful elite of law firms, whereby previously uncontested features of lawyering, including the criteria for partnership, the sustainability of such positions, the nature of consumer/client relationships and the growth of sophisticated marketing as an integral part of law firms' work have all seen radical change.[66]

Such changes suggest that, in exercising control over entry into a large sector of the legal profession, the entrepreneurial character of the elite firms do not seek to safeguard the collective status of the profession. Rather, it is concerned with the individual firm's position within a highly competitive marketplace that dictates the emphasis of selection criteria for training contracts.[67]

In clear contrast to the developing commercialised professionalism espoused by a significant proportion of the hiring law firms, part time students in our interviewed sample demonstrated an awareness and acceptance of what Paterson has identified as the *traditional* model of legal professionalism.[68] Many of the traditional model's key values, such as competence, access, the service ethos, public protection and high status figured highly within the sample. Moreover, in their initial discussion of the images of lawyering shown to them, the students also assessed characters' behaviour through an evaluative perspective based on the merits of objectivity and emotional detachment. For example, when shown a clip of the lawyer in the film, *The Sweet Hereafter*, who sought to enlist bereaved parents in a class action on a no-win, no-fee basis, the groups were swift to condemn him as an 'ambulance chaser' and 'unprofessional'. This general disapproval of what was seen as the lawyer's greed also chimes with the broader equivocation of the questionnaire sample regarding the prospect of a better income as a reason for doing the LLB. The apparent neutrality towards material gain might suggest a connection to Abel's account of capitalist society's 'considerable ambivalence about the explicit pursuit of material gain' that the legal profession has (historically) used to its advantage in restricting competition whilst enhancing the collective profession's status:[69] 'If he was doing it for the money [operating on a no-win, no-fee basis], I don't think that's very professional.' (C2) 'He was like Jaggard in *Great Expectations*.' (C6)

---

65 Abel, 1988; Glasser, 1990; Smith, 1994; Hanlon, 1997.
66 Hanlon, 1999.
67 See, generally, Lee, 1999.
68 Paterson, 1996, p 140.
69 *Ibid*, Abel, p 293.

Similarly, in commenting on the attachment between a female lawyer and a young boy in *The Client*, the groups, whether men or women, frequently found the relationship inappropriate for a professional. This surprising response to an ostensibly sympathetic character may be explained by these students' ready internalisation of the profession's traditional ideological values.[70]

While it is difficult to generalise from such a small sample, the themes identified in this section point towards a view of the part time student body as out of step with a contemporary conception of legal professionalism. The sample showed sympathy and identification with a model of Law Society-led professionalism that Abel suggests is declining and Paterson argues is evolving.[71] Access to legal higher education is widening and the social composition of the legal profession is changing.[72] It is ironic that, as these changes are occurring, part time students may still find themselves disadvantaged by their background and their lack of exposure to what is required of modern legal practitioners.

CONCLUSION

In this study, we found that both the students we spoke to and the staff who taught them were enthusiastic and dedicated individuals. In speaking to the students, we could not fail to be impressed by their openness to our research and their determination to succeed in whatever path they had chosen. It is our greatest hope that the difficulties and obstacles that we suggest will face part time law graduates will prove to be unfounded and that the changes required within the academy and the legal profession to release their potential will take place soon enough to benefit them and not just those who will follow.

However, at the time of writing, it is our belief that serious obstacles will stand in their way. In line with the Dearing Report's finding, we believe there is still a need to improve the level of information about 'the non-'A' level route in higher education'.[73] Problems inherent in the structure and delivery of a part time law degree and in the lives of the students must be accorded greater recognition, and efforts to remedy them intensified. We found from

---

70 Cain (in Carlen (ed), 1976, p 223) conceptualises the components of legal ideology as reification, reverence, righteousness and rectitude and discusses the profession's use of these strategies. See, also, Schlag's witty but incisive discussion of the dichotomous thinking necessary to sustain legal culture's pre-eminence in society (1996, pp 3–13).

71 Abel, 1989; Paterson, 1996.

72 Cole, 1998.

73 Dearing Report, 1997, Main Report, p 109.

our sample that the students were keen to be more greatly involved in this process. Our initial findings also raise concern that part time law students may be misinformed about the possibility of entry into the legal profession. In the increasingly competitive market for training contracts, both law schools and the profession must shoulder some responsibility for improving prospects and creating opportunities.

Rees, Thomas and Todd explicitly challenge the larger law firms to widen their recruitment net and broaden their criteria for selection.[74] Our research supports this challenge and would welcome increased opportunities for all law graduates from all educational backgrounds. However, at the heart of our argument is a challenge to law schools to be more open about their own priorities in opening access to LLB study. Providers of part time legal education must respect students' needs and expectations of practice. Otherwise, the potential of modern legal education, integrating both vocational and academic requirements, might emerge as only a fraction of its anticipated value: an education for education's sake. As a limited study, this research makes no claim to present a definitive picture of the state of part time legal education in England and Wales. However, we believe that these findings may have a broader applicability for other institutions and therefore merit further research. Without continued efforts by the legal academy and the profession, we are concerned that for the majority of those part time students who do aspire to join the ranks of the profession, a university legal education may be all that they achieve.

---

74 Rees, Thomas and Todd, 2000.

CHAPTER 4

WOMEN IN THE LAW SCHOOL – SHOALS OF FISH, STARFISH OR FISH OUT OF WATER?

Fiona Cownie

INTRODUCTION

The position of women in the law school is a complex one. It is not true that women are excluded from law schools; far from it, since they make up more than 50% of the undergraduate body, and nearly that proportion of law postgraduates. Women also make an important contribution to the law school as academic staff; although they constitute a small proportion of law professors, they form a significantly higher proportion of other senior academic staff and nearly half of all junior lecturers in law schools.[1] The figures alone suggest that the position of women in the law school is not a straightforward one.

Interesting though they are, however, numbers alone do not tell us the whole story. Do women in fact play an important part in law school life, or are they excluded from it? Are women integrated into the law school, or are they treated in such a way that they are made to feel unwelcome, or at least ignored? Do women only feel comfortable in the law school if they behave like men? This chapter explores the complex world of women in the contemporary law school and offers some tentative observations intended to contribute to the ongoing debate about their role and status within that institution. In doing that, it will seek to avoid the dangers of 'essentialism' (the assumption that all women feel, behave and react in very much the same sort of way).[2] Like Brooks, I am interested in exploring the 'diverse and contradictory way [*sic*] women experience power'.[3] Women's experience of the law school, whether as undergraduate, postgraduate or member of academic staff, is not a homogeneous one, but is dependent on a large number of social, economic and political factors which intersect differently in relation to different individuals. It is in an effort to acknowledge these elements of diversity that I have begun by referring to 'the complex world' of women in the law school, and it is that world to which we now turn. It is inevitable that in order to

---

1   Precise figures relating to these categories are discussed below.
2   For further discussion of the concept of essentialism, see, eg, Evans, 1995, Chapter 6.
3   Brooks, 1997, p 5.

move the debate on, it will be necessary to refer to women in the law school as a group, but that should not prevent the reader from appreciating the necessity for caution when reading such analysis.

THE STATISTICS: SHOALS OF WOMEN

Women are highly visible in the contemporary law school. The number of women undergraduates entering law schools has shown a steady increase throughout the 1990s. The Law Society's annual statistical reports show that the percentage of female law undergraduates rose from 49.7% in 1987 to 58.6% in 1997. Even as postgraduate students, women play a significant role, with the Harris and Jones survey reporting that 45% of law postgraduates are female.[4]

Both these sets of figures reflect a national trend; data from the Higher Education Statistics Agency also show a steady increase in the number of women participating in higher education, so that by the academic year 1998–99, the latest year for which figures are currently available, women make up 55.8% of the undergraduate student population.[5] They also form 50.8% of the postgraduate student body, though it is likely that there are considerable differences between their participation in different types of programme, with female students making up a significant majority of non-degree level postgraduate programmes (which are dominated by postgraduate certificates of education), but a minority of taught postgraduates courses and research students (that being the case when separate data were available).[6]

Anecdotal evidence suggests that women are also highly visible in the law school as secretaries and as cleaners. Firmer data are available about their position as academic staff, although the picture they give is quite ambiguous. While Clare McGlynn's survey suggests that women form 40% of all legal academics (and 49% of lecturers), it is noticeable that they account for only 14% of professors and 22% of readers.[7] However, even these figures are open to a reasonably positive interpretation since, as she points out, women hold only 8% of chairs across the university sector as a whole.[8] Though, as she also notes, while the 14% figure is cheering when compared to the sector as a whole, it remains the case that 63% of law schools have no women professors[9] and the position is even worse in Scotland, where all three women professors

---

4   Harris and Jones, 1996, p 91.
5   See student data on the Higher Education Statistics Agency website (www.hesa.org.uk).
6   *Ibid.*
7   McGlynn, 1999, p 75.
8   *Ibid*, p 77.
9   *Ibid.*

hold posts at one university.[10] Nevertheless, it is difficult from the figures alone to justify an argument that women are obviously treated in a discriminatory fashion in the contemporary law school, especially when the position of senior non-professorial staff is taken into account, since women form 40% of this cohort.[11]

The position of women legal academics largely reflects the position of professional women in society. Women employed in management and the professions provide reasonable comparators for female legal academics; in both those sectors, according to the Equal Opportunities Commission, women's share of employment is steadily increasing, so that by 2006 it is predicted to be just over 40% in both sectors.[12] However, although the overall gender pay gap narrowed throughout the 20th century, the gap still remains, and this is as true in higher education as it is in other sectors.[13] In comparison with the legal profession, female academics appear to be making greater inroads into senior positions than their peers; statistics relating to the number of women in the judiciary, for instance, show that, in 2000, there are no women judges in the House of Lords and only two in the Court of Appeal; further down the judicial ladder, women constitute 7.9% of High Court judges, 9.3% of Recorders and 13.5% of district judges, while in the same year 12.8% of those appointed as QCs were women.[14]

Overall, there appears to be evidence that women legal academics, while not having gained equality with their male counterparts, are nevertheless making strong inroads into their chosen profession, and there certainly seems little to suggest that they are in a worse position than their peers in comparable modes of employment. As far as sheer numbers are concerned, there are, indeed, shoals of women in the contemporary law school, and their numbers are steadily increasing in much the same way as is the case with comparable professions.

WOMEN SUCCEEDING: THE STARFISH

Law students

As far as students are concerned, there are some aspects of the experience of women in law schools which can be celebrated, revealing, as they do, women

---

10   McGlynn, 1999, p 85.

11   *Ibid*, p 80.

12   Equal Opportunities Commission, 2000.

13   *The Times*, Higher Education Supplement carried reports on 31 March 2000 (p 3) and on 19 May 2000 (p 1) that female academics earn on average £4,300 a year less than their male colleagues.

14   Figures taken from the Lord Chancellor's Department website: www.open.gov.uk/lcd/.

who are making a success of their academic career. Not only are women entering the law school in large numbers, but, once admitted, they are achieving considerable academic success. Statistics from the Law Society's cohort study show that women now form the majority of undergraduate students awarded upper second class degrees and above in law (although women are slightly less likely than men to gain a first, they are more likely to gain an upper second, thus bringing them out ahead overall).[15] In terms of first class degrees, it is at least possible that women have a greater chance of achieving a first at a new university than an old one (that being the case when separate data were provided), though there is no available research to provide an explanation for this phenomenon.[16]

Law staff

As far as women staff are concerned, one area which might be cause for some optimism about the position of women legal academics is their rate of participation in the influential positions in academic life – as members of professional associations and public bodies. Women's achievements in this area are not uncontested. McGlynn argues that a major problem for women legal academics is that peer review and professional support from those in senior positions play very important roles in academia, determining, for example, teaching requirements, sabbatical leave and promotions, as well as invitations to conferences and to contribute to collections of essays. Her main point is that these gatekeepers are mostly men, who tend to make choices which are advantageous to those in their own image – other men.[17]

However, McGlynn goes on to concede that 'slowly there are more women occupying positions of power and influence'.[18] This is perhaps to understate the position of women legal academics. While it is true that women do not command the majority of powerful positions within the academic legal world, it is, nevertheless, arguable that the female gatekeepers who do exist form an influential cohort. It is not merely that there are currently a considerable number of women legal academics in powerful positions, but the picture of the legal academic world is changing so rapidly that current postholders may well herald a period of considerable change in gender politics within the legal academic world. Below, I examine the rate of participation by women in two public arenas: as members of professional

---

15 Shiner and Newburn, 1995, p 25.

16 McGlynn, 1998, pp 18–19. It is unclear why women overall obtain fewer first class degrees than men, and this is an issue which needs further analysis.

17 This is also the implication behind the open letter written to *The Times*, Higher Education Supplement, by Professor Celia Wells concerning the appointment of an all-male law benchmarking group by the QAA (see Wells, C, letter (1998) *The Times*, Higher Education Supplement, 19 June).

18 *Ibid*, McGlynn, pp 49–50.

associations and as members of 'quality control' bodies, in order to try and estimate whether, indeed, women are, in terms of the 'public life' of academic law, 'starfish' or 'fish out of water'.

Professional associations

The Association of Law Teachers (ALT), the Society of Public Teachers of Law (SPTL) and the Socio-Legal Studies Association (SLSA) are the three main professional associations to which academic lawyers belong. In order to estimate the significance of the role of women within these organisations, I have examined the constitution of their executive committees over the last 10 years.

The ALT

Between 1990 and 2000, 40% of the chairs of the Executive Committee were women.

In the same period, the Association has had two secretaries, both holding office for periods of five years; one was male and one was female. The treasurer has been a man for the entire period.[19]

The SLSA

In the 10 year period since its foundation in 1990, 60% of the chairs of the SLSA have been women, as have 80% of the vice chairs and 30% of the treasurers; the position of secretary (stereotypically a woman's job) has always been held by a man.[20]

The SPTL

Since 1990, the SPTL has had 10 presidents, of whom 20% have been women. The posts of secretary and treasurer have both been filled by men for the whole of the relevant period.[21]

In terms of professional associations, while it remains true that, over the 10 year period in question, these have been dominated by men, that domination is not as overwhelming as some might have expected. Women have actually played a greater role than men in the newest association, the SLSA, which, despite being the 'new kid on the block', has proved itself to be a major player in the academic legal world.[22] In addition, women have played a very

---

19 I would like to express my thanks for this information to John Hodgson, Nottingham Trent University, current secretary of the ALT.

20 I would like to express my thanks for this information to Trevor Buck, University of Leicester, current secretary of the SLSA.

21 See SPTL Directories 1990–2000.

22 See Thomas, 1997, p 10.

significant role in the ALT, filling nearly half of the presidential posts and acting as secretary of the association for precisely half of the last 10 years.[23] It is, therefore, only the SPTL on which women appear to have made little impact. Yet, on closer examination, there is considerable evidence which suggests that the attitude of the SPTL towards women is changing rapidly. Since 1997, the first two women to become president of the SPTL have been elected. One of the joint editors of the society's journal, *Legal Studies*, is a woman, and as a result of recent changes to the constitution of the society, enlarging the Executive Committee, Council (the managing body of the society) is specifically required, in so far as it is practicable, when it is appointing people to the Executive Committee, to 'procure a reasonable balance in such appointments, taking account of factors such as gender, ethnicity, regional representation, type of institution and subject section representation'.[24] These changes have resulted in an Executive Committee, 42.9% of which is female, contrasting with the position immediately before the changes were implemented, when 15.4% was female.[25] Taken together, these changes point towards a substantial shift in attitude within the SPTL and one which, over the next few years, is likely not only to bring it into line with the other two legal academic associations in terms of equality of participation by women, but at the same time significantly to increase the influence of women in the public arena of legal academic life. Taken overall, the influence of women within professional associations in law is significant; it is certainly an area in which it would be more accurate to categorise women as starfish, rather than fish out of water.

Quality control bodies

The two bodies which have quality control roles in relation to institutions of higher education in England are HEFCE (the Higher Education Funding Council for England) and the QAA (Quality Assurance Agency).[26] HEFCE's periodic research assessment exercises evaluate the quality of research produced by academics in every discipline. The evaluation is carried out by subject panels, composed of distinguished academics within the field; both in financial terms and in terms of the status of the individual law schools involved, the results of the exercise are highly significant, and participation in the exercise as a member of the subject panel is a prestigious occupation.

Research assessment exercises were carried out in 1992 and 1996 and, at the time of writing, the panel for the 2001 exercise has already been

---

23 See figures above, p 67.

24 *Rules of the Society of Public Teachers of Law*, SPTL Directory of Members 2000, para 18.

25 See SPTL Directory of Members 1999.

26 For details of the functions of these two bodies, consult their websites: www.hefce.ac.uk/ and www.qaa.ac.uk/.

appointed.[27] In terms of the participation of women, the picture is mixed. In the 1992 exercise, the law panel was made up of six academics, all of whom were men.[28] In the 1996 exercise, the law subject panel had 11 members, two of whom were women. There are 12 members of the 2001 panel, four of whom are women. The participation by women is, therefore, growing at the rate of 100% per exercise; starting from a base of no participation at all, this still means that only 30% of the panel is female. However, there is room for optimism in the rate of growth, though the interesting question is 'How many women will be appointed to the next exercise?' (if there is one), because, assuming the total size of the panel remained the same, if the numbers of women were to increase at the same rate as in the 1996 and 2001 exercises, this would result in a panel with a majority of women members.

So far, the Quality Assurance Agency does not have a good record in terms of the involvement of female academic lawyers. The agency was created in 1997 to review the performance of institutions of higher education, which it achieves by (a) auditing academic management, and (b) assessing the quality of teaching and learning at subject level.[29] It is mainly the latter activity in which academic lawyers are involved, and in 1997, the QAA set up a number of subject groups to produce 'benchmarks' which will be used for quality assurance purposes in each subject area. The law benchmarking group contained only one woman (who was not an academic, but was nominated by the legal profession in Northern Ireland), a fact which was the subject of an immediate protest by Professor Celia Wells, who, in a letter to *The Times*, Higher Education Supplement, commented that, in appointing the law benchmarking panel, the QAA 'has failed to notice that law schools employ women as well as men'.[30]

So, in terms of the 'public life' of academic law, women are playing an increasing role, and in two of the professional associations (the ALT and the SLSA) they are major players. In terms of quality control bodies, the picture is not so bright, but the steady increase in the participation of women in the RAE panels gives cause for some optimism, showing, as it does, that women are no longer excluded from this highly prestigious activity, concerned with research, which itself is generally regarded as the most prestigious activity within university life.[31]

---

27 The HEFCE website contains detailed information about all of these exercises: www.hefce.ac.uk/.

28 Details of this panel are not on the HEFCE website; the 1992 exercise was carried out by the Universities Funding Council (UFC), predecessor to HEFCE, and details of the Law Subject Panel can be found in UFC Circular 24/92 RAE 1992, Membership of Assessment Panels.

29 See the QAA website for further details: www.qaa.ac.uk/.

30 Wells, C, letter (1998) *The Times*, Higher Education Supplement, 19 June.

31 For a longer discussion of the way in which research is regarded within the academy, see Halsey, 1992, p 207.

The 'private life' of law schools

Another area in which one might find evidence of women as 'starfish' is in their position within the law school, thinking here not so much about the public life of academic law, as what Martin Trow has called its 'private life', that is, 'what actually happens in the classrooms, the libraries, the laboratories, at the desks and in the offices – the moment by moment, day to day activities and interactions of teachers and students engaged in teaching and learning'.[32]

Clare McGlynn is not optimistic about the role of women within the legal academy, arguing that: 'If women students are to learn to act like lawyers, but the only role models they have are junior women, or women who are marginalised, they may themselves be imbued with a sense of the woman lawyer not as authoritative lawyer, judge or academic, but as handmaiden.'[33]

However, while it is true that there is a dearth of women professors, the dearth of women legal academics in general should not be exaggerated. McGlynn's own figures show that there are many women in the law school who can both act as role models and play a significant part in the development of academic law – the 49% of junior lecturers and 40% of senior staff who are women.[34] These are not insignificant figures. It is also important to remember that, in law schools which lack female professors, it is the sub-professorial senior women who necessarily take on many of the roles which might be carried out by female professors elsewhere; their ability to act both as role models and as mentors should not be underestimated.

There is a wider point to be made here, namely that, in evaluating the influence of women within the academic legal world, we should remember that it is not necessary to bear the title of professor in order to wield influence – the current chair of the SLSA, the current chair of the ALT, and four of the six women on the executive committee of the SPTL are not professors, but they nevertheless play important roles in legal academia.[35] Further, the mere existence of a female professor in a law school does not necessarily mean that women will be provided with a positive role model, other than the symbolic one of the mere existence of a female chair-holder.

Research

In the context of considering the position of women within the legal academy, it is particularly interesting to look at feminist legal research; not because all women carry out feminist research (they clearly do not; some men, on the

---

32 Trow, 1975, p 113.
33 McGlynn, 1999, p 87.
34 *Ibid*, p 80.
35 For details of the composition of the relevant bodies, see the 2000 edition of their Directories.

other hand, do), but because the value placed on feminist research is an indicator of the extent to which research associated closely with women is accepted by those belonging to the academic discipline of law.

McGlynn is not optimistic in her assessment of the extent to which feminist research is valued; while she concedes that feminist scholarship is published in established journals and by traditional publishers, she still argues that it is doubtless less valued than non-feminist writing, speculating that research on women legal academics might remain too 'risky' in career terms.[36] Without firm empirical evidence, it is difficult to evaluate this comment, since it is impossible to decide whether writing feminist research is 'risky' or not. It is, at least, arguable that writing feminist research is no more 'risky' than undertaking any other kind of research which is not 'black letter', and that any suspicion about such research arises not from the fact that it is about women, but that it is 'not law'. In other words, what is being questioned is the place of any research in the law school which is not doctrinal. Certainly it is the case that, as far as feminist legal research is concerned, its place in the legal academy was not raised as an issue in the extensive consultation undertaken by the 2001 law RAE panel. Indeed, feminist and gender studies are expressly listed along with other specialisms, such as company and commercial law, property law and tax, as belonging within the 'unit of assessment' for law.[37] In that instance, at least, feminist/gender studies appears to have been unproblematically accepted as part of the discipline of law – contrast the position of legal education, which was the only area of legal research specifically identified as one which might be more appropriately submitted to another unit of assessment (education), rather than being accepted as part of the discipline of law.[38] This may suggest, at least at RAE level, a greater acceptance of feminist research than McGlynn was prepared to acknowledge. This, taken together with the publication of feminist work in mainstream journals, and by mainstream publishers to which McGlynn refers, as well the emergence of specialist journals such as *Feminist Legal Studies*, could provide greater grounds for concluding that feminist research, while still undertaken by a minority of legal academics, has, nevertheless, gained acceptance as part of the mainstream content of the discipline of law. In that sense, at least, feminist research is an aspect of women's participation in the law school by which they might be judged to be starfish, rather than fish out of water.

Optimism about the extent to which feminist legal research will in future be accepted without hesitation as a mainstream aspect of the discipline of law can also be founded on the work of a number of commentators who have written recently about the extent to which doctrinal law is losing its grip on

36 McGlynn, 1998, p 51.
37 See RAE Circular 4/99, Draft Statements of Criteria and Working Methods.
38 *Ibid*, para 2.28.23.

the legal academy. While many might find Bradney's comment that 'The academic doctrinal project ... is now entering its final death throes' somewhat extreme, his analysis of the significant decrease in the power of black letter law, as he points out, is shared by many others, including Hepple, whose inaugural lecture at Cambridge called for law students to study, amongst other things, social sciences, ethics, philosophy and history, Cotterell, whose idea of 'law's community' involves the recognition that a few decades of socio-legal scholarship have produced more valuable knowledge about the phenomenon of law than centuries of doctrinal writing, and Thomas, who, in the introduction to his collection of essays on socio-legal studies, identifies the current growth in socio-legal studies as heralding the emergence of a new paradigm in law schools.[39] Even in a subject like company law, unquestionably part of the doctrinal mainstream for so long, arguments are being made that in the current state of knowledge, a 'black letter' analysis is inadequate. Writing in the *Cambridge Law Journal*, Professor Brian Cheffins argues that there is currently a movement in Britain towards theoretical legal scholarship (which he defines as the study of law from the 'outside', using intellectual disciplines external to law to carry out research on its economic, social or political implications (a definition which, for many, would equate with socio-legal studies).[40] He goes on to argue that the movement towards theory which has influenced law in general has also affected company law, and notices that this includes the development of a feminist corporate law literature, which explores issues of gender which are traditionally hidden by the basic concepts of company law.[41]

The decrease in the power of doctrinalism which is noted by all these writers can only be good for the development of feminist approaches to law, as it is for all alternative paradigms. The less powerful is the doctrinal paradigm, the more space there is for alternative interpretations of the legal world to take root.

THE OVERALL PICTURE: STILL FISH OUT OF WATER?

Despite the relatively positive view of women's experience of, and contribution to, the law school which I have adopted up to this point, there is still a large body of evidence which suggests that, in many ways, the experience of women in law schools, both as students and staff, is not only different from that of their male counterparts, but is also in some ways unfairly or disadvantageously different.

---

39 Bradney, 1998, p 73; Hepple, 1996, pp 481 and 485; Cotterell, 1995, p 296; and Thomas, 1997.
40 Cheffins, 1999, p 198.
41 *Ibid*, p 211.

Law students

The traditional approach to law teaching has been to regard the curriculum as gender-neutral. However, women students' experience of law school is of a legal curriculum whose acceptance of the traditional boundaries of legal specialisms makes it difficult to identify connections and common themes; accounts of rape and domestic violence are commonly split between criminal law courses and family law courses, and if the analysis is confined to a doctrinal approach, discussion can be reduced to analysis of technical matters, drained of any sense of the significance of the issues being discussed.[42] Mary Joe Frug's analysis of the law of contract serves as just one powerful reminder of the extent to which gender suffuses the teaching of law in universities.[43] There is much still to be explored, yet traditional doctrinal analysis is of no help, since it lacks the tools with which to explore gender issues as they affect law and law teaching.

Developing Smart's observation that there are 'mutual resonances' in the constitution of law and masculinities, Richard Collier has argued that there is an overwhelming case for linking the masculine, the rational and traditional legal method.[44] As he goes on to point out, although it has long been acknowledged that traditional law schools offer what Kennedy famously termed 'a training for a hierarchy', the gender dimension of this process is relatively unexplored.[45] Collier's conclusion contains a powerful challenge to law teachers: 'While excluding feminist challenges to the power of law, doctrinal exegetical method entails a systematic negation of questions of subjectivity and the denial of the legitimation of any sexual political engagement which might question the silences of gender ...'[46]

It is in the traditional doctrinal approach to the study of law that the 'silences of gender' are most obvious, but that is not to say that students whose teachers follow a less traditional approach will find that their studies involve deconstructing the gendered nature of law and law teaching. It remains true that this is a relatively unexplored area, and while that continues to be the case, women law students are likely to continue to find that legal education leaves them stranded, at least occasionally, as fish out of water.

So far, my analysis of the legal curriculum has focused on the gendered nature of law and law teaching, and the contribution those issues may make to the way in which legal education is experienced by women students. For women law students, it is also important to look specifically at the issue of

---

42 For further discussion of women and the law school curriculum, see Cownie and Bradney, 1996, pp 131–32.
43 Frug, 1992.
44 Collier, 1991, p 431.
45 *Ibid*, p 441.
46 *Ibid*, p 447.

feminist legal studies. Arguably, this is one area of the curriculum where women students might feel at home. Whether that is the case will partly depend on the extent to which this subject is regarded as legitimate by the legal academy. McGlynn's survey suggests that, at her census date in 1997, about 30% of law schools offered courses entitled 'women and the law', 'gender and the law' or something similar, while just under half (45%) of law schools said they offered at least one course which offered a gender/feminist perspective (given the survey relied largely on reporting by heads of department, it is possible that it suffered from some under-reporting – this was certainly the case in my own institution).[47] Arguably, McGlynn's data suggest that feminist approaches to law are gaining ground; the earlier Harris and Jones survey showed that, in 1995, 20% of law schools taught a subject described as 'gender and the law', while 6% taught feminism and law (and there may be some double-counting here).[48] However, even taking the more optimistic later data, evidence of the existence of one specialist course, or one topic within a course, in a minority of law schools, does not suggest that feminism has moved into the mainstream of the legal curriculum. The treatment of issues relating to women in the legal curriculum is not, it appears, nearly as positive as the legal academy's treatment of feminist/gender research, and thus the extent to which its appearance on the curriculum enables women students to feel fully accepted by the legal academy is arguably not as great as might have been expected.

Support for the proposition that law schools are far from comfortable places for women law students also comes from the work of Margaret Thornton, whose analysis of Australian law school culture leads her to conclude that law schools are, in general, hostile, masculine places, where all students are expected to be docile and subservient to the 'technocratic' legal knowledge they are being taught.[49] Although it is the case that there are considerably more women entering law school than there have ever been before, Thornton reports that the majority of her interviewees found the experience of law school 'profoundly alienating in respect of its culture, the nature of legal knowledge transmitted and the pedagogical style' and that they found the law school classroom 'physically, socially and emotionally threatening'.[50] She concludes that, while women now constitute approximately 50% of law students, they are not accepted on equal terms with male law students, even though they perform at least as competently in academic terms. 'Women are generally not taken as seriously as male students by either staff or male students themselves ...'[51]

---

47 McGlynn, 1998, Appendix 2.
48 Harris and Jones, 1996, p 52.
49 Thornton, 1996, Chapter 3.
50 *Ibid*, p 89.
51 *Ibid*, p 104.

Thornton's arguments are powerfully put, and provide the reader with much food for thought about the ways in which women, while physically present in large numbers, might nevertheless effectively be excluded from the contemporary law school. However, her arguments are framed in the context of Australian law schools, and it would be dangerous to assume that a direct analogy can be drawn with the situation of women in UK law schools. One of Thornton's main points is that the law taught in law schools is doctrinal and that this legal positivism, with its assumption of right answers, discourages any kind of critical analysis or alternative interpretation of legal phenomena:

> With the exception of some optional subjects, the vast body of legal rules still tend to be taught primarily as intellectual exercises, so that scant critical attention is paid to the social contexts in which they operate. I use the term 'technocentrism' to capture the centripetal pull of rules rationality and the way in which it disqualifies other forms of knowledge.[52]

The problem about applying this analysis to all UK law schools is that, as we have already seen, there is no clear evidence that pure doctrinal analysis, in the form described by Thornton, is as dominant in the UK context as it appears to be in Australia. Thornton reports that, in Australia, there is '... an increased focus on technocratic law within legal education, a focus that comports with the economic rationalism of the 1990s ...'.[53] This contrasts with the position in the UK, where the move appears to be away from dominance by doctrinal law to a much more pluralistic approach.[54] This does not, of course, mean that female students in the UK find law school a comfortable and congenial experience, but it does mean that they are not faced with precisely the same situation as that which Thornton describes.

But this is not to deny that problems remain. One such area concerns the type of subject which women choose to study. It would appear that women at law school are already identifying with the 'caring, sharing' subjects, which tend to be regarded as being of less status than the heavy commercial subjects. The Law Society's cohort study found marked differences between men and women in terms of areas of interest. Men were more interested in the commercial subjects, whereas women were very much more interested in family, matrimonial, welfare law and human rights. The significance of the data becomes even clearer when they are seen in relation to the study's findings on the factors which are important in career choice, which revealed that women are less likely than men to prioritise salary as a factor in their career choice, but more likely to prioritise factors such as the value of work to the community.[55] As the authors of the study comment:

---

52 Thornton, 1996, p 76.

53 *Ibid*, p 103.

54 See Bradney, 1998; Cotterell, 1995; Thomas, 1997; and Hepple, 1996; also Brownsword, 1999, p 26.

55 Shiner and Newburn, 1995, p 60.

Taken together, these findings strongly suggest that the men are acting to select themselves into the more lucrative commercial areas of law, while the women are tending to select themselves into the relatively poorly paid areas of law that are presently dominated by legal aid work. Clearly, if these divisions continue into professional life then they imply the maintenance or further development of high levels of gender segregation within the legal professions.[56]

Since year 4 of the cohort study showed that there is a generally high correlation between the areas of law in which trainees expressed an interest and those in which they actually obtain work, this suggests that segregation on gender lines may be a feature of the legal profession.[57] Attitudes displayed by female law students whilst at university may therefore have far reaching consequences, such a possibility being further reinforced by data from the cohort study about career choices, which suggests that women are more likely than men to choose to work in the less glamorous parts of the legal profession, such as central or local government, the CPS or the magistrates' court service.[58] These findings reflect the contrast between law schools in the UK and those in the USA, where all students tend to gravitate towards a male norm, many women changing their position from an initial interest in welfare law or public interest work to the male interests in commercial/political subjects.[59]

Overall, there is sufficient evidence to suggest that women's experience of legal education is different from that of men. While that remains unacknowledged and is ignored in terms of curriculum content and delivery, there are good reasons for thinking that female students in a law school may feel like fish out of water.

Law staff

Margaret Thornton's research also helps to raise questions about the extent to which the contemporary law school is a comfortable place for female academic staff. Her view is that 'the contemporary university is a modern corporation organised among bureaucratic lines ...' and that there is a clear congruence between bureaucratic power and masculinity.[60] Thornton's central argument is that bureaucracy bears differently upon men and women, so that, generally, men dominate academia, occupying most of the powerful and prestigious positions: 'Not only do they lunch and drink together, but

---

56 Shiner and Newburn, 1995.
57 Shiner, 1997, p 82.
58 *Ibid*, p 65.
59 See, eg, Guinier *et al*, 1994, pp 1–110.
60 Thornton, 1996, pp 106 and 108.

they nominate each other to important decision making positions so that they are able to vet candidates and promote policies that accord with the organisation's "mission", as they have designed it.'[61]

Women are generally found in the lower echelons of university bureaucracies; if they are appointed to positions of authority, their authority will not be regarded as being the same as the normative male. They also face continual difficulties of either being seen as 'men in drag' or, if they adopt a softer management style, of being ignored or seen as non-authoritative; either way, women in leadership positions are likely to face considerable resistance.[62] All women in bureaucracies, argues Thornton, are meant to be 'dutiful daughters', carrying out caring roles such as assuming responsibility for student welfare, or other institutional caring and housekeeping roles, such as conference organising. 'Dutiful daughters also find themselves assigned to a plethora of relatively unimportant and time-consuming advisory committees so the academy can present an appearance of gender neutrality and collegiality'.[63]

Thornton's analysis of academia is not unproblematic. Apart from the fact that her empirical work was carried out in Australia, so that we need to be cautious in applying her conclusions in the UK context, Thornton's central idea of the university as a bureaucracy is also problematic. The extent to which it is accurate to equate universities with modern corporations is fiercely contested. Trow, for example, would clearly reject such an interpretation. Commenting on the Dearing Report, Trow takes issue with the report's assumption that, in universities, 'management' can unproblematically impose its will on individual academics. Dearing's eighth main recommendation was that 'with immediate effect ...' institutions should give high priority to developing and implanting learning and teaching strategies which focus on the promotion of students' learning.[64] Trow commented:

> I like particularly the intensifier 'with immediate effect': the phrase suggests how strong is the committee's illusion that universities are organised like firms, bureaucratically, with clear lines of authority that can ensure the instructions down the line will be obeyed 'with immediate effect'.[65]

While it is not possible here to enter fully into the debate about the nature of universities. it is important to note other competing analyses of the university which some readers, at least, might find more appropriate. These would include, for example, analyses which focus on the organisational dynamics of

---

61 Thornton, 1996, p 109.
62 *Ibid*, p 110.
63 *Ibid*, p 114.
64 National Committee of Inquiry into Higher Education, 1997, para 8.10.
65 Trow (1997) *The Times*, Higher Education Supplement, 24 October, p 26.

universities (the 'political university'), or which conceive of universities as 'organised anarchies'.[66]

In questioning Thornton's wholehearted adoption of the notion of the university as bureaucracy, I am not, however, seeking to diminish the general point she is making about the importance of analysing university law schools as sites of masculine power. This is an area of great significance which has generally lain unexplored, and Thornton's work remains immensely valuable in raising important issues for consideration. Her analysis of the culture of academia, leading to the conclusion that women legal academics may still, in some senses, be 'fish out of water' in the law schools in which they work, is not to be lightly dismissed.[67]

Further evidence that women legal academics may indeed be 'fish out of water' comes from a number of different sources. Leighton *et al*, in their survey of legal academics, found that male and female staff had significantly different attitudes towards research and teaching. More males (81%) than females (67%) reported that they were engaged in research;[68] while more women (80%) than men (57%) considered teaching and contact with students an 'essential' part of their job[69] and the reverse was true of research, with 63% of men and 47% of women considering that research is an essential or important part of their job.[70] This data confirms the findings of a large number of surveys carried out in the USA, which have found that considerably more women than men list teaching as their principal activity.[71] Given the heavy emphasis frequently placed on research in terms of promotion, it would seem, to say the least, that women's interest in teaching (and disinterest in research) means that they are out of tune with the prevailing culture. There is copious evidence to suggest that universities have a strong research culture, and the comment in the Dearing Report that 'research and scholarship are defining purposes of higher education ...' reflects a mainstream view.[72] This is not to say women are wrong to value teaching (indeed, I have argued strongly elsewhere that it is essential for academics to take teaching seriously),[73] but the dissonance between their concerns and the norm suggests that, particularly at reader/chair level, where

---

66   See Bargh, Scott and Smith, 1996, p 32.
67   Apart from Thornton, few writers have addressed such questions; a notable exception is the work of Richard Collier (see Collier, 1991). See, also, McGlynn, 1998 and 1999 and Cownie, 1998, pp 102–16.
68   Leighton, Mortimer and Whatley, 1995, p 38.
69   *Ibid*, p 50.
70   *Ibid*, p 51.
71   This research is discussed in Collins *et al*, 1998, p 108.
72   National Committee of Inquiry into Higher Education, 1997, p 75. See, also, Cownie (forthcoming). For similar views in the USA, see Dunkin and Prescians, 1994, p 85 and in Australia, see Dunkin, 1991, p 115.
73   Cownie, 1999, pp 41–59.

there is most emphasis on research output as a criterion for promotion, women are not going to make major inroads until either they change their attitudes or the prevailing norms are altered, so that teaching activities are valued more highly.

When the data above is combined with further data from the Leighton study on attitudes towards the concept of flexible working, we see another area of dissonance between male and female legal academics. Leighton *et al* found that 49% of women, but only 39% of men, regarded flexible working as an essential aspect of their job.[74] Flexible working hours are undoubtedly beneficial for those who have to care for young children or elderly relatives. It appears likely that women legal academics, just as in society as a whole, remain the primary carers, and it is arguable that law schools, like other institutions in society, need to think more carefully about flexible working patterns if they are to allow women, at all stages of their lives, to participate as fully as possible in their academic career and stop them finding themselves fish out of water.

Further evidence of the likelihood of female academic lawyers feeling like fish out of water comes from work on teaching styles. Heald's essay on academic social relations is a classic example of 'status inconsistency' or 'role conflict' theory, which holds that men and women incorporate different traits and that these differences are sex-typed, so when women are placed in a situation that is sex-typed male (such as a university law school), they experience status inconsistency, because their female sex status is inconsistent with their occupational status as a legal academic. As Statham et al point out, this theory suggests that women will experience extreme role conflict in such situations, because the demands of the two different roles (female and legal academic) are contradictory. As a result, structural role theory predicts that women will encounter difficulty functioning in traditionally male-dominated occupations such as academia and that their female sex-typed behaviours will detract from their competence.[75] Heald's essay explores the way in which dominant discourses impose forms of identity which are tightly circumscribed and exclude many people.[76] She argues that these discourses do not merely constrain us, they actually constitute who we are and how we know who to be, defining identities and setting the limits of what can be done within that subject position by whatever incumbent:

> Thus there can be said to be an 'education subject': a mythical figure who tells us who students and professors are meant to be. The subject constructed in educational discourse claims neutrality ... but this subject is recognisably white, male, middle-class, heterosexual, able-bodied and rational. Other elements which appear as 'neutral' aspects of education include a separation of

---

74 Leighton, Mortimer and Whatley, 1995, p 50.
75 Statham, Richardson and Cook, 1991, p 123.
76 Heald, 1991, p 129.

knowledge and opinion, a belief that the only proper and useful knowledge is rational knowledge ...[77]

These are among the features which currently serve to define the boundaries of current educational discourse. They invite certain ways of being a teacher and a student, and, more significantly, discourage other ways of being those things. Certain expectations are created, into which women may not easily fit. 'As a professor', writes Heald, 'I am supposed to have authority, as a woman I am not'.[78] She goes on to quote extensively from work by Paula Treichler, which graphically illustrates the way in which women academics, merely by being themselves, may find that they are 'fish out of water':

> Studies of teachers find that, at every educational level, women tend to generate more class discussion, more interaction, more give-and-take between students and teacher and among students. In direct relation to the degree to which this is true (1) students evaluate these classes as friendlier, livelier, less authoritarian, and more conducive to learning, and (2) students judge the teacher to be less competent in her subject matter. Thus behaviours judged as traditionally male – a lecture format, little student give-and-take, the transmission of a given body of content, little attention to process – seem also to signal professional competence.[79]

Statham *et al*'s US study of 167 male and female academics and their students in a large Midwestern university provides good evidence of the different teaching styles to which Heald refers, but goes on to provide a theoretical analysis of these differences which suggests that the picture is not as bleak as Heald and Treichler might appear to suggest.[80] Statham *et al* found striking differences between teaching styles of male and female academics. Broadly, women tended to focus more on the student as the locus of learning, men on themselves. Women took pains to involve students and to receive more input from them. They reported that their teaching satisfaction came from students relating to each other, developing their own ideas and coming prepared to participate in class discussion. Men tended to regard student participation as a requirement, or sometimes as a 'time waste'. Women's efforts to nurture independent thinkers seemed to be successful, since the researchers observed students presenting material of their own more often, and independently soliciting more information, in women's classrooms.[81] This aspect of the research in question confirms work by the American researchers Aisenberg and Harrington, who found that, regardless of the extent of their scholarly interests, female academics tend to spend more time with students than male academics; they suggest that, far from arising out of some innate nurturing

---

77 Heald, 1991, p 137.
78 *Ibid*, p 144.
79 Treichler, p 86, quoted in *ibid*, p 144.
80 Statham, Richardson and Cook, 1991.
81 *Ibid*, p 127.

ability, this is because women see learning as a tool for personal empowerment, and that this is their goal both personally and in relation to their students.[82]

In Statham's study, students rated men and women as equally effective instructors, though generally, adherence to a gender-appropriate role was rewarded with higher evaluations, so, for example, women's competence ratings were higher the more they interacted with students, by checking their understanding, acknowledging their contributions, responding to requests for information. Men's ratings were higher the more they used their 'teacher is expert' style.[83]

Statham *et al* argue that, according to a structuralist perspective, women academics feel required to adopt an interactive approach to teaching partly because of prior socialisation and partly because of perceived role pressures and students' demands to conform to more sex-typed behaviour. Yet they also perceive that they will be judged as incompetent if they do so. Consequently, a great deal of role conflict and status anxiety are generated, as women academics try to engage in strategies which enable them to adhere to traditional female role expectations while enacting the role of university lecturer. This is a balancing act men do not have to master, because most traditional male role requirements mesh neatly with the 'academic' role.[84]

The conclusions, here as elsewhere, are complex. While it appears that men and women do use different teaching styles in the classroom, and that the reasons for this are not 'fair', in the sense that women have to negotiate their way through a much more complex set of social relations than men, nevertheless, Statham et al are clear that the approach of women academics has many strengths, and cannot be regarded as less effective than that of male academics, since they achieve equally desirable outcomes. Nevertheless, they also point out that, when teaching is evaluated, it is important that indicators of good teaching are not based exclusively on the male model. It is also important that the pressures of role conflict experienced by women are also managed properly; for instance, it is possible that women may easily become overburdened by too much contact with students.[85] This cautious approach is supported by Basow, whose analysis of the literature on student evaluation of teaching leads her to conclude that, depending on the methodology used, the gender-typing of the discipline and the types of questions asked, female academics may receive significantly lower ratings than male academics, especially from male students.[86]

---

82 Aisenberg and Harrington, 1988.
83 Statham, Richardson and Cook, 1991, p 129.
84 *Ibid*, p 133.
85 *Ibid*, p 153.
86 Basow, 1998, p 136.

This is yet another area, I would argue, in which it is impossible to draw a clear-cut conclusion that women's ways of doing things are unacceptable; rather, the picture is of a different way of doing things. As with all studies carried out in a different geographical location to our own, we cannot assume the results found in the American surveys would be exactly replicated in the UK, but, nevertheless, their analysis provides an interesting perspective on the debate as to whether women in the law school are 'fish out of water'.[87]

CONCLUSION – LIBERATING THE STARFISH

Despite arguing that it is important to acknowledge the real contribution currently being made to the legal academy by female students and staff, and a concern that the very real achievements of women should not be ignored or disregarded, I still share some of the reservations expressed more strongly by some of the researchers whose work I have discussed above.

If we are to understand the position of women in the contemporary law school, there is much work to be done. I have argued elsewhere that researching women legal academics might tell us much about the nature of the academy and the discipline of law, as well as challenging the apparently hegemonic nature of masculinity within law and the law school.[88] I want to explore here the possibilities inherent in a wider research agenda, one which includes students as well as staff.

Behind the idea of 'fish out of water' lies the work of Carol Gilligan, and in particular *In A Different Voice,* the seminal work in which she argued that psychological theory has systematically misunderstood women's motives, commitment and psychological development.[89] Gilligan's work has proved extremely controversial, since her work is easily open to the essentialist interpretation that all women reason differently from men.[90] Yet Gilligan herself is ambiguous on this point. While her study was prompted by her observation of different ways of speaking about moral problems and

---

87 Statham, Richardson and Cook's 1991 study involved a sample of 167 university lecturers of all levels of seniority, including equal numbers of men and women in all departments. Semi-structured interviews were carried out with a purposive sample of 15 matched pairs of academics (matched for all relevant factors except gender) to gather qualitative data; observations of teaching style were made using trained observers who used a time-unit method of observation, which involves the coding of activities that occur in each five seconds of class time. The researchers also administered a questionnaire to gather data on students' responses to their teachers' behaviours.

88 Cownie, 1999.

89 Gilligan, 1982.

90 There is a large amount of literature which discusses Gilligan's work; see, eg, Frug, 1992, Chapter 3; Menkel Meadow, 1985; Rhode, 1988.

describing the relationship between other and self which largely corresponded to male and female voices, she makes it clear in her introduction that:

> The different voice I describe is characterised not by gender but by theme. Its association with women is an empirical observation, and it is primarily through women's voices that I trace its development. But this association is not absolute, and the contrasts between male and female voices are presented here to highlight a distinction between two modes of thought and to focus a problem of interpretation rather than to present a generalisation about either sex.[91]

The evidence discussed above in relation to women in the law school feeling like fish out of water suggests that we should at least explore Gilligan's thesis further in the context of the law school. The research which has already been carried out on gender and the law school provides a basis from which to embark on further explorations of the ways in which law, masculinity and education may combine to suppress the feminine voice in the contemporary law school.

A number of different literatures might influence the necessary research: education (particularly the sub-discipline of higher education studies), anthropology, gender studies and sociology, to name but a few. In terms of female students, we need to build on the work which Thornton has carried out in Australia, by gathering qualitative data on the lived experience of female students in law schools. While women undergraduates are performing extremely well, there remains a question mark over their inability to gain as many first class law degrees as men (or why they do not achieve more than men, given their superior numbers). If we give Gilligan's work even the smallest amount of credibility, there also remains the question about whether law schools cater for the 'different voice' of female law students. In terms of staff, we are left wondering why, at the beginning of the 21st century, there is still such a dearth of female professors in an academic discipline where 49% of senior staff are women. In this context, it would be interesting to explore further Chrisler's analysis of work carried out by social psychologists, which suggests that women academics frequently lack self-confidence, and that this arises because the successes of women are often attributed to unstable factors, such as luck or hard work, whereas the successes of men are generally attributed to stable factors such as ability. Since women's success is attributed to unstable factors, they will not expect continued success in the future, and to make matters worse, they tend to attribute any failure they experience to stable factors, such as lack of ability, whereas men's failures are generally attributable to unstable factors, such as lack of effort. This cognitive pattern is most likely to be found when the activity involved is one which is

---

91   Gilligan, 1982, p 2.

stereotypically considered masculine, such as scholarship.[92] Looking at the quantitative data on women legal academics, it is difficult not to see a 'glass ceiling', but its existence, and its nature, need to be thoroughly researched.[93] Only then will women legal academics have a real possibility of achieving equality with their male colleagues.

As I have argued previously, very little is known about women academics in general, and still less about women *legal* academics.[94] There is an equally strong case for researching female law students. The evidence suggests that there is still a 'fight to be fought' here. But, it is a complex battle. If we are to make real progress in increasing the participation, in the broadest sense, of women in the legal academy, we need more qualitative research, to identify precisely what their current experience is, where the barriers lie, how they are created and what can be done to overcome them. Gender is a greatly under-explored, but essential aspect of the culture of law schools. As Delamont has pointed out on several occasions, much sociology of higher education has failed to use gender as an organising principle.[95] That was certainly true of Becher's seminal study of the culture of disciplines, *Academic Tribes and Territories*.[96] His work is of enormous value in pointing to the significance of the social aspects of the organisation of knowledge communities (including academic law), but he did not collect any data specifically related to the position of women within different academic disciplines, so that his work does not directly contribute to our understanding of women in the law school. Having carried out his research, Becher writes that, if he were to start again, he would want to build in some systematic exploration of gender differences; an acknowledgment, from a leading scholar, that exploration of the lived experience of women in the context of the academy is likely to be a fruitful area of research.[97] Delamont notes, with some apparent surprise, that 'there is, today, no solid body of data on the ethnography of higher education, and few attempts to study the occupational cultures of those who work in higher education ...'.[98] She speculates that this may be because higher education is so familiar to researchers that they just fail to notice what interesting things are going on: '... higher education does have a particular kind of familiarity which makes it especially tough to make its occupational cultures anthropologically strange.'[99] Until we have this information, not only about

---

92   Chrisler, 1998, p 116.
93   For a more detailed discussion of the notion of a 'glass ceiling' as it relates to women academics, see David and Woodward, 1998, p 14.
94   Cownie, 1999, p 102.
95   Delamont, 1996, pp 145–56; Delamont, 1989, pp 51–57.
96   Becher, 1989.
97   *Ibid*, p 174.
98   Delamont, 1996, p 146.
99   *Ibid*, p 147.

the lived experience of women in the law school, but about all that goes on in law schools, we shall not be able to understand the phenomenon of the law school sufficiently well to ensure that the women within it are enabled to be starfish and not fish out of water.

CHAPTER 5

YOUNG, GIFTED AND BLOCKED!
ENTRY TO THE SOLICITORS' PROFESSION

Michael Shiner

INTRODUCTION*

Solicitors constitute an elite professional group with high status, substantial earning potential and a key role in applying and administering the law. The process by which individuals enter such a group is of considerable practical and ideological importance. The most obvious concern relates to the degree to which selection into the profession is meritocratic. While it raises issues of fairness and equal opportunities, the process by which people enter the profession has implications which go far beyond the 'rights' of individual applicants.

Laws are not created or administered in a cultural vacuum and it may be argued that the legal profession should broadly reflect the composition of the society that it serves. Opponents of such a view may reject it on the grounds that it is idealistic or even naïve. It is, however, important to distinguish between a situation in which the skewed composition of the profession reflects broad social forces (for example, those pertaining to access to higher education) and that in which biases from within the profession create, or reinforce, inequality. If certain communities face discrimination in the process by which the legal profession recruits its members, then how legitimate are any claims that the profession may make in terms of representing these communities? Equally, in such circumstances, what confidence can these communities have in the broader services provided by the legal profession.[1]

This chapter is based on a Law Society funded study of entry into the legal profession. The study examined the experiences of a cohort of law students who were due to complete the *academic* stage of their legal training (a law degree or the CPE)[2] in the summer of 1993. Its primary aim was to uncover

---

* The study on which this chapter is based was funded by the Research and Policy Planning Unit at the Law Society. I am indebted to many people for their help with the study, especially Gerry Chambers and Carole Willis, both of whom are former members of the RPPU.

1 Bhatti, 1992; McConville and Mirsky, 1988; Young and Wall, 1996.

2 CPE is an abbreviation for the Common Professional Examination and has been used throughout this chapter to describe all postgraduate conversion courses in law. Although some such courses have the title 'Postgraduate Diploma in Law' they have, for convenience, been included under the term CPE.

and explore those factors that affect patterns of entry into the legal profession in England and Wales. A longitudinal design was employed: members of the cohort were surveyed regularly and this provided for a detailed analysis of their attempts to progress along the pathway leading to a career as a qualified solicitor.

METHODOLOGY[3]

This study was made up of six surveys during the period 1991–99. The first and second surveys sought to establish a representative sample of law students. For the first survey, questionnaires were distributed to a random sample of approximately *half* of the law undergraduates in England and Wales who were in the penultimate year of their course. The second survey included these same students and *all* CPE students who were due to complete their course in the summer of 1993.[4] This first phase of the study was very successful, as the vast majority of sampled institutions co-operated with the research and an estimated 76% of eligible students responded.[5]

The process by which data were collected underwent an important change following the second survey. Questionnaires were subsequently sent directly, by post, to members of the cohort. In order to boost the response rates, telephone interviews were conducted with those who did not respond to the postal survey.

Weighting was used to improve the representativeness of data collected via the surveys. This corrected for the relative over-sampling of CPE students, all of whom were included in the sample compared with half the law degree students. It also corrected for different rates at which individuals in different types of institution responded to the study.[6]

This chapter is based on the first five surveys in the study and details relating to the administration of the third, fourth and fifth surveys are given in Table 1. The numbers included in each of these surveys varied. Not all of

---

3   For more details about the overall design of the study and the separate surveys please refer to Halpern, 1994; Shiner and Newburn, 1995; Shiner, 1997 and 1999; Duff, Shiner and Boon, forthcoming.

4   The second survey also included students on the external LLB degree course offered by London University, an estimated 600 of whom were expected to take final year exams in 1993. It proved very difficult to find a reliable way of contacting these students and very few responded (see *ibid*, Halpern). Consequently, they were subsequently excluded from the study. Similarly, due to a low level of response, those in the cohort who had been overseas students were excluded from the study following the third survey. Neither overseas students nor external LLB students were included in the analyses described in this chapter.

5   *Ibid*, Halpern.

6   *Ibid*, Shiner and Newburn; Shiner, 1997.

those who responded to the first two surveys provided an address at which they could subsequently be reached. Consequently, the number included in the third survey is slightly lower than the number in the cohort as a whole. Fewer still were included in the fourth and fifth surveys, and this reflected a process of attrition. Some members of the cohort asked to be excluded from the study and, for some, information was received that they could no longer be contacted via the address they had given.

Table 1: Survey details (numbers, unweighted)[7]

	Number who responded	Number included in survey	Response rate	Number in cohort
Third survey	2,944	4,011	73%	4,062
Fourth survey	2,637	3,933	67%	4,062
Fifth survey	2,202	3,703	59%	4,062

Although the overall response rate had fallen considerably by the time of the fifth survey, those members of the cohort who constituted the key focus of this survey responded in good numbers. Thus, 72% of those who had started or arranged a training contract at the time of the previous survey responded to the fifth survey. Furthermore, the longitudinal design of the study meant that it was not necessarily appropriate to view each survey as being separate from all of the others. Analyses frequently drew on data from a range of surveys. Thus, for example, that relating to the allocation of training contracts was based on data from the third, fourth and fifth surveys. Eight out of 10 members of the cohort responded to one, or more, of these surveys.

Respondents to the third, fourth and fifth surveys were reasonably representative of the cohort overall in terms of their demographic profile and orientations to a legal career.[8] Nevertheless, women consistently responded at a higher rate than men, and whites responded at a higher rate than ethnic minorities. Ethnic differences were particularly striking, and the lowest response rate came from African Caribbean[9] members of the cohort: in part,

---

7   Those members of the cohort who had been overseas students and those who had studied the external LLB degree offered by London University were excluded from the figures presented in this table.

8   See Shiner and Newburn, 1995; Shiner, 1997 and 1999.

9   Throughout this chapter, the term African Caribbean has been used to describe those members of the cohort who described themselves as black African, black Caribbean or black other. Distinctions between these categories were not maintained, as the numbers in the cohort could not sustain such detailed analysis.

this reflected a greater tendency within this group to have moved away from the address given at the start of the study. Although the low response rate from ethnic minority members of the cohort was important, it did not prevent meaningful analysis. Thus, for example, more than half (55%) the African Caribbeans responded to the third, fourth or fifth survey and were included in analyses relating to the allocation of training contracts.

ANALYSIS, DIFFERENCE AND DISADVANTAGE

The analysis presented in this chapter was crucially concerned with *difference* and *disadvantage*. The notion of *difference* is straightforward and, in the context of this chapter, it largely refers to the proportion of candidates in different groups who secured a place on a course or a job as a trainee solicitor. *Disadvantage* is conceptually more complex and concerns the extent to which a difference may be the result of bias in the selection process. It may be, for example, that male applicants are more likely to gain a job than female applicants are. This *difference* may be based on legitimate criteria: male applicants may, for example, be better qualified. Alternatively, *differences* may persist even when legitimate selection criteria are taken into account. Female candidates may, for example, be less likely to gain a job than similarly qualified males, thus pointing towards the existence of a bias in the selection process.

Differences can be identified by comparing the proportions in various groups that manage to secure a job or a place on a course. Establishing a difference is, however, complicated by the concept of *statistical significance*. Surveys are typically based on a sample or subgroup within a population; because samples do not include all the people of interest, the estimates that they generate are likely to be somewhat different from the actual figures in the overall population. Statistical theory takes account of this uncertainty and allows us to make judgments about the relationship between a sample and the population from which it is drawn. Statistical tests are used to evaluate how likely it is that a difference in a sample may simply be produced by chance: if it is considered unlikely, then a difference is said to be *statistically significant* and can be safely generalised to the population[10] from which the sample was drawn.[11]

In order to establish the role of *disadvantage*, more complex, multivariate forms of analysis are required. The term 'multivariate' is used to describe

10 Probability, or p, values estimate the likelihood that a difference in a sample is simply the result of chance. A probability value of 0.05 means that a difference at least as large as the one observed in the sample would have occurred by chance in no more than five out of 100 samples. Following statistical convention and unless otherwise stated, all the results described in this chapter were significant at the 0.05 level or below (ie, $p < 0.05$).

11 de Vaus, 1990; Altman, 1991.

procedures that take account of multiple variables (that is, more than one) in an attempt to explain something such as a difference in the rate at which applicants secure a job. These techniques have the advantage that, in estimating the influence of a given characteristic, they control for (or hold constant) all the other variables included in the analysis. Thus, in the example given above, multivariate analyses can compare the chances of success for male and female applicants while controlling for (or holding constant) their qualifications. In doing so, they isolate the specific 'effect' associated with a candidate's sex. Once again, tests indicate whether or not an effect is *statistically significant*. The form of multivariate analysis on which the results described in this paper were based is known as 'logistic regression'.[12]

The notion of *disadvantage* is related to that of *discrimination*. The use of the term disadvantage reflects the limitations of the analysis. While evidence of disadvantage is consistent with an interpretation based on the notion of discrimination, it does not prove its existence, as it remains possible that differences are due to factors that were not included in the analysis. Furthermore, although multivariate techniques are relatively sophisticated, they do not identify the mechanisms which lie behind disadvantage. While explanations which focus on discrimination may be 'highly plausible', it is rarely, if ever, the case that no other interpretation is possible.[13]

LAW STUDENT PROFILE

The legal profession is often characterised as being made up of white, middle aged, public school, Oxbridge educated men.[14] Bearing this in mind, the composition of the cohort was generally very predictable, although it did contain one or two surprises.

The pathway leading to legal education is generally a very direct one. The law undergraduates in the cohort were, on average, aged 21 during the final year of their degree courses. The CPE students were somewhat older and were, on average, 23 during this phase of their training. More than three-quarters of those in the cohort were classified as being conventionally aged (78%) and only 10% were considered to be mature students.[15]

---

12 Altman, 1992; Liao, 1994; Stata, 1997.

13 Cheng and Heath, 1993, p 164.

14 (1999) *The Guardian*, 9 October.

15 For the analysis described subsequently, respondents were classified as conventional students, late starters or mature students. Law undergraduates were considered to be conventional if they were 23 or younger during the final year of their degree, as late starters if they were between 24 and 28 and as mature if they were 29 or older. CPE students were considered to be conventional if they were 25 or younger during this phase of their training, as late starters if they were between 26 and 30 and as mature if they were 31 or older.

The social class profile of the cohort was highly predictable. There can be little, if any, doubt that law students tend to be recruited from well qualified families with a tradition of employment in high status occupations:

- *Parental education*: combined data from the 1988, 1989 and 1990 *Labour Force Surveys* (LFS) indicated that 11% of British men aged 40–60 (the probable age range of students' parents) and 4% of British women of this age had a degree. The cohort study indicated that 31% of law students' fathers were graduates and that a further 19% were professionally qualified. Of their mothers, 18% had a degree and the same proportion had a professional qualification, although they lacked a degree.[16]

- *Parental occupation*: by 1990, the LFS showed that 51% of working men had manual occupations. According to the cohort study, only 14% of law students' fathers were employed in manual occupations and only 12% of their mothers were so employed. Furthermore, 70% of law students' fathers and 44% of their mothers belonged to the service class which was the highest stratum in the schema being used.[17]

The privileged nature of law students' social class backgrounds was also evident in the types of school they attended at age 14 (see Figure 1). According to Halpern, pupils from independent school were over-represented among law students approximately five fold. He also noted that law students were more likely than those who were studying other subjects at university to have attended an independent school. Thus, while there is a large body of literature attesting to the privileged backgrounds of students in higher education, law students appear to form a particularly privileged group.

While the cohort contained few surprises in terms of its age and social class profiles, its ethnic and sexual composition was more challenging to the traditional image of the legal profession. It indicated that the majority (57%) of those who were due to complete the academic stage of their legal training in 1993 were women,[18] and that a shade more than one in 10 (11%) were from ethnic minority communities.[19] Indians constituted the largest minority group within this body of students, accounting for 4% of the total. African Caribbeans made up 2%, as did the combined categories of Pakistanis and Bangladeshis. This left 3% who described their ethnic heritage as 'other'. Comparisons with 1991 census data for 15–25 year olds indicated that ethnic minority groups were over-represented among those studying law.[20]

---

16 Halpern, 1994; Shiner and Newburn, 1995.

17 *Ibid*.

18 Women are in the majority among those studying law and those entering the profession (the Law Society, 1996). The degree to which this is the case, however, was somewhat exaggerated by the cohort study due to a response bias whereby women were more likely than men to participate in the study.

19 It should be borne in mind that figures quoted in this chapter relate to home students only, as overseas students were excluded from the analysis.

20 *Ibid*, Halpern

Generally, while this trend is evident in relation to higher education,[21] law is a particularly popular choice for ethnic minority candidates.[22]

Figure 1: Type of school attended by law students at age 14

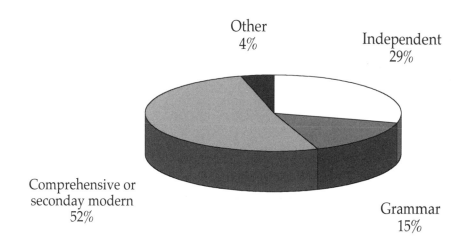

Other
4%

Independent
29%

Comprehensive or
seconday modern
52%

Grammar
15%

Source: Law student cohort (Shiner and Newburn, 1995)   *(n = 4,053)*

When discussing the backgrounds from which law students are recruited, it is important to consider the distinction between the law degree and CPE and between the different types of institution at which these courses may be studied. Although the CPE has enabled graduates from other disciplines to become solicitors, it has led to a narrowing of the social base from which the profession is recruited (see Table 2). CPE students were more likely than law degree students to be white, male, from well qualified family backgrounds and educated at independent school.[23]

---

21 Modood, 1993; Modood and Shiner, 1994; Modood *et al*, 1997.

22 Halpern, 1994.

23 CPE students' privileged backgrounds were also reflected in the types of institutions from which they graduated. While 19% of CPE students had taken their first degree at Oxbridge, only 8% of law degree students were studying at such an institution. Furthermore, while 49% of law degree students were studying at new universities, only 14% of CPE students had graduated from such institutions.

Historically, British higher education was a split between universities and polytechnics, although this distinction disappeared in 1993 when polytechnics and colleges of higher education were granted university status. Polytechnics had traditionally sought to widen the social basis of participation in higher education[24] and this was reflected within the cohort study. Particularly striking differences were evident in relation to age, ethnicity and social class background. Older students, those from ethnic minority communities and those from less privileged social class backgrounds tended to be concentrated in the new university sector[25] and were particularly poorly represented at Oxbridge.[26]

Table 2: Profile of law degree and CPE students (percentages)

| | Type of student | |
	Law degree	CPE
Sex**		
Male	40	49
Female	60	51
Ethnicity**		
White	87	92
African Caribbean	2	1
Indian	6	2
Pakistani or Bangladeshi	3	2
Other	3	3
Type of school attended**		
Independent	24	42
Grammar	13	17
Non-selective	59	38
Other	4	4
Parents' education**		
Degree and professional qualification	7	10
Degree only	24	34
Professional qualification only	21	21
No degree or professional qualification	4	35
	$n = 1,919$	1,020

**

$p < 0.01$

Source: Law student cohort (Shiner and Newburn, 1995)

24 Thompson (1999) *The Times*, Higher Education Supplement, 14 May; Major (1999) *The Guardian*, Higher, 1 December; Modood, 1993; Modood and Shiner, 1994.

25 Throughout this chapter, the term 'new universities' has been used to describe those institutions which were granted university status in 1993.

26 Shiner and Newburn, 1995.

FROM GRADUATION TO TRAINING CONTRACT

In the pathway that leads to a career as a solicitor, the *academic* stage of legal training is conventionally followed by the *vocational* stage. While the Law Society Finals (LSF) traditionally formed a key element of this phase of training, the period on which this study focused witnessed something of a shake-up. In 1993, the LSF was replaced by the Legal Practice Course (LPC), and this constituted an important watershed in a number of ways. First, it saw the introduction of a significant element of skills-based work into this element of legal training. Secondly, and more importantly from our point of view, it marked the end of the monopoly enjoyed by The College of Law as the sole provider of the LSF. Sixteen institutions were validated to provide the LPC in its first year and this diversification involved a marked increase in the number of places available for this stage of legal training.

The expansion of the LPC was not matched by an increase in the number of training contracts. As a result, more people were chasing the same (or approximately the same) number of training places (see Figure 2). While the mid 1990s were a particularly bad time for would-be trainees, the period of heightened competition engendered by the expansion of the LPC was fairly short-lived. This was primarily due to a notable downturn in the take-up of LPC places (in 1996–97 and 1997–98 approximately a quarter of places were unfilled), although it also reflected an increase in the number of training contracts that were available. Towards the end of the 1990s, overall levels of competition had fallen below that which existed at the start of the decade: in 1991–92, there were 1.4 LSF graduates to every registered training contract and, while the respective figure for 1994–95 was 1.6, in 1997–98 it fell to 1.2.

Figure 2: Competition for LSF/LPC places and for training contracts[27]

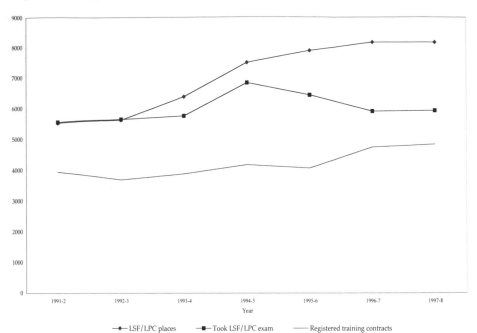

Source: Jenkins (1993; 1994), Jenkins and Lewis (1995), Lewis (1996), Cole (1997 and 1998)

THE LEGAL PRACTICE COURSE

According to the cohort study, approximately four-fifths (80%) of those who complete a law degree or the CPE apply for a place on the LPC. Despite this level of popularity, securing a place does not appear to constitute much of a barrier to qualification as a solicitor. Of those in the cohort who applied to start the LPC in 1993, for example, 92% were offered a place.

---

27 This figure shows recent trends in the availability of LSF/LPC places, the number of candidates taking the LSF/LPC exam and the number of training contracts registered each year. The figure for the number of candidates taking the LSF exam in 1992–93 has not been published. For the purposes of this illustration it has thus been estimated by taking the mid-point between the 1991–92 figure and the 1993–94 figure.

Reflecting this very high rate of success, there was relatively little evidence of disadvantage in the allocation of LPC places: applicants' chances of securing a place did not appear to be affected by their sex, disability status or social class background.[28] Nevertheless, the process by which places were allocated was not entirely meritocratic. Some differences persisted when academic qualifications (and other factors) were taken into account. Candidates who had taken the CPE, for example, had an advantage over those who had taken a law degree, and there was evidence of slight biases against candidates who attended a new university, either as law undergraduates or CPE students, and applicants from ethnic minority groups. It was estimated that, for an average candidate, attendance at a new university increased the probability of being left without an LPC place from 0.01 to 0.05. Similarly, being from an ethnic minority group increased it from 0.02 to 0.03.[29]

While most applicants have little difficulty securing a place on the LPC, paying for the course constitutes a notable barrier to qualification. LPC students can expect to have to find upwards of £8,000 to pay for this element of their professional training and the financial implications of this were highlighted by the cohort study: nearly three-quarters (73%) of LPC students were in debt at the end of the course and the average level of debt at that time was £5,000. The role of finance as a barrier was particularly evident among those in the cohort who had not pursued their legal training beyond the academic stage. A shade more than half (51%) of those who had not applied for a place on the LPC or the Bar Vocational Course for barristers indicated that they could not afford to do this element of legal training. Furthermore, 15% of those who secured an LPC place did not take it up and this clearly reflected financial barriers. Of those who declined a place, 55% indicated that they could not finance their participation on the course and 51% cited the financial insecurities of starting the course without a training contract.[30]

---

28   For the analyses described in this chapter, respondents' social class backgrounds were assessed on the basis of the type of secondary school they attended and on their parents' qualifications. This reflected difficulties that are associated with measures of social class based on parents' occupations. It should also be noted that these measures were strongly associated with parents' qualifications.

29   The analysis on which these results are based tended to overestimate the probability of success. These probabilities are slightly different from those presented in Shiner, 1997, as they were estimated in a somewhat more sophisticated way. The probabilities presented throughout this chapter were generated using the models presented by Shiner (1997 and 1999) and were based on the characteristics of a statistically average application. The mean value of each significant variable was used to estimate the probability of success.

30   Shiner and Newburn, 1995.

Table 3: How students paid for the LPC[31]

	% contributed for	
	fees	maintenance
Source		
Parents	30	47
Commercial loan (bank or building society)	28	15
Professional sponsorship	26	14
Local Education Authority grant	6	3
Savings	4	5
Partner/other relative	4	7
Scholarship/bursary	2	1
Work in term	n/a	4
Holiday work	n/a	2
	n = 1,945	1,934

Source: Law student cohort (Shiner and Newburn, 1997)

In order to make sense of the levels of debt incurred by LPC students and to understand the extent to which money constitutes a barrier to qualification, it is important to appreciate the way in which participation in the LPC is financed. The cohort study generated estimates of how students financed their way through the LPC: separate estimates were made for course fees and maintenance costs (see Table 3). While students drew on a range of sources of income to pay for the LPC, it is clear that parents constituted the single most important source of finance: it was estimated that they met almost a third of the cost of course fees and almost half the maintenance costs. That participation in the LPC is so dependent on parental support means that discrimination is woven into the very fabric of the process by which students train to become solicitors. Clearly, not all students, or potential students, have parents who can support them to the extent required.

The legal profession itself made a sizeable contribution to financing students through the LPC in the form of sponsorship. This source of support is particularly important as it has the potential to counterbalance some of the biases that are inherent in any system of finance that is largely dependent on

---

31   Figures were rounded to the nearest whole number and thus do not total 100.

private finance and parental support. That it largely failed to realise this potential, however, was clear from the rule of inverse need that was evident in its allocation: 'Students who were already most likely to be disadvantaged – ethnic minorities, mature students, women – were the least likely to have received money from the profession in the form of sponsorship.'[32]

ALLOCATION OF TRAINING CONTRACTS

The training contract is key to the process by which people enter the solicitors' branch of the profession. As well as largely controlling who gets in, it plays a pivotal role in relation to the early stages of solicitors' careers once they have qualified. There was a very strong degree of continuity between solicitors' training contracts and the early stages of their post-qualification careers. To a large degree, the training contract defined the type of firm or organisation in which solicitors worked once they had qualified. In addition, it also tended to set the level at which they were paid.[33]

The cohort study indicated that, of those law students who applied for a job as a trainee solicitor, 72% were offered a position. Almost one-fifth (18%) of those who completed the LPC, however, were left without a training contract.[34] The rate at which offers were made varied according to a range of characteristics and it is evident from Table 4 that applicants enjoyed particularly high levels of success if they were young, white, male, from privileged social class backgrounds and were not disabled. Ethnic differences were particularly striking: a little less than a quarter of African Caribbean applicants secured a position as a trainee and this compared with almost three-quarters of white candidates.[35]

---

32 Shiner, 1997, p 35.

33 Shiner, 1999; Duff, Shiner and Boon, forthcoming.

34 Shiner, 1999. These figures are based on the third, fourth and fifth surveys. The 72% of applicants who had secured a training contract included those who indicated that they had been successful in response to the third, fourth or fifth survey. The 28% who had not secured a training contract included respondents to the fifth survey who had never received an offer and those who did not respond to the fifth survey but indicated in an earlier survey that they had not received an offer. Figures relating to the period up to the fourth survey were based on responses to the third and fourth surveys. In order to examine disadvantage, multivariate analyses took account of different patterns of response to the study.

35 While the precise figure for African Caribbean applicants should be treated with some degree of caution, owing to the small number of cases included in the analysis, the broad trend of reduced success for ethnic minority candidates is clear.

Table 4: Allocation of training contracts by social characteristics[36]

	% of applicants who were successful	n
Age	*	
Conventional	73	2,067
Late starter	68	301
Mature	66	195
Sex	**	
Male	75	1,087
Female	70	1,486
Ethnicity[(1)]	**	
White	74	2,261
African Caribbean	24	46
Indian	58	131
Pakistani or Bangladeshi	61	52
Other	71	78
Disability status	*	
Disabled	58	64
Not disabled	73	2,241
Parents' education	**	
Degree and professional qualification	78	209
Degree only	77	740
Professional qualification only	77	535
Neither degree nor professional qualification	65	1,079
School	**	
Independent	81	818
Grammar	73	350
Non-selective[(2)]	66	1,316
Other	72	83

** $p = <0.01$ * $p = <0.05$ ns not statistically significant

(1) Success rates did not vary significantly between black Africans, black Caribbeans and black others or between Pakistanis and Bangladeshis.

(2) This term includes comprehensive and secondary modern schools.

Source: Law student cohort (Shiner, 1999)

36 The results presented in this table were based on all respondents who applied for a training contract. The percentage of applicants who received an offer is presented, along with the number of cases included in the analysis (these figures are presented under the column heading 'n').

The rate at which applicants secured positions as trainee solicitors also varied according to the route they had taken through the academic stage of legal training and according to the institutions they attended during this phase of their training. Applicants who had taken the CPE enjoyed a higher rate of success than did those who had taken a law degree although, for both groups, Oxbridge graduates were particularly successful and new university graduates were relatively unsuccessful. The apparent difficulties faced by candidates who had attended a new university were also evident in relation to the CPE. While 11% of applicants who had taken the CPE at The College of Law or an old university were left without a training contract, this compared with 29% of those who had attended a new university.

Table 5: Allocation of training contracts by type of course and institution

	% of applicants who were successful	n
Law degree or CPE	**	
Law degree	67	1,640
CPE	81	932
Degree institution: law graduates	**	
Oxbridge	89	132
Old university	69	748
New university	69	761
Degree institution: CPE students	**	
Oxbridge	95	139
Old university	81	522
New university	69	103
CPE institution	**	
College of Law	89	380
Non-Oxbridge old university	75	94
New university	71	458
** $p = <0.01$	72	2,572

Source: Law student cohort (Shiner, 1999)

For those applicants who successfully arranged a training contract, it is important to consider their destinations within the profession. The cohort study indicated that 95% of trainees worked within private practice: 3% trained in a government agency (central or local), the Crown Prosecution Service or the magistrates' courts service and 2% trained in a commercial or industrial company. This left less than half of one percent who trained in a law centre, a legal advice centre or some other type of organisation. There were very few differences between trainees in private practice and those based elsewhere, although women were more likely to be training outside of this sector than were men: 7% of female trainees compared with 3% of males trained outside of private practice.

Figure 3: Distribution of trainees within private practice

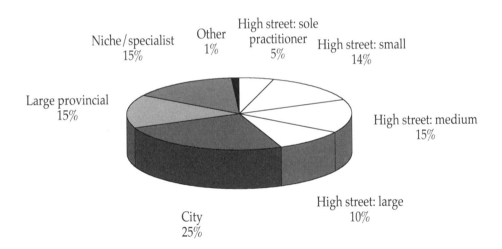

Source: Law student cohort (Shiner, 1999)   *(n = 1,198)*

Within private practice, high street firms were the biggest employer of trainees, followed by City firms, large provincial firms, niche/specialist firms and other firms (see Figure 3):[37]

Trainees' destinations within private practice varied according to a range of socio-demographic characteristics (see Table 6). Although there were no apparent differences according to trainees' sex, there were significant age, ethnic and social class variations. Mature trainees, those from ethnic minority groups and those from less privileged backgrounds (as indicated by the type of school attended and by parents' educational background) tended to be concentrated in high street firms. Furthermore, within high street practice, older trainees and those from ethnic minority groups were particularly concentrated in small firms.[38] Ethnic differences were particularly striking in this regard, possibly indicating a tendency whereby ethnic minority trainees are employed by 'Black' firms.[39]

---

37 This classification was developed in close consultation with the Research and Policy Planning Unit at the Law Society. The term 'high street firm' describes those that were defined as such by trainees or were defined as being legal aid firms. This reflects a blurring of the distinction between these types of firm. Within high street practice, firms with four partners or fewer have been described as 'small', those with between five and 10 partners as 'medium' and those with between 11 and 25 partners as 'large'. Firms with 26 partners or more that were located in the City of London have been defined as 'City firms' and those of this size that were located elsewhere have been defined as 'large provincial firms'. The term 'niche firm' applies to those that were so classified by trainees, had 25 partners or less and were not described as being high street or legal aid firms. Firms that did not fit into any of these categories were defined as being 'other'.

38 Henceforth, the term 'small firms' includes sole practitioners.

39 See Shiner, 1997.

Table 6: Trainees' destinations within private practice by social characteristics[40]

	% of trainees in private practice who were based in the following types of firm		*n*
	High Street	City	
Age**			
Conventional	42	27	
Late starters	45	25	
Mature	73	9	
Sex ns			
Male	–	–	
Female	–	–	
Ethnicity**			
White	43	25	
Ethnic minority[1]	56	22	
Parents' education**			
Degree and professional qualification	35	38	
Degree only	33	33	
Professional qualification only	46	24	
No degree or professional qualification	55	16	
School**			
Independent	28	37	
Grammar	52	24	
Non-selective	55	16	
Other[2]	26	48	
** $p = <0.01$ * $p = <0.05$ ns not significant			*1,198*

(1) The numbers in each of the minority categories were insufficient to support the more detailed ethnic breakdown used previously. There were only seven African or African Caribbean trainees working in private practice (two worked in high street practice, two were in City firms and three were in large provincial firms), 44 Indians (32 worked in high street practice, five were in City firms, four were in large provincial firms and four were in niche firms), 19 Pakistanis or Bangladeshis (12 worked in high street practice, three were in City firms, two were in large provincial firms and three were in niche firms) and 28 whose ethnicity was described as other (10 worked in high street practice, 12 were in City firms, four were in large provincial firms and three were in niche firms).

(2) Schools described as 'other' were primarily overseas schools.

Source: Law student cohort (Shiner, 1999)

40 The number of trainees in private practice who described themselves as disabled was insufficient to support meaningful analysis ($n = 19$).

City firms recruit trainees from particularly privileged social backgrounds. Trainees whose best qualified parent had a degree and a professional qualification were more than twice as likely to be working in a City firm than were trainees who came from families where neither parent had a degree or a professional qualification (38% and 16% of trainees from these respective backgrounds were working in City firms). A very similar pattern was evident in relation to the type of school that trainees had attended.

There was no evidence that trainees' destinations within private practice varied significantly according to prior contact with the profession, either in the form of having close relatives in the profession or of having carried out previous legal work experience. Their destinations did, however, vary significantly according to the route that they had taken through the academic stage of legal training and the type(s) of university they had attended. Trainee solicitors who had taken a law degree were more likely than those who had taken the CPE to be working in high street practice (53% compared with 33%). Conversely, those who had taken the CPE route were more likely to be working in City firms (31% compared with 20%), large provincial firms (19% compared with 13%) and niche/specialist firms (17% compared with 14%). Among those working within high street practice, however, the size of firm that trainees were based in was not significantly associated with whether they had taken a law degree or the CPE.

Table 7 shows how trainees' destinations within private practice varied according to the types of university they attended. The most striking differences related to the contrast between high street practice and City firms. Oxbridge law-graduates were roughly 10 times as likely as new university law-graduates to be working in a City firm. They were also three times as likely to be working in a large provincial firm. Conversely, new university law graduates were almost seven times as likely as Oxbridge law graduates to be working in high street practice. The over-representation of new university law graduates in high street practice was particularly marked in small firms.[41]

The links between Oxbridge and City firms and between new universities and high street practice were also evident among trainees who had taken the CPE. For trainees in high street practice who had taken the CPE, however, there was no significant link between the size of the firm that they were working in and the type of university at which they had studied their degree or CPE course. Similarly, among trainees in high street practice who had not received an offer until after they had started the LPC, the size of the firm they were based in did not vary significantly according to the type of institution they attended to study this course.

---

41 See Shiner, 1999.

Table 7: Trainees' destinations within private practice by type of university

	% of trainees within private practice in the following types of firm				n
	High Street	City	Large Provincial	Niche/ Specialist	
Degree institution (law graduates)[**]					
Oxbridge	11	63	23	3	64
Old university	44	24	15	17	353
New university	75	6	8	12	272
Degree institution (CPE students)[**]					
Oxbridge	7	54	20	19	108
Old university	36	28	20	16	329
New university	63	8	15	15	48
CPE institution[**]					
College of Law	16	50	19	15	228
Old university (non-Oxbridge)	38	24	28	10	50
New university	49	14	17	20	218
LPC institution[1] ns	–	–	–	–	436

[**] $p = {<}0.01$ ns not significant   *1,198*

(1) The association between the type of institution trainees had attended to study the LPC and the type of firm they were based in was only assessed for those who received a training contract offer after they had started the LPC. Those who received an offer prior to starting the LPC were excluded from this analysis.

Source: Law student cohort (Shiner, 1999)

EVIDENCE OF DISADVANTAGE
– MULTIVARIATE ANALYSIS

So far, discussion about the training contract has focused on *differences* rather than *disadvantage*. Distinctive patterns have been identified in relation to the rate at which candidates secured a training contract and in the type of firm or organisation in which they were based. Although important, such *differences* do not necessarily indicate *disadvantage*. Procedures that are considered to be meritocratic may produce differences between groups that reflect the impact of legitimate selection criteria.

Allocation of training contracts

It may be that training contracts were allocated at different rates because of variations between groups in terms of their qualifications. The rate at which candidates secured a training contract certainly increased markedly with better qualifications[42] and applicants' academic profiles did vary according to a range of key characteristics.[43] Academic differences were taken into account via a series of multivariate analyses which also identified other factors which continued to have an independent effect on applicants' chances of securing a training contract. For reasons explained elsewhere,[44] analyses were conducted separately for 'early' and 'late' offers. Early offers, defined as those received by applicants before they started the LPC, were considered on the basis of all members of the cohort who had applied for a training contract. Late offers, defined as those received by candidates after they had started the LPC, were considered on the basis of applicants who had not secured a training contract before they started the LPC.

Multivariate analyses confirmed the importance of academic qualifications in the selection of trainees. Good degree and/or CPE grades increased candidates' chances of success in relation to both early and late offers. Furthermore, while the probability of early success was further improved by good 'A' level grades, for late offers, the influence of 'A' levels was replaced by the LPC. The effect of candidates' academic qualifications on their chances of securing a training contract varied according to the route they had taken through the academic stage of legal training. In relation to both early and late offers, there was a discernible bias in favour of applicants who had taken the CPE.[45] While this indirectly disadvantaged ethnic minority candidates and those from less privileged social backgrounds (as they were poorly represented among those who took the CPE), there was also evidence of more direct forms of disadvantage.

Why some applicants were successful and others were not could not wholly be explained with reference to the standard of their qualifications and whether they had taken a law degree or the CPE. Once these factors had been taken into account, a range of other variables continued to be associated with applicants' chances of securing an early and/or late offer of a training contract (see Table 8).

Work experience plays an important role in the process by which employers identify and select trainees.[46] This was most apparent in relation to late offers. For an average applicant, the probability of securing a late offer

---

42   Shiner, 1997.
43   Shiner and Newburn, 1995.
44   See *ibid*, Shiner.
45   *Ibid*.
46   *Ibid*, Shiner and Newburn.

stood at 0.44 if they did not have any legal work experience. Having gained holiday work experience with a solicitor increased this probability to 0.65. The use of work experience to identify and select trainees may seem reasonable: after all, willingness to gain such experience may indicate a commitment to becoming a lawyer and, as a result of doing it, candidates may acquire skills which give them a competitive edge over other applicants. However, ethnic minority students, students from less privileged social backgrounds and those who attended new universities experienced particular difficulties gaining such experience.[47] As a result, work experience both masks and amplifies existing patterns of disadvantage in the process by which training contracts are allocated.

Table 8: Non-qualification variables associated with an 'independent' effect on applicants' chances of securing a training contract[48]

	Model A Early offers	Model B Later offers
Sex	●	○
Ethnicity	●	●
School type attended at age 14	●	○
Parents' education	●	●
Type of university attended	●	●
Legal work experience	●	●
Close relative in the legal profession	●	○

● = statistically significant   ○ = not statistically significant

The following variables were not statistically significant in either Model A or Model B: age, disability status, subject(s) studied at degree level.

Source: Law student cohort (Shiner and Newburn, 1995)

---

47 Shiner and Newburn, 1995.

48 In estimating the influence of each variable or characteristic, multivariate techniques take account of all of the others included in the analysis. In doing so, they isolate the specific effect associated with each variable. Thus, each of the variables shown in this table was associated with an effect that was independent of all of the others in the analysis, including those related to academic qualifications. We can, eg, therefore be confident that ethnic differences in access to training contracts were not due to differences in applicants' qualifications, in the route they had taken through the academic stage of legal education, in the type of school or institution(s) of higher education that they had attended or to any of the other variables included in the analysis. In addition, further variables were included in the analysis to take account of differences that may have resulted from respondents' patterns of response to the surveys.

Work experience was not the only form of prior contact with the legal profession that appeared to be influential in candidates' chances of securing a training contract. Having a close relative in the profession also helped, although it appeared to be the case that, if family links were of a sort which could help, then their influence was generally felt early on. Having relatives in the profession increased the probability of receiving an early offer (from 0.34 to 0.46), although no such effect was apparent in relation to subsequent offers.

Even when the effects of work experience and of having a close relative in the profession were combined with those associated with candidates' qualifications and the route they had taken through the academic stage of legal training, the remaining variables shown in Table 8 continued to have an important role in the process by which training contracts were allocated. While the multivariate analyses sought to isolate the effects associated with specific variables, individual applicants clearly displayed a range of characteristics, many of which were interrelated. Thus, for example, law students who had been educated at independent school also tended to come from well qualified families. Equally, students from particularly privileged backgrounds tended to be concentrated in old universities and were well represented at Oxbridge. In addition, there was an important ethnic dimension to these patterns, as ethnic minority students had less privileged social class backgrounds than whites and were more likely to have attended a new university.[49] The joined-up nature of these characteristics meant that the disadvantage that they stimulated tended to be mutually reinforcing and it is, therefore, appropriate to think in terms of multiple disadvantage and multiple advantage.

For an average applicant who was a white, independent-school-educated male with a graduate or professionally qualified parent and who had attended an old university as a law undergraduate or The College of Law as a CPE student, the probability of securing an early offer was 0.70. For a black[50] woman, whose parents did not have a degree or a professional qualification, who was educated at a non-selective school and who attended a new university as a law undergraduate or CPE student, but who otherwise had an identical profile to our previous applicant, the probability of having received an early offer fell to 0.11. Equally, in relation to late offers, an average applicant's chance of success varied from 0.41 to 0.62 depending on their ethnicity, their parents' qualifications and the type of institution they attended to study the LPC.

The specific effects associated with ethnicity and type of university were particularly striking. For an average applicant, attendance at a new university

---

49 See Shiner and Newburn, 1995.

50 In this context, the term 'black' has been used interchangeably with the term 'ethnic minority'.

during the academic stage of legal training reduced the probability of receiving an early offer from 0.45 to 0.28. In relation to late offers, the institution attended by candidates to study the LPC overrode the effect of the institution they attended during the academic stage of their training.[51] Nevertheless, the bias against new university students was, once again, apparent: for an average applicant, attendance at a new university to study the LPC reduced the probability of receiving a later offer from 0.62 to 0.55.

The influence of university type was more complex than the simple divide between old and new universities implies. For early offers, separate analyses were conducted for candidates who had taken a law degree and those who had taken the CPE. These analyses included a more detailed breakdown of degree institution and, while supporting the conclusion that new university students were disadvantaged, they also pointed to a significant Oxbridge bias. This bias was apparent regardless of the route that candidates had taken through the academic stage of legal training and, for those who had taken the CPE, regardless of the type of institution they had attended during this course (see Figure 4).

In contrast to the consistency of the Oxbridge effect, that associated with new universities varied according to the route that candidates had taken though the academic stage of legal training. Having studied for a law degree at a new university rather than a non-Oxbridge old university significantly reduced the probability of receiving an early offer. Among those who had taken the CPE, the institution they attended during this course overrode the distinction at degree level between non-Oxbridge old universities and new universities. The extent of the disadvantage faced by applicants who had taken the CPE at a new university did not vary according to whether they had attended a new university or a non-Oxbridge old university as an undergraduate.

---

51 In the model for late offers, the type of university attended as a law degree or CPE student was not statistically significant.

Figure 4: Predicted probability of an early training contract offer by degree institution

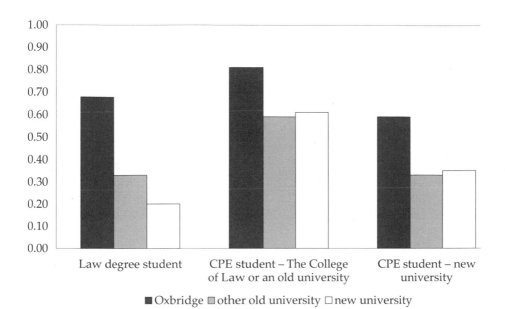

■ Oxbridge ▨ other old university □ new university

Source: Law student cohort (Shiner and Newburn, 1995)

Bias against ethnic minority applicants was evident in relation to early and late offers, although it was particularly striking in relation to the latter. The probability that an average candidate had of receiving an early offer was 0.38 if he or she was white and 0.23 if he or she was from an ethnic minority group. For late offers, the respective probabilities were 0.60 and 0.47. These effects are illustrated in Figure 5, along with those associated with candidates' sex and social class background (measured by school type and parental education).

The influence of school type on the probability of receiving an early offer lay principally in the distinction between independent schools, on the one hand, and grammar and non-selective schools on the other. Having attended a grammar school rather than an independent school reduced the probability of receiving an early offer from 0.43 to 0.36 and having attended a non-selective school reduced it to 0.32. Coming from a family where neither parent had a degree or a professional qualification reduced the probability of receiving an early offer from 0.39 to 0.32 and of receiving a late offer from 0.62 to 0.54. Finally, in relation to Figure 5, being female reduced the probability that our average applicant had of receiving an early offer from 0.39 to 0.34.

Figure 5: Effect of ethnicity, sex and social class background on the probability of being offered a training contract

Source: Law student cohort (Shiner and Newburn, 1995)

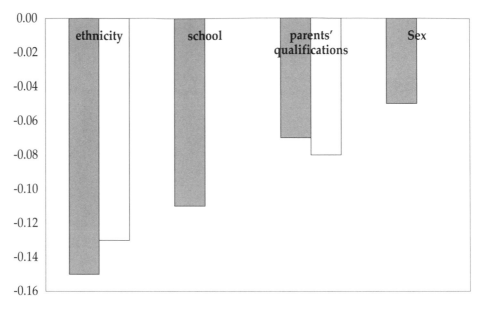

■ early offers □ late offers

Although there was no evidence that disabled applicants were directly disadvantaged in the allocation of training contracts, it does appear that they were indirectly disadvantaged by the way in which postgraduate legal training is financed. Among applicants who did not receive an early offer of a training contract, disabled candidates were significantly less likely to have taken up an LPC offer than were their non-disabled counterparts (75% had done so compared with 90%). There was no such difference among applicants who had secured an early offer of a training contract. Thus, it would appear that disabled people are less willing and/or less able to take the financial risk of starting the LPC without having arranged a training contract.

Destinations within the profession

Having established that applicants for a training contract were disadvantaged on the basis of a variety of characteristics, including their ethnicity and social class background, it is important to consider whether the biases that underpinned these patterns of disadvantage were evenly distributed throughout the profession. While trainees' destinations within the profession varied according to a range of social characteristics, it remains possible that this simply reflected differences in their qualifications and career aspirations.

Multivariate analyses relating to destinations were primarily concerned with private practice because, as already noted, there were few differences between trainees within this sector and those based outside it. Nevertheless, further analyses were conducted in order to examine why there was a particular concentration of female trainees outside private practice. Although women showed slightly less interest than men in working in this sector, such a finding did not wholly explain their different destinations. Furthermore, while this sex difference was relatively small (see above, p 102), it is noteworthy given the finding that female applicants were disadvantaged in the allocation of early training contract offers but not late offers.[52] When combined with the greater propensity of women to be training outside private practice, this suggests that, having experienced initial difficulties in securing a training contract, women enjoyed greater success once they channelled their applications away from this sector.

Trainees' destinations within private practice varied according to their qualifications and the multivariate analysis confirmed the importance of this link. Higher 'A' level and degree grades were associated with an increased probability that a trainee was working in a City firm or a large provincial firm and a decreased probability that they were working in high street practice. For niche/specialist firms, there was no clear pattern.[53]

In order to identify the way in which biases within the profession may push trainees in particular directions, it was important to take account of candidates' preferences and their patterns of application. At the same time, however, it should be noted that preferences are not developed in a vacuum and may reflect external factors that limit the choices that are available. Discrimination was widely anticipated by applicants,[54] and it may be that, for some, their preferences were based on the levels of discrimination that they anticipated in the different types of firm.

Applicants' orientations to the various types of private practice firm were fairly polarised. Interest in City firms tended to imply interest in large provincial firms (and vice versa), although it was inversely related to interest in high street practice. At the same time, while interest in niche/specialist firms appeared unrelated to attitudes to high street practice, it tended to be matched by interest in large provincial firms and lack of interest in City firms. Trainees' destinations within private practice varied markedly according to their orientations to the various types of firm and the multivariate analysis

---

52 Shiner, 1997.
53 See Shiner, 1999.
54 Shiner and Newburn, 1995.

confirmed that applicants' levels of interest continued to be a significant predictor of their destinations even when other relevant factors had been taken into account.[55]

Trainees' destinations did not simply reflect their qualifications and orientations to the various types of firm. Even when these factors had been taken into account, the following variables continued to be significant predictors of their destinations within private practice:

- the type of institution they had attended as undergraduates and the subjects they had studied;
- whether they had close relatives in the profession and the nature of the work experience they had gained;
- their social class background and, within high street practice, their age.

The multivariate analysis indicated, however that the following were not significant predictors of the type of firm that trainees were based in: their sex, ethnicity,[56] the grades they had gained on the CPE and the LPC and the institutions they had attended to take either course.

City firms and niche/specialist firms seem to place a particular value on foreign languages.[57] For an average trainee, having studied a language or part language degree increased the probability that they were based in a City firm from 0.16 to 0.26 and that they were based in a niche/specialist firm from 0.24 to 0.35. While it left the probability of being based in a large provincial firm unchanged, it decreased the probability of being based in the high street from 0.45 to 0.25.

While having a close relative in the profession appeared to have clear implications for trainees' destinations, variations according to work experience were fairly ambiguous. Having family links with the profession appeared to be particularly influential in relation to City firms and large provincial firms. For an average trainee, such links increased the probability of being based in a City firm from 0.15 to 0.23 and of being based in a large provincial firm from 0.14 to 0.19. Although they had little impact on the probability of being based in a niche/specialist firm, they were associated with a reduced probability of being based in high street practice (from 0.45 to 0.35 for an average trainee). Although the extent and nature of applicants' work experience was significantly associated with their destinations, there was no clear pattern to this effect.[58]

---

55   See Shiner, 1999.

56   Because of the small number of trainees from some minority groups, the ethnic breakdown used for the analysis simply distinguished between white trainees and those from minority groups.

57   Joint law degrees were most commonly combined with language subjects: 30% of students who took law as part of a joint degree also studied a language. Among CPE students, 12% had taken a language degree.

58   *Ibid*, Shiner.

Biases on the basis of social class background and type of university attended were particularly marked in relation to City firms. The Oxbridge bias within the profession was, for example, driven by City firms and, to a lesser extent, large provincial firms. For an average trainee, having attended Oxbridge as an undergraduate was associated with an increase in the probability that they had a training contract with a City firm from 0.15 to 0.23. It was also associated with an increase in the probability of having secured a contract with a large provincial firm from 0.14 to 0.22. While studying at Oxbridge had minimal effect in relation to niche/specialist firms, it was associated with a reduced probability of having secured a position in high street practice (for an average trainee, this reduction saw a fall from a probability of 0.46 to 0.27).

The particular social class bias of City firms was apparent in the type of school that trainees had attended and in the education level of their parents. Figure 6 illustrates that, for an average trainee, having attended a non-selective school (that is, a comprehensive or secondary modern) reduced the probability that they had a training contract with a City firm from 0.23 to 0.11 and increased the probability that they had one with a high street practice from 0.38 to 0.48. Coming from a family where neither parent had a degree nor a professional qualification reduced the probability that an average trainee had a contract with a City firm from 0.19 to 0.12 and increased the probability that they had one with a high street practice from 0.41 to 0.47.

Although the ethnic bias within the profession did not appear to be any stronger in one type of firm than another, the biases described above did have an ethnic dimension. The orientation of City firms and, to a lesser extent, large provincial firms towards Oxbridge graduates and trainees from particularly privileged backgrounds indirectly disadvantaged ethnic minority applicants. Furthermore, as already noted, law students from less privileged social class backgrounds tended to be concentrated in new universities and were particularly poorly represented at Oxbridge. In view of this, it is important to note that the particular social class and institutional biases within the profession tended to reinforce each other. For an average trainee, having a graduate or professionally qualified parent, having been educated at a school other than a comprehensive or secondary modern and having attended Oxbridge as an undergraduate increased the probability that they were based in a City firm from 0.08 to 0.35. This set of characteristics was also associated with an increase in the probability of an average trainee being based in a large provincial firm from 0.13 to 0.20. While it had little discernible effect in relation to niche firms, it decreased the probability of an average trainee being based in high street practice from 0.55 to 0.21.

Figure 6: Effect of social class background on trainees' destinations within private practice (estimated probabilities)

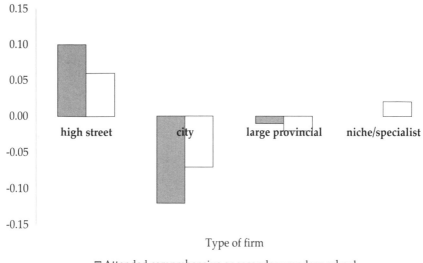

Type of firm

■ Attended comprehensive or secondary modern school
□ Parents did not have a degree or professional qualification

Source: Law student cohort (Shiner and Newburn, 1995)

Within high street practice, there was very little evidence of particular biases. To a large extent, the size of the high street firm that trainees were working in reflected their preferences as applicants. Once these preferences had been taken into account, the only effects that were significant were those linked to trainees' ages and their 'A' level grades. Although the probability that a trainee was working for a medium or large high street firm increased with good 'A' level grades, the age differences that were evident did not constitute a clear trend.[59] While the particular concentration of ethnic minority trainees in small high street firms could not be explained with reference to 'A' level grades alone, such ethnic differences ceased to be significant once their orientations to the different types of firm had been taken into account. It should, however, be noted that ethnic minority trainees tended to be poorly paid and that this reflected a certain degree of disadvantage, as differences persisted even when type of firm and geographical location were taken into account.[60] Such disadvantage may indicate that ethnic minority candidates are recruited to less prestigious firms or to less prestigious positions.

---

59 Shiner, 1999.

60 *Ibid.* There was also evidence that disabled trainees were disadvantaged in terms of salary levels although the small number of cases included in the analysis means that little confidence can be placed on the results.

CREATING AN ELITE WITHIN AN ELITE AND REINFORCING PATTERNS OF DISADVANTAGE

City firms and, to a lesser extent, large provincial firms have something of an elite status within the solicitors' profession. They pay the highest salaries[61] and tend to recruit the most highly qualified candidates from the most prestigious institutions. It is, however, evident from the detailed analysis described above that the particular profile of trainees within these firms cannot be explained simply in terms of their qualifications and orientations to the various types of firm. It is, therefore, worth considering how these firms manage to maintain their elite status. A key part of this relates to when training contracts are offered. City firms and large provincial firms tend to make early offers: 82% of trainees in City firms and 62% of those in large provincial firms had arranged a training contract before they started the LPC. In contrast, 62% of trainees in high street practice and 47% of those in niche firms did not receive an offer until after they had started the LPC.

Analyses relating to trainees' destinations within the profession and the timing of training contract offers highlight an important part of the process by which training contracts are allocated. They indicate that City firms and, to a lesser extent, large provincial firms are able to cream off the best qualified candidates as a result of their greater ability to finance trainees through the LPC and, where relevant, the CPE. This interpretation was clearly supported by analysis of which trainees had received professional sponsorship to finance their way through the LPC. Trainees from City firms were the most likely to have benefited from professional sponsorship, and those in high street firms were the least likely to have done so. While 75% of City trainees received professional sponsorship to pay their fees and/or maintenance costs, this compared with less than 5% of high street trainees.

When combined with the particular biases of City firms and large provincial firms, these patterns of professional sponsorship go a long way to explaining the rule of inverse need that was noted earlier. To an extent, the lack of access that some groups had to professional sponsorship was a function of the difficulties that they had in securing a training contract. This, however, is only part of the story, as applicants from disadvantaged groups who successfully arranged a training contract were concentrated in those firms (high street firms) which tended to make late offers and rarely provided sponsorship.

---

61   Shiner, 1999.

CONCLUSION

It is clear that the pool from which the legal profession recruits its members is not representative of the general population. To some degree, this reflects broad social processes by which education reproduces existing patterns of advantage and disadvantage.[62] Nevertheless, while the social class profile of the law student body is predictably privileged, its sexual and ethnic composition is more challenging to the traditional image of the legal profession. Women are in the majority among those studying law at university and ethnic minority communities are also well represented.

While a university education is often viewed as a 'stepping stone to higher level occupations',[63] the attempts of some applicants to become solicitors were hindered by multiple forms of disadvantage. Although more women than men are currently entering the profession,[64] there was evidence of a slight bias against women in the allocation of training contracts. More striking patterns of disadvantage, however, were evident in relation to ethnicity, social class background and type of university attended. Ethnic minority candidates, those from less privileged social class backgrounds and those who had studied at new universities gained entry into the profession at a very low rate and this could not simply be explained by the standard of their qualifications. The biases that were evident within the profession on the basis of these characteristics tended to be mutually reinforcing, and this heightened their impact.

Although overall levels of representation are important, attempts to ensure equality should look beyond the general composition of the profession and consider the sectors and type of firm in which people are working. While City firms and, to a lesser degree, large provincial firms may be viewed as forming something of an elite within the profession, it is these firms that appear to be the driving force behind the institutional and social class biases described above. City firms, in particular, had a strong bias in favour of Oxbridge graduates and trainees from privileged social class backgrounds. Although ethnic bias in the allocation of training contracts did not appear to vary between the different types of firm, the particular social and institutional biases of City firms and large provincial firms did have an ethnic dimension. Furthermore, ethnic minority trainees were disadvantaged in relation to pay, and this may indicate that they were concentrated in less prestigious firms or less prestigious positions.

The biases of City firms and large provincial firms are particularly important because of the financial arrangements that surround the LPC.

---

62 Roper, Ross and Thomson (2000) *The Guardian*, Education, 2 May; Davies (1999) *The Guardian*, 14–16 September.
63 Cheng and Heath, 1993, p 151.
64 The Law Society, 1996.

Students are rarely supported by local education authorities during this phase of their legal training and finance constitutes an important barrier. Although LPC students draw on a variety of sources of income to pay their way, parents constitute the single most important source of financial support, followed by commercial loans and the legal profession itself. The importance of professional sponsorship is heightened by its potential to counterbalance some of the biases that are inherent to a system of finance that is largely dependent on private finance and parental support. City firms and large provincial firms constitute the major sources of professional sponsorship. While this enables them to cream off the most highly qualified trainees, their particular biases mean that professional sponsorship tends not to go where it is most needed.

In order to challenge the patterns of disadvantage that have been highlighted by the cohort study, a comprehensive review is required of the financial arrangements that surround the LPC and of existing recruitment practices within the profession. This poses the obvious question: does the goodwill exist for such a review? Findings from the study have had a mixed reception. The public response from the Law Society has largely been considered and positive[65] and the patterns of disadvantage highlighted by the study are alluded to in the society's model anti-discriminatory policy:

> As a result of continuing evidence of discrimination faced by job applicants of ethnic minority origin (particularly for training contracts), the Law Society has introduced a policy of setting targets for the number from ethnic minorities to be employed by solicitors' firms. The figures aim to give ethnic minority trainee and qualified solicitors as fair a chance of employment as their white counterparts ... These are not enforceable quotas which would be contrary to the law, but targets to reach as good practice. The Law Society expects firms to participate wholeheartedly in this policy.[66]

Although official response to the study has been positive, one need look no further than to a former president of the Law Society for evidence of defensiveness and complacency. Martin Mears implied that the research on which the study was based was 'bogus'[67] and, according to an article that appeared in the *Law Society Gazette*:[68]

> He is deeply sceptical of the evidence produced in the Policy Studies Institute report which points to direct discrimination against ethnic minority students seeking articles ... Mr Mears is disgusted with the ease with which Council members have been willing to believe solicitors are racist. 'Isn't some healthy scepticism in order?' he asks. Personally, he does not believe that solicitors are racist. 'Racism is to be found in West Ham and on football pitches' but not

---

65 See Dyer (1994) *The Guardian*, 14 September; Sweet, 27 October 1995.
66 The Law Society, 1999, p 171.
67 Mears, 1994.
68 Gilvarry, 1994.

within 'our learned profession'. He thinks it equally 'laughable' to suggest that solicitors discriminate against homosexuals, viewing the sexual orientation clause in the anti-discrimination rule as 'an insult to the profession'.

Somewhat later, having been elected President, Mr Mears went on to argue:[69]

> I was asked to explain why it was that minorities were under-represented among trainees ... During a recession, training contracts are more likely to be offered on the basis of personal contacts. To take the most obvious example, a small firm might not intend to offer training contracts at all, but would make an exception for the son or daughter of one of its partners or valuable clients. To do this is not to 'discriminate' against anyone.

If such views, and the practices that they imply, go unchecked, then the legal profession may pay a heavy price. Symbolically, the role of legal representation rests on the notions of equality, fairness and impartiality. If the legal profession continues to be seen to violate these principles, then it runs the risk of destroying the foundations on which its own legitimacy is constructed.

---

69   Mears (1995) *Law Society Gazette*, 29 November.

CHAPTER 6

HEARING BLACK AND ASIAN VOICES –
AN EXPLORATION OF IDENTITY

*Sumitra Vignaendra, Marcia Williams and Jerry Garvey**

All marginal groups in this society ... are faced with the peculiar dilemma of developing strategies that draw attention to one's plight in such a way that will merit regard and consideration without reinscribing a paradigm of victimization.[1]

They cannot 'speak' until they have been 'asked'.[2]

The 'non-essentialist black subject ... opposes the notion that a person is born with a fixed identity – that all black people, for example, have an essential underlying black identity which is the same and unchanging. It suggests instead that identities are floating, that meaning is not fixed and universally true at all times for all people, and that the subject is constructed through the unconscious in desire, fantasy and memory.[3]

Thus immigration policies, and especially the socio-political legislation which accompanied them and was intended to define the nature of British nationality (identity) as a means of limiting the entry of British subjects from the commonwealth (that is, 'blacks'), contributed to a new kind of 'race' politics in modern Britain, the politics of identity.[4]

INTRODUCTION

In February 2000, the African Caribbean and Asian Lawyers group hosted a debate, the title of which was 'Is It Worth It?', which was an acknowledgment of the difficulties faced by some Black and Asian solicitors and barristers in making inroads into the solicitors' and barristers' professions and finding spaces there for themselves. The resounding answer to this question was, in fact, 'yes'; however, there was much discussion about the extent to which one's ethnic identity had to be compromised in order to enter the legal profession and then survive once there; specifically, whether compromising one's identity was justified by the ends, for example, by a greater representation of Black and Asian lawyers in the legal profession (on an

---

* The authors would like to thank Judith Sidaway for giving this research her support and for her suggestions, Christine Cooper for her very helpful advice and, most of all, the 15 interview participants who generously gave us their time and trust.
1   hooks, 1995, p 58.
2   Thompson, 1978, as quoted by Harris, 1999, p 403.
3   Hall and Bailey, 1992, as quoted in Owusu, 1999, p 6.
4   Glavanis, 1999, p 58.

altruistic level) and (on a personal level) the procurement of an arguably lucrative job that had status.

While such debates do occur both formally and informally within and between minority ethnic groups, they are not necessarily held within the wider legal profession – public space has yet to be created for this discussion. According to African-American performance artist and political commentator Anna Deavere-Smith, theories around topics that are potentially sensitive – politically and otherwise – seem to need to be well rehearsed before being taken into the public forum. She raises the dilemma of what she describes as 'giving public voice'[5] to 'the private self',[6] the dilemma being that, while public commentators and audience alike expect public discourse to be smooth and free of contradictions by those giving voice to them, well rehearsed theories create no movement or action. They are poor mirrors of real world difficulties and as such, are nothing more than interesting. Their utility is limited.

Such debates also require a certain level of background knowledge of the topic discussed, without which there may be a lack of confidence in engaging in discussion about them in the public domain. In the case of the Black and Asian experience in the legal profession, it is unclear whether the wider legal profession does have the requisite knowledge to engage in debate around this topic, given that such groups have not been documented outside statistical research findings and newspaper and magazine articles on discrimination. There is definitely a place for statistics and, in recent times, they have usefully provided representative findings where, once, none existed. The most recent of the Research and Policy Planning Unit's *Annual Statistical Report*,[7] for example, reports that Black and Asian solicitors are still less likely than their 'White European' counterparts to attain partnership. In addition, they are more likely than their 'White European' counterparts to be in smaller firms and sole practice where financial rewards are less than in large and medium sized firms. As, however, more than one lawyer commented during the course of the research for this chapter, 'statistics are not everything'. These trends only reveal one small part of what is a very large and complex story. Research methods derived from the empiricist research paradigm, such as the written survey, are unable to explore such factors as choice, priorities, motivations, or the individual's changing career aspirations, which both give context to statistical findings and make sense of them.

There are also questions about the culture-specific nature of research tools such as the anonymous written survey. Such tools may be better suited to the mindset of certain sub-groups of British society and not others, which may

---

5   Deavere-Smith, 1999, p 289.
6   *Ibid*.
7   Cole, 2000.

account for why some minority groups seem less inclined to respond to written surveys than their majority counterparts.[8] Certainly, the interviews conducted for this chapter suggest that a great amount of trust first needs to be established before Black and Asian lawyers will consider disclosing any information pertaining to their experiences or before they will discuss their identity. This, in fact, is one of the themes explored in the annexure to this chapter.

As for incidents of discrimination reported by newspaper and magazine articles, such reports may reveal less about the attitudes and behaviours of the people allegedly being discriminated against and more about those allegedly doing the discriminating (in the case of direct discrimination), or more about the changing values and politics of groups/organisations/society or the times, than about the individual for whom rights are being claimed (in the case of indirect discrimination). Also, by linking the Black and Asian experience only to discrimination marginalises these groups and may inextricably link their public identity to deviant and negative behaviours and attitudes not of their own making. In addition, to add to the earlier point on the limitations of the written survey, it is too crude a tool to uncover the complexities and details of discriminatory behaviour.

MOTIVATIONS, AIMS AND STRUCTURE OF THE CHAPTER

Motivations and aims

This chapter is, therefore, an opportunity to begin the process of documenting the views and the experiences of Black and Asian lawyers in the profession and broaden the focus of the Black and Asian experience beyond reports of discrimination. We have done this by making identity our focus, given that it is the recurrent theme of most of the formal and informal debates occurring among and between minority ethnic groups – Black, Asian or otherwise – both within and outside the legal profession. Identity has been described by Oberweis and Musheno as being 'how we recognise ourselves and each other. It is a composite of all the multiple and intersecting subject positions that one actor occupies either by chance or by choice.'[9] Our aim is to focus on two subject positions – ethnicity and occupation – while recognising the importance of other subject positions such as, for example, social class, religion, sex, age and sexuality, all of which, as will be discussed later, are inextricably linked to each other and to the concept of identity.

---

8   As found by the Law Society's *Entry into the Legal Professions Cohort Study of Law Graduates*, Shiner, 1999 and as reported by Shiner, Chapter 5, in this book.

9   Oberweis and Musheno, 1999.

This chapter was informed by interviews with a group of solicitors and barristers of African, African-Caribbean and Asian[10] descent and of mixed heritage backgrounds on the topic of ethnic and occupational identity and the nexus between the two from an individual perspective. The main finding from the interviews was that while the nexus does seem to exist, locating it is not as straightforward. The aim of this chapter is therefore twofold:

- to discuss some of the issues that almost confounded our search for the nexus; and

- to explore the themes that may bring us closer to some understanding of the nexus, the caveats mentioned in the first part of the chapter notwithstanding.

Our purpose in looking for the nexus between ethnic and occupational identity was in large part to uncover the degree of fit that exists between being Black or Asian and working as a solicitor or barrister. In the process, we hoped to learn more about the experiences of Black and Asian lawyers. We do recognise, however, that the degree of fit is an issue that not only concerns Black and Asian lawyers, but all lawyers and all those people in the paid workforce. The world of work does not always resemble other facets of our life. It is arguably more contrived and, therefore, is bound to raise challenges for anyone entering it, be it into the legal profession or elsewhere. Nonetheless, having chosen to focus on the Black and Asian experience, it would be a mistake for us to link and/or contrast these groups with other groups in the legal profession. On the one hand, this would define Black and Asian lawyers solely in relation to other groups and would, therefore, defeat the purpose of this exercise. On the other, it would imply an inherent uniqueness and a role for Black and Asian lawyers in the legal profession with which many of the interviewees would not agree. Furthermore, such links and contrasts are not possible, given that we only interviewed Black and Asian lawyers.

In addition, our purpose is not to cover this topic in its entirety, but rather to begin a dialogue on it in a public space. With such a small and unrepresentative group of research participants, all of whom were living and working in London (although some did have prior experience of working as a solicitor or barrister outside London), this chapter, and the interviews that informed it, could only serve as a pilot study for a much larger project or series of projects.

---

10 The participants described as Asian were all of South Asian descent, except one, who was of South-East Asian descent.

Structure

The structure of the chapter reflects these two broad aims of the chapter. In the first part, we identify the variables that almost confounded the search for the nexus. In the second part of the chapter, we explore the themes raised by the interview participants in part to help us locate them in their respective ethnic groups and thereby help us understand their experiences and identity. These themes bring us closer to some understanding of the nexus.

In addition, a number of issues were raised by the interview process that contributed as much to our understanding of the topic as the interview discussions themselves. We discuss these issues in the annexure to this chapter and very strongly encourage the reader to refer to it. At this point, readers are encouraged to read the section entitled 'Definitions of the ethnic categories' starting on p 146.

THOSE CONFOUNDING VARIABLES

Identity is the forefront of everything I do – one's way of thinking is in the genes.

Trying to cope with [the amalgamation of personas] in a non-constructive, non-integrative way is unrealistic. And it *is* possible to combine it in a constructive way.

I push my identity more than most.

These quotes were responses from three of the interview participants to the topic of this research. It is a useful place to begin documenting the research findings as it highlights the complex and differing takes on the concept of identity, what Brah describes as being '... an enigma which, by its very nature, defies a precise definition'.[11] The interviews reinforced the nebulous nature of identity. They also raised what the difficulties were of locating a nexus between only two subject positions of identity – ethnicity and occupation. These issues are as follows:

- The relationship between socio-demographic characteristics is such that first, ethnic identity occasionally competes with other identities such as sex, class, age, sexuality/sexual orientation and religion on the political arena, where they are 'vying with each other for the scarce resource of public attention ...',[12] as Bauman describes what he terms 'one-issue campaigns ... [that] divide as much as they unite ...'.[13] Secondly, one's social identity, if it is possible to delineate identity in this way, is often an

---

11 Brah, 1996.
12 Bauman, 1996, p 34.
13 *Ibid.*

unquantifiable amalgam of several social characteristics, of which, for some people, certain characteristics dominate. Furthermore, our interviews revealed that, for some people, characteristics could displace one another as the dominant characteristic as individual's age and as experiences change.

- The notion of occupational/professional identity is questionable, particularly in relation to the legal profession in which people practise in a wide variety of areas, sectors and sizes and types of firms and organisations, as revealed by the Law Society's *Annual Statistics Report* (ASR) and *Panel Study of Solicitors Firms*.[14]

- Individual differences play such a large role in the construction of identity that the concept of group identity – ethnic, occupational, or otherwise – may possibly be meaningless.

- The concept of ethnicity requires a certain level of belief and is often linked to theories of difference, such as race and racial difference, differences that have been found to be spurious and based on unsubstantiated research.[15] Others still consider ethnicity to be synonymous with culture, skin colour and/or nationality. All the above makes the concept of ethnicity seem vague. As such, ethnic terms often lack precision and are furthermore subject to constant politically motivated change.

Our aim in this section is to discuss each of these four issues in greater depth. We discuss them individually, although recognise that they are not mutually exclusive.

When socio-demographic factors compete

This topic is worthy of (at least) its own chapter. Given that space does not permit us to cover the total length and breadth of this topic, we will simply illustrate how other social categories interact and/or compete with ethnicity in complex ways, recognising that they also interact with each other in similar ways.

Sex

The interviews revealed that sex could mediate experiences within, and perceptions of one by, the legal profession. To illustrate, one Black participant explained her choice to be up-front about her membership of an ethnic-based law graduate group in a job interview in the following way: 'With Black women, this type of membership was seen as an indication of character, while with Black men it might have appeared militant.' Similarly, another

---

14 Sidaway, 1996.
15 Montagu, 1999.

participant commented: 'If I was a bloke they would see me as a threat.' A third participant explained that '[if you are] a woman … they find it charming that you are different'.

None of this means that there was a consensus that Black and Asian men, particularly African-Caribbean men, who are more disproportionately under-represented in the legal profession than any other ethnic group,[16] have greater difficulties getting into and surviving in the legal profession than any other group (although other anecdotal evidence suggests that this may, in fact, be so). It does suggest, however, that the interaction of sex and identity mediates experience such that women and men from Black and Asian backgrounds have qualitatively different experiences. Fredman explains this relationship (she refers to 'race' rather than 'ethnicity' in her explanation): 'The complexity of the race-sex interaction derives largely from the fact that the lines of domination are not horizontal. White women are in the dominant racial group although not in the dominant gender group.'[17] In this case, Black men may be part of the dominant gender group, but not the racial one, yet the disadvantage experienced by Black men according to Fredman's explanation (used by her to describe the situation of Black women) 'is not merely the result of adding [or subtracting] racism to [or from] sexism and vice versa; it is synergistic'. So, for example, discrimination against Black men can exist, even in the absence of discrimination against Black women and White men.

Sexuality and sexual orientation

Sexuality and sexual orientation was a theme that was implicitly alluded to by half the interview candidates, usually in reference to what they thought was the interaction between ethnicity and sex. Sexuality was considered by some to mediate the perception of Black men and women especially. To illustrate, one Black female candidate observed that her White male colleagues seemed to take an interest in her partly because they were curious about Black women, with whom they had limited contact. She also added that her attractiveness worked in her favour – she knew other Black women not perceived to be attractive by their White male colleagues who did not receive the same support that she did.

Many interview candidates, both men and women, thought that the stereotype of Black male sexuality possibly featured in the way Black men were perceived. To illustrate, one Black male candidate, when describing what it was like being gay in the solicitors' profession, commented: 'The danger of the Black male was not there, I'm sure, because they knew I was gay.'

This same candidate also added that his sexual orientation was more important to him than his ethnicity as he had experienced greater hurdles in

---

16   Lewis, 1996; Cole, 1997, 1998 and 2000.
17   Fredman, 1997.

relation to the former than the latter, although not just in the solicitors' profession.

Age

In the same way that sexuality and sexual orientation mediated the relationship between sex and ethnicity, age was also a mediator, and also competed with both gender and ethnicity as the dominant characteristic that defined the individual in both the profession's eyes and in his/her own. For some considered to be outside the demographic norm (for example, women from the minority ethnic groups who commenced their law degrees as mature aged students), the relationship between ethnicity, gender and age was synergistic. For others, it was a case of a triple disadvantage of sex, ethnicity and age which, in some cases, manifested itself financially: for example, extra financial commitments in the form of dependants. Yet, as one interviewee with children noticed, her fellow students were paradoxically better placed to secure the more lucrative jobs. Another interviewee with the similar demographic characteristics but without children commented: '... it seems that in the opinion of many firms or chambers, an older woman is a greater risk and not a worthwhile investment [in part due to the perception that] ... she may have ideas of her own and be more difficult to mould ...' Another candidate, also sharing the same demographic traits saw that 'this supposed triple disadvantage ...' could be used to one's advantage; however, as she mentioned more than once in the interview: '... I had the comfort of having financial support so I was able to plug at it ...' and in her case, find a niche in which her age, sex and ethnicity were bonuses.

Class

The relationship between social class and ethnicity for certain ethnic groups in the UK is largely historical. African-Caribbean people migrated to the UK in large numbers in the 1950s and South Asian people migrated to the UK in large numbers in the 1960s (from South Asia) and in the 1970s (from East Africa).[18] These migrants tended, largely, to join the wage-earning labour and the service occupations and their incomes largely and predictably determined where they lived and where their children went to school. As such, it was assumed that they would share largely the same working class experience with many White people; however, Fenton describes this understanding as 'not so much wrong as incomplete and potentially misleading'.[19] On the whole, these groups were seen as competition by the working classes and, therefore, stood at the edges of both the class system and the politics

---

18 Cashmore, 1997.
19 Fenton, 1999, p164.

commonly associated with this class. The children of these migrants, however (and all but one of our interview participants could be described as such), responded differently to this situation:

> Unlike their parents, the second generation of Black youth did not see themselves as 'temporary guests' of Her Majesty's government. They were not here to work and eventually return 'home' to the Caribbean or Africa. Britain was their home, and according to one of the symbolic political slogans of the time, they were 'Here to Stay!' Consequently, they had little choice but to engage the class- and race-laden structures of British society.[20]

For these reasons, some interview participants thought that their working class experiences and identity were an equal or a greater disadvantage to them than their ethnicity, especially given what they saw to be 'the middle class values' of the legal profession. Others still, thought it was arguable whether Black and Asian migrant groups have even been partially incorporated into the entrenched class system in the UK. When told that some participants had felt that minority ethnic groups were not completely integrated into the class system and, therefore, did not share the politics of their White counterparts in the working classes, one participant (who had described himself as working class during the course of the interview) conceded that migrants were possibly unlikely to actively take part in class-related politics. He offered that this may have been due, for example, to an unwillingness to invite trouble by standing out: '... ethnic minorities realised that they need to blend in and not cause trouble to survive ...' In addition, some migrants who moved into working class jobs and areas, for example South Asians from India and East Africa, often came from a class and/or caste in their 'home' countries that shared similar attitudes, privileges and status to the middle class in the UK. Taken together, these patterns suggest that, unlike their White counterparts, the children of migrant groups have arguably a greater readiness than children of non-migrant groups to re-invent themselves, be classless or be class mobile. They arguably also have a greater potential to locate themselves and their children in a class of their own choosing. The desire for class mobility, or the freedom to locate themselves in a class of their own choosing, partly motivated some interviewees' decision to study law. Class mobility/class selection was conceived by some participants as being a continuation of the pioneering mentality that brought Black and Asian migrants to this country in the first place.[21]

---

20 Owusu, 1999.

21 For some involved in this class mobility, especially for those who came from, or whose parents came from, the equivalent of the UK middle class 'back home', this may be where the nexus between ethnic and occupational identity lies. It is in the merging of the occupation's class and individual's ethnic-class values, which could arguably be called small 'c' conservative.

That some Black and Asian people achieved class mobility (by choosing to study law, for example) had the effect of further strengthening the class system within the Black and Asian communities.[22] Such a class system within minority ethnic groups did already exist at the time of entry into the UK, but it was arguably qualitatively different or less noticeable than now.

There is, therefore, clearly an inextricable link between the concept of class and the concept of ethnicity, but this link is not always clear or straightforward. Each can allow the other to be transcended, or each can reinforce the other to the advantage or disadvantage of the individual. The experiences of the interview group suggest that, for each individual, whichever turns out to be the case seems largely to be dependent on opportunity and circumstance. This, in turn, determines whether ethnic identity is more or less (or equally) important to the individual than class-based identity.

Religion

The link between ethnicity and religion was best illustrated by the comments of one interviewee, who did not see herself as South Asian British (as we had described her, given that both her parents were born in South Asia) but rather as Muslim:

> I was brought up as a Muslim but not necessarily Asian. There are some overlaps but there is not a huge amount in common when you look at the details. The Muslim culture overrides the Asian one ... Being Muslim is me – the way I think, behave and often the way I work. It is an essential part of who I am which overrides whim. If I thought of doing something reckless, my conscience would kick in and my conscience is Islamically driven.

This illustrates a trend in the UK in which religious identity is chosen in favour of an ethnic identity, or in some cases, religious identity is chosen as an ethnic identity.[23]

The above participant was not the only interview participant, however, whose religious identity/spirituality defined her concept of self (although she was the only one whose religious identity displaced her ethnic one). More than half the group referred to their religious and spiritual identity in the interviews. While, for some, their religion/spirituality and ethnicity were strongly linked (one participant commented: 'Black people tend to be more spiritual in our way of life'), for others, their religious/spiritual beliefs were

---

22 'As cities went up in flames and the State responded with various reform initiatives, a new Black career stratum, some "spokespersons" of the community, others sponsored by race and equal opportunities programmes, climbed through the ranks of the city halls ... and corporate establishments, intensifying the class divisions within the black communities.' (Owusu, 1999, p 11.)

23 Weller, 2000, p 16.

independent of their ethnicity, though no less important. As one interviewee expressed it: 'I am not religious, but my religious practice features in my daily routine and therefore makes up who I am.' Spiritual identity manifested itself as The Survivor/The Philosopher/The Individual: '... your [ethnic] group can give you support and it's good to have them to turn to, but in the end you have to be responsible for yourself ... my Buddhist practice gives me the strength, courage and confidence I need ...'

Notions of occupational identity

Ethnicity, therefore, is arguably fluid, very much in the eye of the beholder. Occupational identity, however, can be linked to qualifications, registration and/or membership. Nonetheless, ethnicity could describe the whole person – apparent before one is introduced and also visible from afar – while occupational identity only describes the individual in a particular context and/or may require more information than the person's presence. It does not visibly announce itself. Given the predominance we give to sight for identifying and placing people and objects in our environment, this is not insignificant. There are few tangible markers that announce occupational identity and the few that exist are ambiguous. All these points raise questions about the ways in which occupational identity and ethnic identity are linked. For example, are they linked? Or are they parallel constructs that never interact?

In addition, as will be discussed under the next sub-heading, while ethnic groups are not easily defined and are subject to constant change, notions of occupational or professional identity may be untenable even despite qualification, registration and/or membership:

> ... professional identity is assumed to be associated with a sense of shared experiences, understandings and expertise, common ways of perceiving problems and their possible solutions. The identity is produced and reproduced through shared and common educational background and professional training, by similarities in work practices and procedures, by shared ways of perceiving and interacting with customers and clients ... [however] ... diversity within the profession should be given more prominence in analysis ... Most professions are moving from a position of comparative homogeneity to a state of increased specialisation, and perhaps fragmentation.[24]

This is particularly true of the legal profession, the diversity within which is well documented. The diverse areas of work, the different sectors in which solicitors and barristers can work, the differing nature, type and size of the firms and/or organisations in which they work (which may, in turn, call for

---

24 Evetts, 1998, p 57.

different skill sets) only account for part of the challenge to define occupational identity. Another part of the challenge is created by the link between this diversity and social categories such as ethnicity, class and sex, whereby certain social class groups, ethnic groups and women are more likely to be found working in certain areas of work and in certain types of firms/organisations or sectors.[25]

The importance of individual differences

That individual differences were important can almost be left unsaid; it is, arguably, a given. That individual difference was important to the participant group was highlighted by the fact that some interviewees described themselves differently from how others around them had described them. Ethnic and occupational tags, for example, were not always used in interviewees' descriptions of themselves, nor were they tolerated in some instances. Some interviewees did not see the relevance of such pigeon-holing – they did not want assumptions made about them. Others still did embrace both their ethnic and occupational identity, but claimed to give such tags something other than their historical meanings.

The varying importance given to individual differences is best illustrated by the responses to the question that usually ended the interviews and effectively summarised the discussion: 'How do you describe yourself?' These were the 13 responses (two interviewees were not asked this question):

At the individual level, I am a man who knows his mind and is at peace with himself and seeks to be at peace with his neighbour's nature. At the political level, I am a man, a black man. There is a great divide between the people of colour and the people of no colour. There is a colour dimension to being black, but there are also value systems ... we are natural conservatives.

I never thought of my ethnic and occupational identity as being separate; however, first I am a person, an individual.

How I describe myself depends on whom I am speaking to ... I am a British Muslim solicitor ... I have married my ... identities in a way that is satisfactory to me.

If I have to describe it succinctly, I am an Asian lawyer with an emphasis on Asian which is the pride I have in my [states ethnic] identity, although I recognise that my professional identity is important to the outside world. Notice that I did not say that I was an Asian [states area of law] lawyer.

I am opinionated and ambitious.

How I describe myself is context-dependent. I am a young lawyer. If I were asked to qualify this, I would describe myself as being a young, female lawyer. Race would not enter into the description.

25 As found by the Law Society's *Entry into the Legal Professions Cohort Study*, Shiner, 1999, and reported by Shiner, Chapter 5, in this book.

Depends who's asking. For the purposes of this research, I am a [states nationality] lawyer. I would give a longer description of this to my clients as they have little knowledge of what lawyers do.

I am an individual.

I do not think about such things.

Being a lawyer is not a big part of my identity ... It does not feature at home, outside the office. I am a fair, open-minded person [to] anyone and everyone ... reasoned in everything I do. It is important not to assume too many things about others and not to be prejudicial and assume that you are better than anyone else or that anyone else is better than you. Have pride and self-respect, but also respect others. If you show others respect, you will always get it back ... If used in context, I would not mind others using an ethnic tag to describe me, but otherwise labelling is unhelpful.

The question and notions of identity are bogus ones ... People overrate identity issues ...

To a complete stranger, I would describe myself as being a legal researcher. To more interested parties and at a deeper level, the key words would be difference, courage, anxious.

I'm a prosecutor ... This would not vary according to the person I am speaking to ... I would not mind others using an ethnic tag to describe me depending on the context and their reasons.

Race v ethnicity: terminology

As discussed in the first section of the annexure to this chapter, the interview group labelled itself using a variety of ethnic, racial and culture-related terms, each with varying levels of inclusiveness – for example, 'Black', 'Asian', 'black', 'people of colour', 'ethnic minorities'. What is of consequence is that the term (and the level of inclusiveness of the term) favoured by the wider legal profession to describe individuals considered to be outside the majority ethnic group – 'ethnic minorities' and, among equalities practitioners, 'minority ethnic groups' – was a term/level of inclusiveness that was only sometimes used by interviewees. Interview participants tended to prefer 'Black', 'Asian' or 'Black and Asian' to describe themselves. That 'Black and Asian'[26] was favoured over umbrella terms such as 'ethnic minorities' and

---

26 'In the UK, the separation of black to Black and Asian (and other groups) is recent and has largely been a result of a recent shift in politics: the transition to the political doldrums of the early 1990s also saw a noticeable shift away from the grand globalising themes of the previous decade: "Black Britishness", "Black art", "the struggle", "anti-racism", etc – indicators of a certain readiness to embrace political alliances across nationality and ethnicity ... Stuart Hall believes that it is no longer possible to mobilise "Afro-Caribbeans and Asians" under "a single political category" (Black). It is imperative that we should recognise "the complex internal cultural segmentation. The internal frontlines which cut through so called Black British identity".' (Owusu, 1999, p 9: he uses 'Black' and 'black' in the opposite way to us.)

'black' hints at an implicit belief that there exists occasionally named, but largely unnamed, important differences between minority ethnic groups. Perhaps for this reason, the small group within the participant group who thought the difference was irrelevant also separated black into 'Black' and 'Asian', as an acknowledgment that other Black and Asian solicitors and barristers mostly grouped themselves separately.

To some extent this difference may be grounded in primordialism, which Fenton describes as being 'a fundamental attachment grounded in early socialisation ... this term has persisted as a focal point of a debate about the very nature of ethnicity as a social bond and identity'.[27] Primordial terms, however, have been subjected to continuous social reconstruction, giving them enough flexibility and elasticity to allow individuals to pick and choose membership of an ethnic group or, what's more problematic for the individual, allow others to place them in an ethnic group without consultation. A very good example of this is the Muslim solicitor, mentioned above, whom we, the researchers, labelled South Asian British. The absence of agreed-upon definitions of ethnic groups therefore allows the opportunistic and/or non-negotiated use of ethnic tags. It also contributes to the nebulous nature of ethnic terms, ones fraught with a multitude of meanings that make conversations about ethnicity somewhat difficult and not easily generalisable.

The second problem with the use of tags such as Black and Asian, aside from the mixing of colour with geography, is that race and ethnicity become inextricably linked. As such, fundamental identifiers of so called racial categories – which Gilroy importantly describes as being dangerously outmoded[28] – are also seen to be identifiers of ethnicity. This is particularly true of physical appearance. It is not so much that race and racial difference are reified, so much as race forms the basis of difference; for some, ethnic tags are refined racial ones, whereby dimensions of class, culture, experiences, language and/or religion are added, thereby allowing for 'race' and 'ethnicity' to be used almost interchangeably. While Bashi draws the distinction between race and ethnicity – 'race is a classification that is typically assigned or externally imposed while ethnicity is internally asserted ... race is a power relation while ethnicity has none of these connotations'[29] – this distinction does not seem to be made by the general public. It is uncertain to what extent lay theories of ethnicity and race coincide with 'academic' theories, which at least have the advantage of being debated in the public domain rather than accepted almost unquestioningly. Further to this, there are some for whom, as

27   Fenton, 1999.

28   'In an era where colonial power had made epidermalising into a dominant principle of political power ... "race" might be best approached as an after-image – a lingering symptom of looking too intently or too casually into the damaging glare emanating from colonial conflicts at home and abroad.' (Gilroy, 1998, p 845.)

29   Bashi, 1998.

Bashi points out, 'racial identities are obtained not because one is unaware of the choice of ethnic labels with which to call oneself, but because one is not allowed to be without a race in a racialised society'. In addition, Gilroy comments that racial terms are used 'by those whose oppositional, legal and even democratic claims have come to rest on identities and solidarities forged at great cost from the categories given to them by their oppressors' (the term 'black', for example, is a term that is steeped in racial meaning and colonial-centred thinking and history).[30] Such terms have been reclaimed by some of the people who historically have been named such and given different connotations. Others, however, especially those outside these groups, use tags that are grounded in lay racial definitions, which lack scientific validity, but contain historical ones.

Furthermore, Gilroy argues that by using ethnic and racial tags, one buys into the notion of separate camps, of 'us' and 'them' and the dangers that accompany these distinctions, not only between majority and minority groups, but also between minority groups.[31] As one interviewee who argued against the public/common use of ethnic tags described it: 'It's best to say you are British first and then Black. If you point to the differences first, then you cannot blame others for treating you differently.'

There are, of course, important reasons for using ethnic tags. The separation of 'Black' and 'Asian', for example, highlights the qualitatively different experiences of the two groups and the perceived differences in perception of the two groups by the wider legal profession. This seems a complex relationship that has both resulted in and has been mediated by the differing responses to the legal profession by Black and Asian lawyers and vice versa. However, as one participant in particular felt, the separation of Black and Asian has led to the two groups acting as comparators for one another in often unhelpful ways.

HOW DIFFERENT AM I? WHAT IS THE STRENGTH OF GROUP IDENTITY?

At this point in the chapter, we tentatively bring ourselves closer to the nexus by taking a look at the commonality of attitudes and experiences of the 15 interviewees. Notwithstanding the four provisos and caveats discussed in the last section, there did exist a degree of commonality, especially around the notion of difference. Most participants were conscious of being different from most of their colleagues in the legal profession. This difference was a result of

---

30 Gilroy, 1998.
31 *Ibid*; Gilroy, 2000.

their ethnicity for most, their class for some and their religion for one in the group. The degree to which this difference was embraced was not as predictably varied as we expected given the variety of cultures, experiences and attitudes within the participant group. For almost all in the group, this awareness of being visibly the minority in the profession resulted in the seeking out, mainly through membership of ethnic-specific groups such as the ACA (African Caribbean and Asian Lawyers Group), SAL (Society of Asian Lawyers) and SBL (Society of Black Lawyers), others who shared their experiences.

In this section, we unpack what participants thought made them different (even if only at one level), and what made them similar to the people they sought out through membership of ethnic-specific groups or via other means. Our aim is to raise questions about, but not answer (given the smallness and unrepresentativeness of the group), *where* the nexus between ethnic and occupational identity could lie for Black and Asian solicitors and barristers.

Being visibly different

Almost all the interview participants spoke about being visibly different and for some, this in turn meant that they were not seen to have ownership of the legal profession. As one interviewee expressed it: '... the legal profession was one of the last bastions of the white male'. Some subscribed to this notion with comments such as 'this is their profession, not ours' ('their' was reference to White people of English heritage). One interviewee qualified this by saying:

> ... the general climate is important – people have changed their attitudes towards ethnic minorities, except the layer of the right wing. People are now more warm, more interested. Our culture is no longer taboo. In fact, it is now seen as something positive ... We have moved on a great deal, at all levels, younger and older.[32]

Nonetheless, this interviewee also thought that Black and Asian lawyers were perceived to be outsiders in the legal profession as a result of being visibly different.[33] Other interviewees who also shared this view felt this difference was not only located in skin colour and physical features, but also partly

---

32 This same interviewee admitted to hiding her identity while at school: 'As a child, I would not promote my identity at school by talking about my weekend activities, religion or being vegetarian. When I was asked what I did outside school, I used to make it up ... I lived in a working class area at the time of Enoch Powell ... I became more confident about my identity as I grew older.'

33 A few participants did buy into this notion of Other, which came out in discussions about the terms 'British' and 'English' and the perceived difference between the two. 'English' was not a term that anyone used to describe themselves, even those participants from a mixed heritage background where one parent was English. As one participant put it: '"English" is a heritage to which I can lay no claim.'

linked to the unfixed, unrecognised heritage of minority ethnic groups in this country. They would remain outsiders (the Other) for as long as the majority did not incorporate certain groups in their thinking of what is British,[34] and more specific to this chapter, what constitutes the legal profession in England and Wales.

For more than half the group, being the Other was not confronted for the first time on entering law school or the legal profession. They had, in fact, been one of the few Black or Asian children at their primary and/or secondary school. They were, therefore, used to being different and, in the instance of two in the group, used to confronting the stereotype of a black person. For others in the group, law school was their first experience of being a visible minority in an institutional setting and therefore 'fitting in' became one of the many challenges of studying and practising law.

How participants managed their difference was in part dependent on where they saw 'home' to be. Some who saw 'home' as being a country other than the UK (because either he/she and/or his/her parents were overseas born) to some degree had a pragmatic acceptance of being treated differently, voicing 'we are, after all, not in our own country'. That they saw the legal profession as being one of the 'last white bastions' was more reason for these interviewees to accept differential treatment; they saw the barrier created by their ethnicity as being inevitable, even if disheartening. Nonetheless, experiences of being marginalised was in fact what prompted some participants to defer to the concept of Other and to not call themselves British (and certainly not English). As such, they look to their country of birth (or their parents' country of birth) for their identity. How they were treated within and/or outside the legal profession determined the level to which they were willing to take ownership of things British, including the legal profession.

Use of ethnic tags

While we raised questions about the validity of the use of ethnic tags in the last section, the consistent use of these terms by all but one participant nonetheless hinted at the importance of such terms to the participant group. Even those participants who did not use an ethnic tag to describe themselves, used ethnic tags to describe others. So, while Gilroy provides cogent

---

34   This touches on a broader theme that is currently being debated in the wider public arena; what is 'British', 'Britishness' and British identity? As mentioned by Maya Jaggi in her article in (1999) *The Guardian*, 3 November, it is a debate that the powers that be also recognise needs to be had: 'Chris Smith, the cultural secretary, opened a debate yesterday whose purpose is to redefine not just the seemingly quaint notions of heritage, but the very heart of British identity.' Andrea Levy in her article in (2000) *The Guardian*, 19 February, wrote about the irony and frustration of being viewed as a foreigner in one's country of birth, extended also to immigrants to the UK who have lived here most or all of their lives.

arguments for moving away from what he terms 'racial' tags, the reality is that people do use such tags in relation to themselves and/or others. This is not to say that every participant was always comfortable using such tags and one made the point that: '... there's no necessity to go around saying that you are a Black solicitor. It is sufficient to say that you are a solicitor.' There was, however, an implicit recognition that sometimes, and to most people, ethnic tags were important shorthands to explain experiences and attitudes. Participants used the terms Black and Asian with a degree of certainty to demarcate boundaries of ethnicity and/or race and thereby allow themselves the opportunity to assess their own experiences against the experiences of others in the profession to whom they thought they were most similar. Expectations about their survival and success within the legal profession were an inevitable result of such a demarcation process.

Also the use of specific ethnic terms such as 'Black' and 'Asian' in place of broader banner terms highlights to the others, including the legal profession, the diversity covered by the term 'ethnic minorities' or 'minority ethnic groups'. (Some within the legal profession may be ignorant of these important differences.) The thinking was that if 'Black' and 'Asian' are problem terms for the breadth of differing peoples and cultures they cover, then 'ethnic minority' is even more so. To cite an example, in a recent meeting with law firms about the recruitment of African-Caribbean men into law firms (a group that is particularly under-represented in the legal profession),[35] recruitment staff at one large City firm spoke about using 'ethnic minority' solicitors at their firm to attract African-Caribbean candidates from the law student pool. They complained, however, that this method failed to achieve the desired effect and concluded that African-Caribbean men were not interested in working at their firm. It transpired, later, that the 'ethnic minority' solicitors they took with them to recruit African-Caribbean law students were South Asian.

Shared experiences

Ethnic tags were shorthands that were used by interviewees to identify other individuals on the route into or in the legal profession who shared similar experiences. This was particularly true in relation to recruitment: based on their own and/or the experiences of others who shared their ethnic tag, most participants concluded that there was the potential for ethnic identity to be given a premium over ability and educational qualifications in the recruitment of trainees, qualified solicitors and pupils. Or, if ethnic identity was not directly a barrier, it was indirectly one, as it was recognised that ethnicity was

35   Cole, 2000.

closely linked to other perceived barriers such as type of university attended.[36] Consequently, participants noticed that, while they were no different to their peers in terms of qualification/s and potential, they were in the minority in terms of their potential success at securing the more desired jobs.

What is interesting about this is that, despite most interviewees having undergone great difficulties to get to where we found them (for example, 10 of the 15 interviewees reported making between 200 and 600 applications for training contracts and/or pupillages), most of them were at pains to point out that they had faced no discrimination. They were really quite reluctant to use this word in relation to their own experience. We call this the 'discrimination as taboo' phenomenon and discuss it further in the concluding section of the chapter. Such a view usually resulted in the modification of expectations at each successive point on the route to entry into the legal profession, a modification governed largely by pragmatism and an acceptance of the reality. Modifying expectations was, however, not the only measure taken by the interviewees who faced difficulties entering the legal profession. A range of measures were explored and employed, including undertaking further study or obtaining extra qualifications, obtaining experience within another jurisdiction ('I went back to my home country to practise'), moving some distance from their home city/town to find training contracts (in one case, uprooting the whole family of which she was the sole parent), becoming a member of a black law group and/or seeking a support group that would provide practical careers advice. Some participants observed that, while such strategies were not unique to Black and Asian experience, their anecdotal experience seemed to suggest that many more Black and Asian graduates were doing this (or, at the very least, had the expectation of having to be this pragmatic).

The benefits of being so strategic were not lost on participants, however, and most recognised that it provided them with the necessary attitude to work and survive in the legal profession. As expressed by one participant:

> ... irrespective of one's identity, working as a lawyer is dehumanising. The firm is not interested in you beyond how much money you bring in. This fosters an unhealthy competition and places a burden of responsibility for which the newly qualified lawyer is not prepared ... Learning to survive is important.

It also led to a recognition that 'playing the game' was very much a part of successful entry into, and survival within, the legal profession. One interviewee described it in terms of masks, whereby the mask he puts on for

---

36 This is interestingly borne out by statistics – the Law Society's *Entry into the Legal Professions Cohort Study* (Shiner, 1999) found that, in the allocation of training contracts, there was a bias against those graduates from the new universities, also reported by Shiner, Chapter 5, in this book.

the profession bears no resemblance to his own 'ethnic' self. Others spoke about learning to reveal only parts of their identity – by suppressing the full expression of their ethnic identity, for example – to suit the situation. Some participants spoke about this level of pragmatism taking its toll: the identity that was considered acceptable by the legal profession overriding the individual's ethnic identity. As one interviewee put it: 'The mask becomes the face.' It was interesting that all participants with children remarked that they would not want their children to enter the profession. For them, society was not necessarily an unknown or unacceptable place to be within, but the legal profession had too many unspoken rules that, first, needed to be interpreted and secondly, did not allow the expression of their ethnic self.

Interviewees therefore felt that it was not only in trying to enter the legal profession that Black and Asian solicitors and barristers faced hurdles. Once in the profession, there were other hurdles in the form of the trimmings. To some participants, these trimmings constituted the previously mentioned unspoken rules that determined one's success within the legal profession: in a profession where, traditionally, entry and survival was linked to patronage and relationships, moving up the hierarchy is somewhat dependent on socialising with colleagues and clients. What created problems for most interviewees was not only learning about this in time, in the absence of any road maps, but also feeling comfortable participating in such extra-curricular activities, especially when alcohol was involved. Most respondents reported that drinking alcohol was not a part of their culture. Also, such socialising also usually required a knowledge of, and a level of comfort with, a community dissimilar to their own at the socio-cultural level: '... you need to know how to make small talk, which we don't do in our community. Black people hate small talk. They either say what they mean or are quiet ...' Participants also felt that this unmeritocratic process further compounded their disadvantage: 'I have been told that Black and Asian people have to work twice as hard to get half as much. I don't mind this, but I thought hard work was enough.'

Stereotypes

Shared experiences also extended to dealing with ethnic stereotypes. Most participants claimed to be unfazed by their difference, but they found the stereotypes held by others about their ethnic group was at the heart of their challenges. Being mistaken as the client or the social worker in court was one way in which the stereotypes manifested for Black participants, for example. More damaging, however, was when one's ethnicity led to one being perceived as being aggressive or exotic or an acceptable exception of one's ethnic group. Participants thought the first two characteristics implied irrationality and ineffectuality respectively, and were characteristics that were looked upon disdainfully by the legal profession. As such, being perceived to have such qualities affected one's chances of moving up the hierarchy. Being considered to be an acceptable exception of one's ethnic group, however, was considered to have the opposite, more positive career consequences. However, participants thought it came at a huge psychological cost.

Ethnic stereotypes were therefore considered to have a twofold effect. First, they prevented the individual from emerging from their ethnicity as an individual. In addition, it pushed ethnicity to the forefront of the individual's thinking in possibly unhelpful ways. For example, while few participants had any proof that their ethnicity contributed to their difficulty in obtaining training contracts or pupillage, the suspicion that their ethnicity was a contributing factor was a nagging thought and, therefore, potentially debilitating. As one interviewee put it:

> I don't like thinking that things going wrong are beyond my control. I would rather think that it was due to my grades, etc. Yet there were people in my year who were fairly mediocre who were getting on better than me ... These people knew the right people and would have been seen as fitting in ... If you get a first then perhaps ethnicity ceases to be a problem ... It's difficult to know ...

Secondly, stereotypes make the individual simultaneously invisible and visible: invisible in the sense that one's individual difference/personal attributes are not acknowledged, and yet visible in the sense that one's physical traits – skin colour, hair, features – make one noticed.

For most participants, the decision to study law was not motivated by the desire to challenge the stereotype of their respective ethnic group, but rather was made despite this stereotype. In fact, their reasons for choosing to study law were a combination of social, intellectual and practical ones and, thus, probably no different from the reasons offered by people who are not Black or Asian. In continuing along the path into the legal profession and making their way up the hierarchy, however, confronting ethnic stereotypes became more commonplace for some and difficult to ignore. The most extreme version of this was described by one participant in the following way: 'My identity was not an issue for me [at the time of making the decision to study law]. It did become an issue for others in the system, however, who noticed that I was only one of a few Black people studying law ... I probably went to the Bar for the wrong reasons – to prove people wrong.'

Pressures from within – coconuts[37] and bananas[38]

Despite the hurdles, the potential for hurdles and the stereotypes, all interview participants made the decision to enter, and then remain in, the

---

37 The direct definition of which is black on the outside, white on the inside: the implication that one is black and trying to be white.

38 The direct definition of which is yellow on the outside, white on the inside: the implication that one is yellow and trying to be white.

legal profession. What motivated them to persist? Thus far, we have mentioned very little about the importance to participants of being a solicitor or barrister, nor discussed their notions of occupational identity outside their notions of ethnic identity and their experiences with the legal profession. This absence reflects the fact that occupational identity on its own was barely alluded to directly, if at all, in the interview discussions. There was definitely some pride around being a lawyer and more than one participant mentioned that it had been their aspiration and/or their parents' aspirations for them since they were young. In the words of one participant: 'Being a lawyer is special.' Some of their reasons for choosing to remain in the legal profession were, therefore, were related to the personal rewards that are gained from practising law.

Nonetheless, given the predominance given to ethnic identity in the interview discussions, personal rewards were alluded to less than rewards to the ethnic communities to which participants belonged (although participants did point out that personal rewards were no less important and in some cases, provided greater motivation for remaining in the legal profession than rewards to the community). Some participants felt they had an obligation to ensure that there was Black/Asian membership in the legal profession. As explained by two participants:

> If you are a black professional in any field, you have an obligation to put something back in the community when you have found success. That has always been with me.

> If you have pride in your identity, you should do everything possible to enhance your own culture. This way you earn greater respect from other communities.

Such comments precipitated broader questions about the role of Black and Asian solicitors and barristers, and this became one of the recurrent themes of the interviews. Should Black and Asian solicitors and barristers assimilate at the expense of their own ethnic identity or ethnic group's identity? Was it possible to do this? Why should Black and Asian solicitors and barristers concern themselves with such questions? These are questions that are, arguably, asked by all groups who are part of a minority whose power within certain contexts is limited. For Black and Asian lawyers, these issues expressed themselves in terms of what it means to be Black, Asian or Black/Asian within the legal profession.

While many in the participant group agreed that what it means to be Black or Asian is up to the individual, some did acknowledge that to some degree, this was negotiated between the individual, the group to which s/he belongs and the legal profession. The danger of being seen as a 'coconut' (or 'banana', for South East and East Asians) is there.[39] A visible display of loyalty to, and

---

39 The negative, disparaging connotations that accompanied these terms implied that it was something to be avoided.

an affiliation with, other Black or Asian colleagues was one way in which participants thought being seen to be a coconut/banana could be avoided. More accurately, in the absence of this loyalty or affiliation, one ran the risk of being perceived as having turned one's back on one's own, or of pretending to be 'white'. As one participant put it, when a Black or Asian person in the legal profession puts his/her head down and 'gets on with it' without any care for others in his/her ethnic group: '... then they may be missing out ... I hope that this happy scenario continues and that it would help them if they do come across discrimination, given that they have not attached themselves to a support network of people who share the same experiences ...' Another responded: '... some have little choice but to be like this if in a white establishment like law but you could at least try to work within and help your own ...'

Those seen to go one step further and mimic the majority group 'to get ahead' were looked on with a mixture of disdain and sadness by a few:

> ... they try to put themselves in [the white person's] clothes and adopt [the white person's] way of life – it's pathetic, they are deluding themselves. When you are doing things on your own ground, you are majestic: you are bringing something unique to the party rather than providing a poor imitation of someone else ...

> People can survive this way depending on the type of lifestyle they want. If you want a middle class lifestyle and to mix with people of your own stature, then you can do it ... Nonetheless, you don't know how these people truly live their lives. And this is up to the individual – not all people have to have a commitment to the community. You have to live the life that is true to you. I would, however, have a problem if every black solicitor had this intention/attitude.

Others were more pragmatic in their response:

> The legal profession is very snooty – it's very much about fitting in and getting on with others. [To a point] you may have to do certain things.[40]

> Everyone does things for individual gain. What a person chooses to do is their own business – it's a personal decision. For some people this is a natural way to go. Work life does change one, perhaps more positively than negatively ... and one's values develop and merge with the firm's values.

> Depends on your career aim ... We've all got to do it our own way ... You cannot judge how another person sees their identity and whether in fact they are compromising their [ethnic] identity. It depends on a number of factors including family needs.

> ... they could be quite revolutionary in themselves ...

> ... when in Rome to a large extent ... each to their own ...

---

40 She was, however, disdainful of people who went as far as to change their names to fit in.

If the term 'coconut' was being applied by a black person to a black person then it would mean nothing – they should know what you are up against.

One participant found the concept of coconuts and bananas, and the prescribed behaviour the use of the terms implied, disheartening:

> I would defend such a person [who is called a 'coconut' by their own ethnic group] against any attack. Being black should be whatever you want it to be because white people have that freedom/liberty of individuality. The biggest disservice black people do to their own is criticise each other in this way – it's destructive. I mean, thank God for Clarence Thomas in a way – it shows that as a group we are complex ... I know some people would not see me as black as I do not share the same ... diet, values ... political ideals. There may be some validity in their claims but it also really infuriates me.

PULLING THE THREADS TOGETHER

A multitude of experiences and attitudes were uncovered by the search for the nexus between occupational and ethnic identity for Black and Asian solicitors and barristers. This range and variety suggests that group identities within the legal profession (that is, Black, Asian or Black/Asian) are not derived from, nor give insight into, the individual identities of Black and Asian solicitors and barristers. These group identities do exist, however, but in highly constructed forms that sit outside the individual Black or Asian solicitor or barrister. The existence of these identities seems largely functional – they are used for purposes of identification and inclusion/exclusion by some Black and Asian solicitors and barristers and by some who lie outside these groups. They are seemingly contingent on general patterns of entry into the legal profession and experiences within the profession being common to a large proportion of graduates who are seen to fall into these ethnic groups. Once such patterns become more disparate within these ethnic groups, the specific group ethnic identities within the legal profession would, arguably, be invalidated.

This is not to suggest that some, most or all Black and Asian solicitors and barristers want to distance themselves from their ethnicity or ethnic make-up. They do, however, seem to want to distance themselves from having an ethnic role in the legal profession, either by choice or by default. It is an extension of Fishman's comment that: '... the phenomenon of ethnicity is not identical to ethnocentrism or racism ...'[41] This is not only because ethnicity is only one component of the individual, but also because to focus solely on ethnicity potentially limits one's understanding of those individuals described solely or mainly in terms of their ethnicity. It was for this reason that many in the

---

41 Fishman, 1996, p 63.

participant group were reluctant to identify themselves as recipients of discrimination – either positive discrimination (*sic*)[42] or negative discrimination.

Many in the group, however, were in favour of positive action and recognised that ethnic identification was a necessary part of creating a level playing field and for group self-help. As one participant described it: '... you need to demonstrate that you can help yourself ... by harnessing resources from within your own [disadvantaged] group ...' The point, however, is that group ethnic identity within the legal profession, in the form of ethnic-specific support groups and other initiatives, is a response to others in the legal profession and not necessarily a choice. Further to the point made in the previous paragraph, group ethnic identities within the profession are important for only as long as there are clear differences in experiences within the legal profession according to ethnicity. The importance of a study on identity, and our aim in making this our focus, is that it shows that theories of self-identity are not always formally or informally linked to group ethnic identity (this accounts for why ethnic tags were used sparingly and why some interviewees felt prompted to describe themselves using an ethnic tag only when asked to describe their experiences). Instead, a substantial degree of belief about the concept of ethnicity and of group ethnic identities – and the 'buying into' such concepts – is required; these are parameters within which the legal profession operates. Yet, such concepts not only can mask the plight of the individual, but force them into a role not of their own making. This is an important point given that the legal profession's policy on, and support and resources for, minority ethnic groups is premised on a belief in group ethnic identities; the profession finds it useful to group people into ethnic categories. Furthermore, the existence of a number of ethnic minority support groups within the legal profession – the ACA, SAL, SBL and, arguably, the MLA (Muslim Lawyers Association), amongst others – suggests that group consensus of group ethnic identities does not even exist amongst Black and Asian minority groups within the legal profession.

These are only our tentative hypotheses. Further research with a greater number of solicitors and barristers from these ethnic groups is required to enable us to comment more firmly on the many themes raised by the search for the nexus between ethnic and occupational identity for Black and Asian solicitors and barristers. The issues that arose from the interview process (discussed in the annexure to this chapter) also suggest that multiple interviews with each interview participant are also necessary, as is the need to begin the research process by narrowing research participant membership according to gender and more specific ethnic categories than Black and Asian. For example, given the greater under-representation of African-Caribbean

---

42 Positive discrimination is illegal in the UK.

men in the legal profession compared to other gender-ethnic groups, we will begin the next stage of our research with this group and only then move on to other gender-ethnic groups; at this stage, we plan to research gender-ethnic groups individually. This will give us the opportunity to have more direct discussions about the meanings and (arguably) the appropriate use of ethnic tags and explore the relationship between at least two of many socio-demographic subject positions that individuals are seen to occupy – gender and ethnicity – more thoroughly. Inclusion of more participants who only have limited or no contact with others in the legal profession from their ethnic group will also be a necessary part of this process. In addition, given the differences in entry requirements and environment of the solicitors' and barristers' profession, and given the number of significant differences between employed work and private practice, narrowing participation membership according to these variables is also necessary. As such, we will begin the next stage of our research by looking first at the largest of these group – solicitors in private practice – and only then extend our research to the other groups.

Finally, we would like to conclude with the words of the President Elect of the American Bar Association, Martha Barnett, who, at the ABA Conference in London in July 2000 said: 'Real success of diversity is not just numbers, but when you listen to what the other person has said and incorporate it in your thinking.'

ANNEXURE: ISSUES THAT EMERGED FROM THE INTERVIEW PROCESS

Our aim in this section is to highlight to the reader how methodological factors impinged on the search for the nexus between occupational and ethnic identity for the groups that we chose for this research. We also explore what we, the authors – Sumitra, Marcia and Jerry – brought to the research process, and why this was important.

Definitions of the ethnic categories

Throughout this chapter, we try to reflect the words and phrases that were used by the interview participants. This was particularly true for the descriptors 'Black' and 'Asian'.[43] 'Black' was used almost uniformly as an exclusive term, comprising all those of African and African-Caribbean descent in Britain and elsewhere, including the USA (although the latter were

---

43 We, the authors, prefer the more inclusive descriptor 'black' or 'minority ethnic', the latter including more than just people of African, African-Caribbean or Asian descent.

sometimes labelled Black American, to distinguish them from Black British, where the interviewee thought this distinction was important). The implied meaning of Asian seemed to conform to Cashmore's discussion of the word:

> The term 'Asian' in a British context usually refers to migrants and their offspring from South Asia, that is, India, Pakistan, Bangladesh and Sri Lanka. It also includes those of Asian descent who previously lived in the East African countries surrounding Lake Victoria: Kenya, Tanzania, and Uganda. The former travelled to Britain as migrants mostly in the 1950s and, especially, the 1960s. The latter were political refugees who fled to Britain following expulsion in the 1970s.[44]

It was uncertain whether South Asians who live in or came to Britain from any other country outside those mentioned in Cashmore's definition (for example, the Caribbean, where in some parts they are known as East Asian), were included in participants' definition of 'Asian'.

The only person who used the term 'Asian' differently was the one South-East Asian interview participant, whose implied meaning of the term included people of South East Asian or East Asian descent but not, interestingly, necessarily of South Asian descent.

Where Black and Asian peoples were occasionally referred to differently by interviewee, it was usually with phrases such as 'people of colour' or 'visible minority', which were terms broad enough occasionally to encompass South East Asian peoples and Islander peoples (that is, all those considered by participants to have 'dark skin'); however, it was uncertain whether East Asian peoples were incorporated by this term. People of East Asian descent tended to be referred to as 'Chinese'. The term 'black' was occasionally also used in this way (that is, as an inclusive term) by some interview participants, but by and large it was 'Black and Asian' – what has almost become a term of art in some communities – that was most commonly used to describe legal professionals who were descendants of either African, African-Caribbean or Asian peoples.

The only participants who actively mentioned individuals from mixed heritage backgrounds (authors' terminology) were those participants from mixed heritage backgrounds themselves, all of whom had one parent who was described as being either 'White', 'European' or both (that is, 'white'). There was no uniform word used to describe people from a mixed heritage background and the words used by participants of this background included 'mixed race', 'Black' and 'mulatto'.

People described by the census as being 'white', were referred to by this word. We, the authors, believe that it a problematic term, as it is unclear which groups of people are incorporated by the term. As mentioned by

---

44 Cashmore, 1997, pp 40–41.

Mason, it is not a term that comes under scrutiny in the same way as the word 'black/Black':

> ... the term 'white' ... is less often seen as a problematic term and serves a useful shorthand function ... It is useful to note, however, that the term is scarcely precise or unambiguous. It is used interchangeably with other terms such as 'European' or 'British' ...[45]

While interview participants rarely used the latter word (that is, British) synonymously with 'White', they sometimes did use the former (that is, European) in this way. Others still, separated 'Europeans' from 'White' and, instead, used 'White' synonymously with 'English'. A third group used it in an inclusive way, in much the same way they used 'black' (that is, as 'white' rather than 'White') – to include all non-black people. The term was therefore not used in a uniform way, including by us, the authors, who sometimes referred to the 'majority group', which we realised was as vague and problematic as 'white'.

The importance of credibility and style

Most of the interview participants were identified by Jerry and were known to both Jerry and Marcia. A few were referred to us by fellow interview participants. Only one person invited to participate in the interviews refused to do so. The willingness of all but this one person to participate was in large part due to Marcia and Jerry being known professionally to interviewees through the course of various Law Society activities – more than half the interviewees made this apparent to Sumitra, who had 'called them cold' (that is, they were not pre-warned about Sumitra's call).

In total, 15 people were interviewed between 13 January and 29 March 2000, inclusive. It was not our intention to interview so many people in the three short months we had to conduct the research and write this chapter; however, two things happened after the first few interviews. First, we began to modify and refine our interview approach in order to draw participants out. For example, over time, two standard questions emerged. The first was attached to a hypothetical: 'Someone of your socio-economic description enters the legal profession and does not make the effort to involve himself/herself with other Black/Asian solicitors/barristers, although this may not be a conscious decision. What would your response be about such a person?' This hypothetical situation was supplied to us by the first interview participant. We tested it out on the second interview participant and found it took us more closely to how he felt about himself and others around him and, therefore, used it in all the interviews to almost the same effect. The

45 Mason, 1996.

hypothetical touched on themes that most participants alluded to before the hypothetical was introduced into the interview, but were reluctant to be explicit about. The second standard question ('How do you describe yourself?') tended to end the interview usefully and allow the participant to feed into the overarching theme more directly and succinctly by their answer to it. All discussions prior to this were a broad and meandering lead-up to this end and their answer usually took the interview a full circle.

Secondly, more often than not, themes emerged from the interviews that we thought should be 'tested out' on other Black and Asian lawyers whom we knew might expand on them or provide an alternative view. There were, in fact, many more whom we could have included in the study to fulfil this purpose – there were certainly many more Black and Asian solicitors and barristers willing to participate – but we eventually ran out of time.

With three exceptions,[46] all interviews were conducted by Sumitra with either Jerry or Marcia. That Marcia and Jerry knew most participants meant that rapport and trust was established before the interview began. Participants were willing to disclose a certain amount about themselves and gave the impression of being in a relatively safe environment in which to discuss their views and experiences openly. The interviews did not follow a formal structure or format and fairly soon evolved into discussions whereby, we, the authors, participated in a discussion with the interview participant on or around the broad overarching theme of the interview. Mostly, however, the interview participant 'had the floor', and we steered them within the parameters of the main overarching issue while allowing them to take us to sub-topics that they thought were relevant to this main issue. If the interview occasionally lapsed into a discussion, it was because we began to recognise after a few interviews that the question and answer mode of interviewing seemed to elicit less than, for example, Jerry's informal style, which included playing the devil's advocate, sharing his views and adopting a friendly and humorous style to explore potentially sensitive topics when he felt it suited. Jerry's insider knowledge of the research participant clearly helped him do this comfortably, and participants felt free to disagree with him and/or tell him that he was putting words into their mouths. It is unclear how successful this style would have been if adopted by a stranger.

Certainly Jerry's style was more in keeping with the culture of the groups from which these interviewees came. There also seemed to be a real mismatch with question and answer style of interviewing and the way the Black and Asian lawyers talk amongst themselves about their identity. The former style seemed too formal and contrived and did not allow for the easy use of culture-specific language and terms, such as 'Bounty bar', 'coconut' and other

---

46   In the first of these, Sumitra began the interview with Jerry and continued it on another day without him. The second was a one-on-one interview conducted by Sumitra alone and the third, a one-on-two conducted by Sumitra alone.

informal shorthands, which the informal style of interviewing elicited. Related to this was the freedom with which such terms were used by these individuals who, in their professional lives, seemed to refrain from adopting such terms. Clearly, the fact we were Black and Asian helped – there was less of a risk that the terms (and, generally, the ways in which their views were expressed) would require explanation and/or seem unusual or offensive. Of interest was the similarity in terminology and a feeling of shared experience (or, at the very least, a feeling of having one's views and experiences understood) despite inter and intra-ethnic differences and despite the fact that Sumitra was still new to the UK at the time of the interviews. This highlighted to us that credibility and/or shared experience were necessary (although in some cases not sufficient – this will be discussed below) for eliciting sensitive information from this group. Therefore, while interview style was crucial, it was clear that the success of the informal style depended largely on the interviewee's perception of the level of shared experience and on the level of trust established between the them and (some of) us prior to the interview.

Furthermore, that one of the interviewers was a policy advisor worked further in our favour. It gave participants the (correct) impression that the research had a clear and immediate practical relevance; the interview process and outcome could directly influence policy.

Conditions and ethics

The length of each interview ranged from one to three hours; the average length was approximately two and a half hours. This did not include pre- or post-interview telephone conversations, some of which were quite lengthy. There was clearly much to say and the interviews often took far more time than participants had set aside for them. Given the busyness of the group, this was not expected, especially by the participants, some of whom, when contacted about the interview, were unsure that they had anything to say on the topic. All interviews took place on weekdays – during work time, lunchtime or in the evening. The venues for the interviews included the Law Society, interviewees' workplaces and, on two occasions, a café/restaurant. While, clearly, most participants had a lot to say, interview length did seem somewhat dependent on the interaction between time and venue. That the amount of disclosure was often dependent on interview length made the venue and time of day in which the interview took place all the more important.

Also, despite the lengthy interviews and the opportunity for pre- and post-interview de-briefing, we realised that we were only touching the 'tip of the iceberg' as far as the topic was concerned. Many more interviews with each participant were required to break down barriers even further and explore the topic in greater depth. Therefore, as mentioned above, while prior contact with Jerry and Marcia usefully broke down some barriers, it was not always sufficient. Even despite prior contact with Marcia and Jerry, participants did not always tackle the main issue immediately, but rather, had to be slowly eased into it, and in some interviews, it was only halfway through the interview that momentum was gained. Some participants made the boundaries of disclosure apparent by the way in which they allowed the discussion to proceed past a certain point (or not, as the case was for some). Some participants also indicated relatively explicitly that certain experiences and views were 'off the record' and that they were not willing to discuss such issues even in their private life aside from, perhaps, with a close circle of family and friends. Establishing trust and assuring confidentiality was, therefore, sometimes not enough.

Related to this, the interviews were probably the first time some participants were rehearsing theories about their own identity. This touches on our main concern about research of this nature. While this was not a counselling exercise, there was a counselling component to the exercise: as researchers, we were effectively unpicking what are carefully constructed identities that every individual develops over time, without any back up for the effects of doing this. While participants were very good at indicating where the boundaries were, for some it was the first time they were hearing themselves outwardly explain and/or discuss their identity. Setting boundaries was, therefore, difficult. Also, contradictions in their concept of their own identity (seemingly common to all people) may not have been evident to some interviews prior to the research exercise, which is bound to elicit these contradictions, quite possibly to the discomfort of the interviewee.

Group diversity

As mentioned earlier, the participant group was made up of individuals from either African, African-Caribbean, South Asian or South-East Asian descent and individuals of mixed heritage backgrounds. The group also could be divided into those born overseas and those born locally, solicitors and barristers, those in independent practice and those in employment (either in the public service or in the corporate sector), women and men, and members of the ACA, the MLA, the SAL and the SBL.[47] Participants also were ranged in age and post-qualification experience.

---

47   All but two of the interview participants had links with lawyers from the same ethnic background as them by virtue of their membership of one of the above organisations. One of the two exceptions in the group had links to what she termed as her 'national group', who formed a large component of her client base.

It was not our intention to have such a cross-section of participants. To some extent, this breadth of representation highlighted the diversity of the Black and Asian group within the legal profession: this is by no means a homogeneous group, and an important fact to bear in mind when embarking and reporting on and reading research on this group. It is also an important fact to bear in mind when writing policy that impinges on this group. In retrospect, although the interview group was by no means representative of Black and Asian lawyers (in that participants were not chosen in a random fashion and because a standard interview format was not adopted), this cross-section of lawyers did bring us closer to identifying and separating individual differences from shared experiences. This distinction, however, still remains hazy. Nonetheless, such a broad cross-section prevented us from exploring the experiences of a specific sub-group – for example, Black solicitors – to any great depth.

Primary and secondary research findings

We considered the interviewees to be co-participants in the research process. As such, they were given the opportunity to comment on their own interview, interview notes and on the research process and outcome.

For reasons of confidentiality, and at the request of the interview participants, the notes taken during the interviews cannot be released. As such, in the section of this chapter in which we discuss the themes from the interviews, the findings reported are secondary findings. They are our analyses of the primary data source: the interviews/interview notes. Having begun the chapter on the need for public voice, our dilemma is that we are giving public voice to the private selves of others. While the interview participants were given the opportunity to correct and/or add to the interview notes we had written, this chapter was written purely by us. Even though some participants were sent copies of the chapter prior to its being published, they were not privy to each other's notes to assess how accurately we had distilled the themes of the interviews from the notes.

As mentioned above, in the writing of this chapter, we used interviewees' words and terminology as often as possible. Nonetheless, we are unable to get away from the fact that our prints are all over the writing. This begs the question: who are we and what are our credentials? As mentioned earlier, we were described by the participant group as being Black and Asian and staff members of the Law Society. This is how we would describe ourselves:

Sumitra manages and conducts research on legal education/training and equal opportunities at the Law Society's Research and Policy Planning Unit. Her formal training was in psychology and in education. She was previously a drug and alcohol counsellor/researcher, then researched legal education/training and the legal profession in Australia. She is an Australian national of Sri Lankan heritage who was born in Malaysia.

Marcia is the Law Society's Policy Adviser specialising in equalities policy for the legal profession and Secretary to the Law Society's Equal Opportunities Committee. Her formal training is in law, particularly in discrimination law issues in the UK and Europe. She was previously a lecturer in law in the further education sector. She is a Black woman born in London; her parents were born in Guyana.

Jerry is co-founder of, and the Law Society's Officer to, the African, Caribbean and Asian Lawyers Group,[48] as well as Equal Opportunities Officer at the Law Society. His formal training was in careers counselling, and he previously worked in the Civil Service. If pushed, he would describe himself as Black British of Caribbean parentage; however, he prefers not to describe himself using an ethnic tag.

---

48 The ACA was set up to provide practical help to Black and Asian students seeking to enter the legal professions. The group has also set up positive action programmes and work placement schemes in association with the Crown Prosecution Service (CPS) and the Government Legal Service (GLS) and works closely with the Bar Council – specifically its Race Relations Committee – and the Lord Chancellor's Department, law firms and barristers' chambers.

CHAPTER 7

PROFESSIONALISM, DISCRIMINATION, DIFFERENCE AND CHOICE IN WOMEN'S EXPERIENCE IN LAW JOBS

Peter Sanderson and Hilary Sommerlad

INTRODUCTION

Substantial evidence now exists that women solicitors[1] are differentially placed to male solicitors in the legal labour market in England and Wales,[2] and that this situation is paralleled in other jurisdictions.[3] Furthermore, the differences which exist indicate that women are disadvantaged in terms of earnings, status and promotion chances. This is in spite of the fact that women enter the profession with academic qualifications at least equal to those of men[4] and that the larger, commercial law firms appear to favour women when hiring at the junior levels.[5] The aetiology of this 'difference' is a complex and controversial subject, not least because of the implications which different explanations have for strategies of redress. This chapter attempts a broad overview of the dimensions of cause and strategic response to women solicitors' disadvantage; a discussion which turns on a consideration of the nature of legal professionalism, and the meanings of difference, discrimination and choice.

---

1   For some time now there has been an extensive and ongoing debate within feminist theory over the use of the category 'woman', on the grounds that it essentialises women and ignores such other identity criteria as race, class and sexual orientation. Furthermore, this critique has been specifically applied to studies of women professionals: '... by ... focusing on aggregate gender differences, the complexity and specificity of women's employment situation tends to be lost.' (Bottero, 1992, p 332.) Whilst fully acknowledging these difficulties with the term, those with the power to ascribe identity and difference continue to do so, untouched by the debate. The very fact that the subordination of women lawyers (of women as a 'class'/group) is a legitimate object of study testifies to the continuing reification of women *qua* women, and the continuing need for the category, if only on strategic grounds (Braidotti, 1993; Jackson, 1993; Bacchi, 1996). We, too, therefore, use the term in this sense, whilst noting that, beyond this commonality, the women under discussion are also deeply divided by numerous other criteria and experiences.

2   Podmore and Spencer, 1986; Reynell, 1997; Sidaway, 1997; McGlynn and Graham, 1995; Ross, 1990; Sommerlad and Sanderson, 1998; Moorhead, 1997.

3   See, eg, Murray, 1987; Rhode, 1988; Harrington, 1992; Hagan and Kay, 1995; Thornton, 1996; Mossman, 1990; Koontz, 1995; Epstein *et al*, 1999.

4   Abel, 1988, p 173, p 476; Halpern, 1994, p 17; Lewis, 1996, p 69.

5   *Ibid*, Sommerlad and Sanderson, pp 156–57.

We will begin, in section 1, by essaying a brief portrait of women's contemporary position within the changing solicitors' profession: first, through a summary of some of the relevant statistical evidence, and secondly, by discussing some of the labour market 'choices' women have made. In section 2, we explore some of the explanatory models of women's difference, and its relationship to the culture of legal professionalism. With others, we argue that this relationship must be seen within the ideology and material circumstances of the public/private divide, and that the 'difference' and disadvantage with which we are concerned is not readily susceptible to redress through discrimination law. This perspective leads us into section 3, where we consider some recent critiques of discrimination law. We do this in the context of an examination both of its recent use by (a handful of) women solicitors and of the discussion of these cases and of equality issues generally by the trade press. Finally, in section 4, we will discuss the potential for the alternative approach of the 'regulatory State' to initiate underpinning cultural change.

(1) The position of women solicitors in the legal labour market in England and Wales

Of all the many changes in the legal profession in Europe, North America and Australasia in the last two decades, one of the most remarked has been the increase in women's participation in legal training and the legal labour market. As Hull and Nelson argue, this should be no surprise, since 'women lawyers stand at the intersection of three major transformations in modern society: changes in the gender composition of traditionally male occupations, changes in the social organisation of professional firms and the markets for professional services, and changes in the role of the law as a vehicle for redressing social inequality'.[6] The particular aspects of the issue which have attracted attention, however, have been the steep incline of the increase, and the fact that it has been accompanied by a tendency for women to be concentrated more heavily in particular segments of the profession, whether these are defined by specialism, occupational status, or earnings. This uneven pattern of participation has been attributed by some commentators to 'discrimination',[7] while others have associated women's advent into the profession with those major structural changes which have increased competition, and accelerated the processes of horizontal rationalisation of legal firms and the stratification of expert labour within firms.[8]

---

6   Hull and Nelson, 1998, p 681.
7   Gibb, 1996; Bahl, 1996, p 19; McGlynn, 1998, p 97.
8   Abel, 1988; Hagan and Kay, 1995.

On all rungs of the professional ladder in England and Wales, from education and training through to practice, women continue to represent an increasingly large proportion of total participants. The proportion of women accepted on undergraduate law programmes increased from 58.6% in 1997 to 60.7% in 1998[9] and in their final degree results women were more likely to achieve a first or upper second than men.[10] Women represented 59.9% of students enrolled with the Law Society[11] in 1998–99,[12] and 56.4% of all traineeships registered with the Law Society in the same period, an increase of 70.7 % over 1988–89.[13]

However, Shiner's longitudinal study of law students and their entry to the profession appears to demonstrate that women are less likely to obtain a training contract than their male counterparts, although gender represented less of a disadvantage in this respect than ethnicity or social class.[14] Women appear, at this stage, to have a greater tendency to be interested in working in a 'High Street' practice than in a City firm, although Shiner notes that awareness of market conditions may have qualified many applicants' choices in that they might 'only have applied to firms that they thought they had a realistic chance of getting a job with, rather than those they particularly wanted to work in'.[15] This issue of the relationship between knowledge and expectations of the market is highly significant. As seen below, Shiner's research suggests that a substantial minority of women feel they have experienced discrimination by the time they enter employment as a qualified solicitor.[16] On the other hand, the Law Society's Omnibus Survey suggested that women were more likely to feel that their expectations in terms of status had been exceeded (21% of women as opposed to 17% of men),[17] and although they were more likely than men to feel that their expectations in terms of salary had not been met (41% of women as opposed to 37% of men),[18] this was not to the extent that one might have expected in view of the experiences of discrimination reported in Shiner, and supported by our own previous research.[19] This finding may be in part due to the younger age profile of Shiner's sample, but an alternative hypothesis is that women are

---

9   The Law Society, 2000, p 55.

10 *Ibid*, pp 56–57.

11 Students on the Legal Practice Course (LPC) and in training contracts are required to enrol annually with the Law Society.

12 *Ibid*, the Law Society, fn 9, p 59.

13 *Ibid*, p 63.

14 Shiner, 1999, pp 11–13.

15 *Ibid*, p 21.

16 *Ibid*, p 67.

17 Cole, 1997, p 8.

18 *Ibid*.

19 Sommerlad and Sanderson, 1998.

indeed aware of the extent of discrimination they may face, and adjust their expectations accordingly.

In terms of the population of solicitors on the roll as a whole, women represent 36.6% of the total.[20] The contrast with the much higher proportion of current new entrants is explained largely by the fact that women's entry did not begin its steep rise until the 1980s.[21] However, the overall proportion of qualified solicitors masks a number of other gendered differences. Women's participation rate (the number of women holding practising certificates (PCs) as a proportion of all those on the roll) is lower than men in all age bands, particularly those bands covering the ages over 30.[22] This is partially explained by the fact that women are less likely to work in private practice. Private practice is the core of the profession (employing 80.5% of PC holders), and women represent 33% of PC holders in private practice as opposed to 35% of PC holders as a whole.[23] Women with PCs are far more likely to work in a number of occupations outside private practice (and since these occupations do not require PCs, their participation rate in these sectors is likely to be even higher). For example, they represent around 60% of qualified solicitors working in advice services, education and nationalised industries, and around 50% in accountancy practice, government funded services and local government.[24] 40.7% of PC holders working in industry and commerce are women.

The distribution of women between the vertically arranged segments of the profession is markedly asymmetrical. While 53% of men working in private practice in 1999 held partnership status and 27.7% were assistant solicitors, for women, the proportions are reversed – only 24% were partners and 61% were assistant solicitors.[25] Human capital theorists (see section 2) might point to women's recent entry into the profession as the major reason for this disparity, although, even when the population of practising solicitors is divided into 'experience' bands (calculated by years since admission), men are still far more likely to achieve partnership in each band).[26] Whilst it is true that lengthy career breaks for reasons of childbearing and childrearing might also reduce the prospects of partnership, particularly in the 0–9 year experience band, our previous research has indicated that most women in practice take relatively short breaks.[27] Shiner's analysis of the transition from training contracts to full employment as a qualified solicitor indicates that

20 The Law Society, 2000, p 9.
21 Abel, 1988; Skordaki, 1996; Sommerlad and Sanderson, 1998, pp 104–05.
22 *Ibid*, the Law Society, p 13.
23 *Ibid*.
24 *Ibid*.
25 *Ibid*, p 17.
26 *Ibid*, pp 18–19.
27 Sommerlad and Allaker, 1991; *ibid*, Sommerlad and Sanderson.

motherhood is, in and of itself, a substantial barrier to obtaining employment.[28] He is unable to identify an exact cause: it could possibly be due to the absence of part time working opportunities, though our previous research indicates that this is not the sole factor, and the evidence from the cohort study concerning discrimination and harassment[29] on the basis of gender supports the broader cultural analysis offered by American and Australian feminist critics of the profession.[30]

We have already noted that women are more likely to work in 'High Street' firms, and are more likely, when employed in City firms, to work as assistant solicitors. It is also worth noting that the units of analysis currently used by the Law Society may mask more subtle forms of segmentation taking place at 'ground level'. In our previous work, we noted the advent of the 'salaried partner' status as a means of absorbing ambitious women without integrating them into the ownership structure of firms:[31] currently, a new mode of lawyering is that of the 'support lawyer', an explicit formulation of the 'backroom' to which many women have complained of being assigned after their return from maternity leave. Whilst this is being trumpeted as an example of firms' flexible (and 'radical') response to the needs of women's domestic role,[32] the consequences for women's career trajectory are obvious in a climate where access to the client interface is becoming an increasingly significant aspect of promotion and earnings prospects.

Women are more likely to specialise in particular areas of legal practice than men. On average, they undertake 2.6 types of work as opposed to the 3.6 types undertaken by men and they are correspondingly more likely to describe themselves as specialists.[33] This is, at least in part, explained by women's younger age profile in the profession, taking into account the impact of structural change on the traditional High Street general practice. Older solicitors were both more likely to regard themselves as generalists and to undertake a wide range of work.[34] Women were more likely to spend a greater proportion of their fee-earning time on personal injury work and family law than men, whilst they were likely to spend less of their fee-earning time on crime, residential conveyancing and business and commercial affairs.

We have summarised the research relating to women's earnings elsewhere,[35] but in considering earnings we immediately meet a conceptual difficulty which is central to this chapter. Earnings' differentials which, at first

---

28 Shiner, 1999, p 57.
29 *Ibid*, pp 66–67.
30 Thornton 1996; Harrington, 1992; Hunter, 1999.
31 Sommerlad and Sanderson, 1998, p 112.
32 Gillies, 1999, p 12.
33 Cole, 1997, pp 17–23.
34 *Ibid*, pp 17–23..
35 *Ibid*, Sommerlad and Sanderson, pp 108–09.

sight, might appear to be associated with biological sex difference may, in fact, be affected by a number of intervening variables. These might include the size or partnership structure of the employing firm, the specific specialism worked in, whether the worker conforms to the professional norm of 'full time plus', the number of billable hours credited, the extent of direct contact with the client base of a firm, or the region in which the firm is located (for example, gross fees per firm, per principal and per fee earner are substantially higher in London than in the North and Wales).[36] A significant difference between women and men on any of these variables might translate directly into an earnings' differential. However, the real question is the extent to which these intervening variables themselves actually constitute the nature of gender, as opposed to sex, difference, and the extent to which the differences can be seen as the product of women's agency. The issues are neatly encapsulated by Hull and Nelson:

> When women lawyers 'choose' to leave the rigours of large-firm practice for legal jobs that allow a better balance of work and family obligations, they are making an adaptive choice that allows them to continue their legal careers. It is a choice constrained by broader structural realities But it is still a choice, and one that might be quite gratifying for many women (and more than a few men).[37]

The notion of 'choice' is, of course, a vexed one, and forms the arena for the conflict between the perspectives of human capital theorists and gender stratification theorists which we discuss in more detail below. However, the existence or extent of this choice is not merely a matter of debate for sociologists, any more than is the degree of structural disadvantage in the workplace. Like sociologists, the judiciary make decisions as to which intervening variable to count or discount, and which group qualifies as the comparator to whom reference can be made in assessing the existence or extent of discrimination. As Fredman notes in relation to the defence of justification, the complexity of both the conceptual and the empirical basis of discrimination law is such that it is possible for progress in this area to be 'rowed back' by apparently slight shifts in stance by the judiciary.[38]

However, *pace* Hull and Nelson, women's situation as delineated above must be set in the broad context of the structural (and cultural) transformation of the profession which has taken place in all Anglo-American and, apparently, most other jurisdictions over the course of the last two decades, and which is ongoing.[39] As other contributions to this book note, the pressures of the commercial market, together with the direct intervention of

---

36 The Law Society, 2000, p 48.
37 Hull and Nelson, 1998, p 702.
38 Fredman, 1997, pp 295–300.
39 See, eg, Glasser, 1990; Hanlon, 1998; Galanter and Palay, 1991; Dezalay and Sugarman, 1995.

the State in both the structures and cultures of firms delivering legally aided services, have resulted in, on the one hand, a horizontal integration of firms, characterised by stratified employment structures,[40] and, on the other hand, a fragmentation of the profession both between different types of firms, and between different specialisms within firms. For instance, during the five years 1995–2000, the 'mega-lawyering' firms (26 partners or more) increased by 11.8%,[41] a growth rendered all the more significant by the partner/assistant solicitor ratios in these firms. Over the same period there was a decrease in the number of small firms (two to 10 partners) of between 3.0% and 7.6%, but a small increase in the number of medium sized firms (1.9% in firms of 11–25 partners).[42] It is important to recognise that the changes consequent on this restructuring are not significant simply in terms of the size of organisations. There are concomitant changes in the value rationality of actors in the various sectors; an increasing prevalence of a long hours culture in response to market pressures, and a loss of autonomy, as the comparatively sheltered environments of the small firms disappear.

Clearly, women's particular position has been, and is being, affected by these changes.[43] For instance, at one stage in their personal biography, and during a particular phase in the evolution of the labour market, women may have decided that a viable strategy was to become sole practitioners (and there is evidence that this was a common strategy not only here but also in the USA,[44] and/or to specialise in publicly funded law work. However, these options may be less attractive now, or even less viable, as the changes in legal aid, and the need for more highly capitalised practices, begin to take effect. So, for example, during 1999, the number of sole practices in England and Wales declined by 1.5%, having grown in the previous five years by 6%.[45] Similarly, the Crown Prosecution Service (CPS) was once seen by women as a more friendly market[46] but, as the pressures generated by the neo-liberal reforms of the public sector[47] result in emulation of the rigours of private practice, including the long hours culture, it has become decidedly less friendly. At the same time, it must be noted that there do not appear to be other 'women friendly' niches developing to take the place of the previous shelters.

Having said this, there is evidence of more women moving into previously virtually all-male preserves, and, further, of some commercial practices adopting policies which appear designed to retain women and enhance their

---

40 Sommerlad, 1999.
41 The Law Society, 2000, p 3.
42 *Ibid*, p 3.
43 See Hagan and Kay, 1995.
44 Seron, 1996.
45 *Ibid*, the Law Society, p 3.
46 Sommerlad and Sanderson, 1998, p 112.
47 Termed by Hood, 1991, the new public management (NPM).

career prospects.[48] In such firms, especially those in the commercial sector, alternative working patterns are becoming more institutionalised, rather than available on an individual, *ad hoc* basis only, and these changes may be viewed as the beginning of a contestation of the dominant conceptualisation of what it means to be professional. Another sign of this is the regularity with which features on the 'quality of life' and on working conditions and firm culture now appear in the legal press,[49] endorsing the acceptability of flexible or part time hours. We will discuss the significance of these features in section 3. Commentators have noted that there is not only a commercial imperative on firms to provide such arrangements, but also 'a growing risk of claims against law firms who persist with an unrelenting culture of long hours'.[50] On the other hand, it appears that these alternative ways of working remain almost exclusively female and damaging to career prospects. Further, we have argued elsewhere, in some firms/legal specialisms, an accentuation of hegemonic masculinism is occurring,[51] whilst the legal press also regularly reports on the growing pressure to work ever longer hours.[52] The increasing length of working hours is an issue also referred to by Lee, Chapter 8, in this book.

Evidently, the decisions women solicitors make about their careers must be set in the context of these complex and shifting configurations of the legal labour market. Let us consider the various models which seek to explain their choices and their position generally in this labour market.

(2) Difference, disadvantage, discrimination – theorising women's position in the legal labour market

As we remarked at the beginning of the preceding section, explanations of the patterns of difference described above have frequently framed the problem within a discourse of 'discrimination'. In particular, studies of solicitors' earnings have, as we also noted, given rise to claims that women's apparent lower earnings are the consequence of discrimination.[53] Similarly, press reports on the position of women lawyers (and other professionals) generally stress the role of individual acts of discrimination as a primary cause of their subordination. A recent article in *The Guardian* on the continuing dearth of women professionals in top positions commented: '... the answer is that men are the gatekeepers.'[54] In response, others have contested the use of the term

---

48 See the legal press, eg, Chambers, 1997, pp 21–24; Tyler, 1998, p 39; Gillies, 1999, p 12.
49 See, eg, Terndrup (2000) *Legal Week*, 15 June, p 22; Gubbay, 1999, p 18; Mullally, 1999, p 7; MacErlean, 1998, p 11.
50 Fox and Stein, 1999, p 13.
51 Sommerlad and Sanderson, 1998.
52 Cheyne, 2000, p 52; Bedlow, 2000, pp 10–11.
53 Gibb, 1996; Bahl, 1996; McGlynn, 1998, p 97.
54 Roberts, 1999, p 7.

'discrimination' to explain women's position. So, for instance, Bundock and Cooper,[55] following the human capital perspective, argue that comparisons of earnings by gender need to take account of other factors which differentiate women and men (such as the type of firm in which they are employed), and criticise studies which argue that average differences in male and female salaries are evidence of 'discrimination'. Feminist analysts of the labour market would counter that this variant of human capital theory precisely fails to appreciate that gender[56] is constituted by the range of factors which serve to differentiate women and men structurally, leading to the ghettoisation of women into the least prestigious firms and/or specialisms.[57]

By contrast, human capital and rational choice theorists[58] argue that difference, whether innate or socialised, leads women to make positive (and unconstrained) choices to deviate from professional norms, with the consequence that their career trajectories are distinct from those of men. Similarly, Hakim discusses women's subordination in terms of women's lesser commitment to full time working.[59] From this perspective, women's reduced chances of promotion to partnership and lower participation rate are entirely explicable in terms of the trade-off which women make between family life and professional life. A more subtle version of rational choice theory accepts some inequality in earnings between genders, but then posits this fact as the rational grounds for women accepting the reduced status at work as a means of maximising family benefit. The 'successful woman' who achieves partnership by either eschewing a domestic caring role or buying in a proxy therefore becomes a symbol of the essentially voluntaristic basis of women's position: '... the woman litigator who adopts the "male" model in order to get ahead should not automatically be regarded as the unwitting dupe of structural forces.'[60]

The 'relational' feminist perspective, which postulates a distinctive female morality, rooted in caring and connectedness,[61] may be seen, to some extent, as a feminist counterpart to this interpretation: it similarly views women as

---

55 Bundock and Cooper, 1998, p 601.

56 It is important to note, however, that the use of the term 'gender' is problematic. Its use, in early 'second wave feminist' work, to convey the social construction of sex, today evokes the same difficulties as does the term 'woman'. Thus, Naffine and Owens, 1997, and the essays in this edited volume have argued that the dichotomy between sex and gender is false, in that it suggests that sex is a natural category (and see Butler, 1990). Nevertheless, just as we have argued (op cit, fn 1) that it is the very fact of women's continuing subordination which retains the usefulness of 'woman' as a category of analysis, so, too, 'gender' continues to be important as, to paraphrase Squires, 1999, a category which can explore what counts as 'woman' and as 'man'.

57 See, eg, Reskin and Roos, 1990; Kay, 1997.

58 Caplow, 1954; Posner, 1987; 1989; Becker, 1991.

59 Hakim, 1995; 1996.

60 Hull and Nelson, 1998, p 702.

61 Gilligan, 1982.

agents who both wish to 'lawyer differently' from men[62] and who may make active choices to embrace their nurturing role. The extent to which women are involved to a greater degree in specialisms like family law within private practice could, in this light, be seen as a positive consequence of women's distinctive and, some might argue, superior morality. This complex and problematic perspective, which one of the authors of this chapter considers elsewhere,[63] thus criticises assimilationist strategies and has generated the equality/difference debate, which we refer to in the following section. Like rational choice theory, it challenges both individual and structural models of women's subordination in the labour market, and provides for judicial consideration a range of interpretations of individuals' cases which negate the conceptions of direct and indirect discrimination.

By contrast, other explanations focus rather on the structure of the legal profession; for instance, Hagan and Kay's research with Canadian law firms leads them to conclude that women are being positioned in a particular way to meet the specific needs of a rationalising labour market.[64] This analysis would explain the high proportion of women in assistant solicitor positions as a function of the need for firms to increase their level of capitalisation through a permanent shift in the partner/assistant ratio. Hull and Nelson neatly summarise this construction: 'more women in law provides the basis for more stratification within the law. Greater openness in entry positions in law practice produces greater inequality among the full set of positions within practice'.[65]

Our own approach has been to work to a model of structured agency which construes cultural phenomena as a key engine in the process of both differentiation and the hierarchical ordering of difference. We begin with the way in which the current conceptualisation of legal professionalism, of the labour market, and of the legal and political order are shaped by, reflect, and in turn reproduce, the division of society into public and private sectors generating the symbolic orders of domesticity[66] and of paid work. Such a starting point underscores the fact that not only women's (and men's) experiences, both domestic and in the labour market, but also their very

---

62 Menkel-Meadow, 1985 and 1995; Bender, 1990; and see Pierce, 1996.
63 Sommerlad, forthcoming.
64 Hagan and Kay, 1995, and see Podmore and Spencer, 1986.
65 Hull and Nelson, 1998, pp 686–87.
66 Williams, 2000.

identities, are patterned by what Pateman has termed the sexual contract.[67] This approach leads us to place gender difference in the legal profession in the context of, first, the very complex relationship between lawyers and their social[68] and cultural capital[69] and, secondly, the labour markets in which they move which, as we have noted above, are subject to rapid change at the current juncture. Along with other authors, we have, therefore, challenged the notion that women's 'choices' can be construed within an entirely voluntaristic framework. Women as a category are conceptualised and treated as different – as deviant professionals. They are, therefore, differentially placed in the labour market even before they make decisions to opt out of a professionalism which is culturally male.

Women's subordination does not, therefore, have to be attributed to either voluntary choice or purposefully authored acts of discrimination, but can be the product of 'subtle and institutionalised constraints'.[70] The legal market is not a static impersonal 'thing', but must be understood as comprising sets of personalist relationships,[71] and, as such, is partly shaped by players' expectations and understandings of the meaning of gender. Thus, the 'subtle and institutionalised constraints' which affect women solicitors can be the product of a professional culture framed in an era of patriarchal domination, where men have created an 'imagined community' to sustain an insider world characterised by exclusionary norms and practices.[72]

---

67 In her discussion of the sexual contract, Carole Pateman writes: 'Patriarchal civil society is divided into two spheres ... The story of the social contract is treated as an account of the creation of the public sphere of civil freedom. The other, private, sphere is not seen as politically relevant ... Patriarchy then appears to have no relevance to the public world. On the contrary, patriarchal right extends throughout civil society. The two spheres of civil society are at once separate and inseparable.' (1988, pp 3–4.) Thus, patriarchal relations in paid work sustain women's general social subordination (Walby, 1986 and 1990); similarly, for Hartmann, 1979, there exists a dynamic interrelationship between women's oppression in the domestic and labour market spheres.

In a sense, this analysis is not entirely incongruent with human capital theory; thus neo-liberal accounts of sex discrimination emphasise the interrelationship between the workings of the free market and existing working (and domestic) arrangements (Becker, 1991). However, whereas we, self-evidently, view these arrangements as neither natural nor benign, but rather part of a complex causality of women's subordination, the human capitalist either condones or even supports patriarchal social arrangements. For instance, for Posner, the resulting asymmetrical relationships between men and women are seen as a price worth paying (1989, p 1316).

68 Seron and Ferris, 1995.

69 Bourdieu, 1987; 1991.

70 Hull and Nelson, 1999, p 7.

71 Granovetter, 1985; Sommerlad and Sanderson, 1998, pp 119–51; and see Hagan and Kay, 1995; Dezalay and Garth, 1997; Hanlon, 1998.

72 Hunter, 1999, pp 7–8, citing Benedict Anderson, has conceptualised the legal profession in terms of an 'imagined community'; Tancred, 1999; ibid, Sommerlad and Sanderson, pp 119–150; Hunter and McKelvie, 1998.

These various dimensions to women's position have a reciprocal, circular relationship one with the others; we may, therefore, term this explanation for women's professional subordination as an 'interactive' approach, in that it is attempting to account for the complex interconnections between them, and hence between structure and agency.[73] If we take this approach, we can see that both the structural and dispositional explanations of women lawyers' disadvantage contain elements of truth; that is to say, in the words of Witz: '... gender is ... both socially constructed and a structuring principle.'[74] This is not, of course, to deny that direct discrimination occurs; on the contrary, it clearly plays an important part both in maintaining hegemonic masculinism[75] and 'assisting' women to make their choices. Nevertheless, this approach, which seeks to unpick the complex interweavings of structure and agency, of macro and micro causation, is more powerfully explanatory than one which attributes women's position to direct discrimination, which can always be countered by pointing to variables other than sex.[76]

However, this explanatory model does not imply any straightforward solution. We, like all theorists, are still confronted by the equality/difference dilemma; furthermore, our attempt to indicate the cultural complexity underlying that 'difference' makes clear that the extent to which the law may be used to ameliorate the disadvantage flowing from this difference is limited. This is not to dismiss its utility completely; on the contrary, the law is both a benchmark of cultural change, as well as contributing to such change.[77] Until recently, however, despite reports of both sexual harassment and discrimination, women solicitors did not turn to legal remedies. Elsewhere, we have argued that this was, itself, indicative of the complexity of women's position.[78] Situated in a profession nominally guided by formal rules (which are predicated on principles of equity and economic rationality), but which is really shaped by an informal culture characterised by personalist bonds and a cavalier disregard for employment law, the likely consequence for women, were they to use the formal law against the unwritten codes of these 'imagined communities', would be instant professional ostracism. Ironically, therefore, it would appear that women lawyers have been especially reluctant

---

73 See Hull and Nelson, 1998.

74 Witz, 1992, p 3.

75 Eg, there is a body of research now which indicates that sexual harassment tends to increase as women enter (in substantial numbers) professions, or sections of professions, which were either all male or dominated by men (Cockburn, 1983, 1985 and 1991; Gutek, 1985; Hearn and Parkin, 1995; Collinson, 1996); it is clear that these directly discriminatory acts function to maintain hegemonic masculinism (see Hunter and McKelvie, 1998, pp 45–46; Schultz, 1998; Hunter, 1999.

76 Bundock and Cooper, 1998.

77 Schultz, 1990.

78 Sommerlad and Sanderson, 1998, pp 130–32.

to use the mechanisms of their trade to help themselves. Nevertheless, it seems that one dimension of women's contesting of the dominant professional paradigm is that a handful of women – notably those who have broken into the elite firms – are beginning to turn to legal remedies.[79]

(3) Women's resistance and discrimination: conceptual and strategic difficulties

In this section, we consider some of the problems of using discrimination law to overcome the disadvantage suffered by women solicitors. We begin by discussing inherent difficulties in the conceptual basis of the law and, in particular, the tension between equality and difference, and between actions for direct and indirect discrimination. This leads us into a consideration of the interplay between the nature and role of the judiciary, and the 'vagueness'[80] which results from this tension. We then consider what kind of problem the law is trying to unravel in discrimination cases involving solicitors: in particular, we are concerned with the law's capacity to address cultural obstacles to women's careers. To develop this theme, we explore some instances of public claims of specific discrimination within the profession in England and Wales, and trace the way in which the legal press is developing a discourse of discrimination which attempts simultaneously to identify 'progress' and to underpin the case against the kind of change in culture and working practices in the law which would render a real transformation of women's choices possible.

It is extremely damaging to women that the law has been used as a vehicle for individual judges to expound misogyny, and to construct, naturalise and legitimise 'women's' qualities and role.[81] Consequently, feminist theory has presented a wide-ranging critique of the law. For instance, it functions as a 'gendering discourse'.[82] It is complicit in the construction and reproduction of the public/private spheres and the sexual contract, since the law is where private patriarchy lives.[83] Feminist jurisprudence has also focused on the gendered underpinnings of law and legal reasoning, arguing that facial neutrality and equality is a mask for the male viewpoint;[84] on the formalism of legal method[85] and on the individualisation of social problems and their

---

79 Keane, 1999, p 10.
80 Endicott, 1997.
81 Sachs and Wilson, 1978; O'Donovan, 1985; Olsen, 1990; Fineman and Thomadsen, 1991; Thornton, 1995.
82 Smart, 1992.
83 To paraphrase Wendy Brown, 1995.
84 MacKinnon, 1983.
85 Bartlett, 1990.

redress. On the other hand, others have argued that the law must also be seen as a complex, multiple field characterised by flexibility and indeterminacy, in which it has, as a result, been possible for women to utilise rights-based remedies.[86]

All these perspectives are relevant to sex discrimination law. On the one hand, not only the law generally, but equality law in particular, functions both as one of the pillars of 'domesticity'[87] and, reciprocally, of normative professionalism. In this, it is part of the cultural system which positions women differently, and which we have discussed in section 2: thus, it is the law itself which, in Bourdieu's words, is the 'quintessential form of the symbolic power of naming things, that creates the things named, and creates social groups.'[88] On the other hand, for this very reason, legal challenges which require both the law and the legal profession to operate according to one of its fundamental principles, equity, are useful as propaganda and may create an alternative professional discourse.

Given the multifaceted nature of the law, the issue of whether 'legal liberalism' can provide the basis for remedies for gender inequality has recently been the subject of considerable debate.[89] At the heart of this debate is the equality/difference dilemma referred to earlier which divides 'second wave' feminism.[90] As we noted in section 2, the principle of difference was originally introduced through the fact of labour markets segregated either vertically or horizontally. In the development of discrimination law, this led to two divergent, but related aims, which correspond to the two conflicting approaches within feminism: the need for women to obtain access to markets which are currently unavailable to them, and the need to obtain equal reward between markets which are comparable, but resist desegregation. In her analysis of the conceptual foundations of discrimination law, Fredman points to the contrasting strengths of direct and indirect discrimination.[91] On the one hand, the rights-based claim for equality of treatment characteristic of 'first wave' feminism avoids the stigmatisation of women as 'different' and domestic; furthermore, direct discrimination allows for no defence of justification, and permits the use of a hypothetical male comparator where no actual comparator exists. However, actions focus directly on the individual woman; moreover, this approach cannot address the material reality of women's lives, and does not comprehend the more subtle institutional constraints which underpin structural disadvantage. Others have, therefore,

---

86 Kingdom, 1991.

87 Williams, 2000.

88 Bourdieu, 1987, p 838.

89 Fredman, 1997; Shaw, 1998; Mossman, 1998; Boyd, 1996; Ward, 1997; and Lacey, 1998.

90 See Naffine, 1990, Olsen, 1990, and Smart, 1992, for discussions of the various phases of the women's movement.

91 *Ibid*, Fredman, pp 287–91.

recognised that strategically, in order to achieve equality of opportunity, normative views regarding employees, which are based on the characteristics and needs of men, need to be challenged.[92] Furthermore (as we noted in section 2), some feminists positively embrace the idea of difference.[93]

Evidently, actions for indirect discrimination do raise such a challenge to the current construction of the world of work, and, therefore, potentially, to the gender division within the private sphere. If we consider Walby's argument that, first, patriarchal power depends on an articulation between male dominance in the domestic sphere and the dominant mode of production,[94] and that, secondly, the causal link between women's subordination goes from the labour market to the family,[95] then the fact that indirect discrimination addresses the power imbalance in the labour market by recognising the impact of the domestic sphere is, potentially at least, disruptive of hegemonic masculinism in both spheres. However, there remains the evident difficulty that the fact that indirect discrimination obtrudes the domestic sphere into the public sphere by introducing the idea of 'difference', effectively reaffirms existing gendered social arrangements;[96] similarly, for Beveridge *et al*, the primary weakness of legal redress is that it fails to tackle the problem of private patriarchy.[97]

Furthermore, Fredman identifies three major presumptions underpinning many judgments in indirect discrimination cases which militate against women achieving legal redress. First, there is the presumption of women's autonomy, or unconstrained capacity to choose, and, as Bartlett has commented, courts 'have proven remarkably reluctant to acknowledge the ways in which employer policies or attitudes shape women's choices'.[98] But, as we have noted above, the career trajectories of women are shaped by cultural phenomena which may have the effect of simply transforming their views of their future, and leading them to 'choose' to withdraw from the profession or accept a 'second class' status. Secondly, there is the requirement that women address the courts as individuals, rather than as members of a category; and finally, the fact that the justification of 'market forces' is especially powerful for a profession which has become characterised by its availability to clients.[99] These presumptions, of course, mirror those of human capital theorists, and their predominance goes some way to negate the

---

92 This essentially pragmatic strategy has been dominant in the UK. See Walby, 1994, p 390.

93 Gilligan, 1982; Bender, 1990; West, 1988.

94 Walby argues that 'the primary mechanism which ensures that women will serve their husbands is their exclusion from paid work on the same terms as men' (1986, p 54).

95 *Ibid*.

96 McGlynn, 2000.

97 Beveridge *et al*, 2000, p 387.

98 Bartlett, 2000, p 756; and see Schultz, 1998.

99 Fredman, 1997, pp 287–300.

capacity of actions in direct discrimination to remedy the problems of structural disadvantage.

In fact, arguably, in both causes of action, proof of discrimination is dependent on the yardstick of the male comparator and, therefore, effectively the labour market is taken as given. For direct discrimination, just as much as indirect discrimination, ultimately perpetuates the ideology of motherhood and leaves intact the notion of an ideal, unencumbered worker. Furthermore, the act of selection for comparison is, as Fredman argues, value-laden and ultimately political.[100] Just as it is accepted that, in sociology, indices of segregation depend on the unit of analysis, so decisions concerning discrimination depend on the selection of an appropriate 'pool' for comparison. Achieving appropriate comparison in cases of disparate impact depends on the granularity of the statistical evidence which is available and on keeping pace with the complex relationship between changing patterns of labour markets in terms of numbers employed, the character of the workplace, the extent of reward and the structure of opportunities. In the case of the solicitors' profession, where we have already noted the rapid change in the partner/fee-earner and solicitor/paralegal ratios, the task is extremely difficult. Unless, therefore, the law can accommodate sophisticated sociological reasoning, empirical data gathering and causal modelling, it will be difficult for it to address structural disadvantage.

Further, whilst individual discrimination may sometimes be manifest, as when an employer sets terms which it is clear that most women, as a class, will find difficulty meeting, on other occasions what women are encountering is a more insidious, complex cultural barrier. As a result, what is being addressed are manifestations of a culture which may be located on a continuum. At one end, it may be clear that the behaviour is exclusionary, and hence discriminatory. At the other end of the continuum, however, the barriers are more opaque, and difficult to establish. The cultural presumptions which exclude women are seen as a part of the 'natural' order of things. As we have argued elsewhere, the pervasive character of these cultural presumptions often leads them to be internalised as an element in the 'doxa' of women themselves.[101] As a result, equality and difference are neither straightforward and neutral, nor the absolutes which the law presents them as, but rather complex, indeterminate concepts, which are unresolved, not merely by the law, but by women themselves.[102] Women differ in the extent to which, and the mode in which, they wish to be equal, and who it is that they wish to be equal to. Equality, therefore, joins a range of other concepts which Endicott characterises as the product of linguistic indeterminacy, or

---

100 Fredman, 1997, p 184.

101 Bourdieu, 1987. As Lacey notes, the presumption underpinning legal redress that what is being complained of is abnormal generates resistance, especially since the foci of such complaints will often be the norm (1998, pp 23 and 38).

102 Mossman, 1998, p 33.

'vagueness'.[103] Endicott notes how the law operates on the basis of bivalent judgments, and this leads some legal theorists to believe that the requirements of the law itself must be unambiguous and bivalent.[104] We have argued elsewhere that this indeterminacy is precisely what enables the legal system both to adapt to changing mores, and to accommodate ideological diversity within the judiciary whilst maintaining the fiction of the law's univocal character.[105] The ambivalence identified above concerning women's work orientation was consistently used by the judiciary in the USA in the form of the 'lack of interest' argument, in order to reject discrimination claims related to segregated workforces.[106]

The consequence is that reform of judicial principles is, as Mossman notes, uneven.[107] To take another example, that of sexual harassment as a form of discriminatory behaviour: it was recognised as such not through statute, but in *Strathclyde Regional Council v Porcelli* ((1986) IRLR 135, Court of Session), and the development of the concept has, as Fredman suggests, been subject to the judiciary's limited view of gendered power relations.[108] The definition of harassment as laid down by the Council of Ministers encompasses the subjective experiences of the victims in the view that it is unwanted and offensive to the recipient, but retains elements of an objective test in the view that it should be unreasonable. Fredman notes how the finding in *Stewart v Cleveland Guest Engineering* ((1994) IRLR 440, EAT), that failure to act to remove a display of pornographic pictures was not discriminatory since a man might have found them equally offensive, is an example of the court's failure to recognise gendered power relations in the workplace.[109] Yet, on the other hand, in *Reed v Stedman* ((1999) IRLR 299, EAT) the Employment Appeals Tribunal judged that the question of whether or not behaviour was unacceptable was a subjective one, and stated that tribunals should not use an objective test in deciding whether an employee had suffered detriment. However, it is conceivable that, if the grounds of appeal had been that the defendant had also sexually harassed men, then following *Balgobin v Tower* ((1987) IRLR 401, EAT) where the equality principle was invoked, it might have been argued that the harassment did not amount to sexual discrimination.

Whilst there is, therefore, ample scope for the judiciary to develop equality law in a way which challenges normative professionalism, a mixture of factors may well cause it to send it into reverse. It is customary, even in the most

---

103 Endicott, 1997.
104 *Ibid*, p 61.
105 Sommerlad and Sanderson, 1998, pp 54–67.
106 Schultz, 1990.
107 Mossman, 1998, p 32.
108 Fredman, 1997, p 322.
109 *Ibid*, p 324.

radical texts, to detach judgments from the personal orientations and opinions of judges. Yet, the normative views discussed above are built both into the fabric of the law, and into the perceptual apparatus of the judiciary. Furthermore, the judiciary is itself the product of exactly those cultural processes which it is being asked to count or discount as evidence of discrimination.[110] This is, therefore, not to argue that judgments which progressive feminist theorists might regard as retrograde are the product of deliberate prejudice (although clearly this may, at times, be the case). Krieger has pointed to the fact that human judgments which produce discriminatory outcomes are the outcome of applying what social judgment theorists describe as judgmental heuristic, rule of thumb approaches, which often depend on the unrepresentative character of an individual's experience.[111] This can become particularly significant when, in evaluating disparate impact, judges make decisions about which pool is appropriate for a comparator. Judges are likely to 'see' situations in the light of the most widely available perceptions of what are 'normal social arrangements' with which the law should not interfere.[112]

Radical transformation of these perceptions can prove extremely difficult. Two examples of this are offered by two cases, both of which were lost by the applicants. In *Symes v Canada*, Elizabeth Symes sought to extend the right to charge child care expenses as 'business expenses',[113] and in *Cast v Croydon College* ((1998) ICR 77, EAT), it was claimed that the refusal to offer part time work following a return from maternity leave amounted to unlawful direct or indirect discrimination. The embeddedness of the normative view of the public/private divide is demonstrated also by the fact that, for obvious reasons, other claims of discrimination precisely rest on the fact that this divide is the organising principle of social life, illustrating the difficulties with this approach.. For instance, in *Meade-Hill and National Union of Civil and Public Servants v British Council* ([1996] 1 All ER 79, CA), it was the acceptance, as common ground, that women were secondary earners that enabled the claim, that the inclusion of a mobility clause in an employment contract constituted indirect discrimination, to succeed. The illustration offered by these cases of the equality/difference dilemma illustrates McGlynn's argument that the European Court of Justice's jurisprudence in relation to equality law is, in fact, predicated on protecting women's motherhood role within the family rather than changing the pattern of working practices in male-dominated institutions.[114] Her point is borne out by employment lawyers Fox and Stein who, writing in the trade press, outline how, because of women's 'greater

---

110 Malleson and Banda, 2000; Hunter and McKelvie, 1999.
111 Krieger, 1995; and see Graycar, 1995.
112 See Mossman, 1998, p 35. As Lacey writes, 'the tribunal's response to the evidence may be affected by the very stereotypes which many of us hoped that the legislation would serve to attack' (1998, p 22).
113 *Ibid*, pp 33–40.
114 McGlynn, 2000.

responsibility for child care', the proportion who can comply with the requirement to work full time is considerably smaller than the proportion of men, so that firms may be obliged to show that this requirement is objectively justified by having regard to firms' business needs, administrative requirements, internal structure, cost of operating part time working arrangements and commercial demands of its clients.[115] For, in addition to the difficulties relating to the question of difference, there is the added problem that judges are likely to be sympathetic to firms' claims of 'business necessity'.[116] Given the pervasive culture of most law firms, and especially when the changes in the profession discussed in section 1 are increasing the pressures on firms, it is unlikely that employers will encounter great difficulties in establishing an economic reason for requiring long hours of work from their employees. As we explore the trade press coverage below, we will see that it reflects the view that the 'business case' for imposing a universal male culture far outweighs any 'business case' for equity policies.[117]

Most of the cases recently brought by women lawyers have involved charges of direct discrimination, and the coverage of these and non-litigated charges of sexual discrimination and harassment in the legal press illustrates the complex interactions discussed above. On the one hand, we may speculate that the increased female presence (especially in what were previously male segments of the profession) may be provoking the accentuation of 'hegemonic masculinism' – including increased incidence of individual acts of discrimination.[118] At the same time, the growing numbers and confidence of women solicitors indicates a change to a climate that allows these matters on to the agenda and that encourages women to begin to seek legal redress. The formal complaints and actions for sex harassment against Cameron McKenna, at the end of 1999, serve as one example,[119] whilst another large commercial firm (Edward Lewis) was depicted by an ex-employee as having 'a poisonous atmosphere of sniggering, sneering and leering from those of the partners who behaved like lager louts'.[120] There have also been some well publicised claims by women lawyers with elite firms for sex discrimination. For instance, at the beginning of 1999, *Legal Week* reported on an action by a senior solicitor (with children) against Goodman Derrick for failing to make her partner, in which it cited the head of the employment department of a large firm as saying: '... it is premature to say that it heralds the opening of the floodgates, but as the number of women in the profession increases, the number of cases

---

115 Fox and Stein, 1999, p 13.
116 And see Bartlett, 2000, p 757.
117 McGlynn, 2000.
118 Filby, 1992; Stanko, 1988.
119 (1999) *Legal Week*, 15 April, p 11.
120 (1999) *Legal Week*, 23 September, p 11.

of this nature will also increase'.[121] Similarly, a former partner of another large commercial firm, Manches, filed a claim for sexual discrimination, claiming that the firm's managing partner was aggressive and abusive towards her when she got married and that the situation had worsened after she became pregnant, when he had also deprived her of some of her responsibilities.[122]

Most famously, an employment tribunal found for Jane Coker against the Lord Chancellor in an application of indirect discrimination relating to an 'insider appointment' of a special advisor (*Coker v Lord Chancellor* (1999) IRLR 396, ET). The particular interest of this case is the way in which it centred on the kind of informal networking and male bonding which we have elsewhere described as characteristic of the traditions of lawyering.[123] It was found that the Lord Chancellor's requirement, that the appointee to the post be personally known to him, represented indirect discrimination even though the post had not been advertised and no application had been submitted, since s 6(1)(a) of the Sex Discrimination Act 1975 made it unlawful to discriminate 'in the arrangements' made to determine who should be offered employment, and that 'arrangements' was broad enough to encompass the informal method of appointment in question. Of course, what is untypical of the case is the fact that the Lord Chancellor was so open about the grounds on which he had made the appointment, and that the plaintiff had little or no prospect of her career suffering direct detriment as a result of the case. Neither of these circumstances is likely to apply to most women solicitors. Nevertheless, the case has been seen as significant by commentators in the trade press, who have warned firms of the implications for partnership selection of procedures which rely on informal soundings.[124]

In addition to reporting discrimination cases, the trade press is increasingly carrying commentaries on discrimination. For instance, Fox and Stein note that both partners and salaried staff are protected under the Sex Discrimination Act 1975 against direct and indirect discrimination and that, if they are unjustifiably refused part time working arrangements to accommodate child care commitments, they may have grounds to claim for indirect sex discrimination against their firm.[125] However, despite this advice and the apparent increased willingness by some women to use the law, the difficulties confronting women taking this course of action should not be

---

121 (1999) *Legal Week*, 21 January, p 1.

122 The penalising and marginalisation of women who become pregnant (and frequently at the point of marriage) exemplifies attitudes to 'deviant' professionalism and is a subject we have discussed in detail elsewhere (Sommerlad and Sanderson, 1998).

123 *Ibid*; and see Hunter and McElvie, 1998; and Hunter, 1999.

124 Fontes, 2000.

125 Fox and Stein, 1999, p 13.

downplayed. The individualisation of both the problem and the solution are clearly problematic, and many women may not have the resources to take such exposed, isolated action. Further, the fact that, to date, no such case has reached trial means that no test case exists to encourage and guide would be complainants.[126]

Furthermore, it appears that the take-up of part time work opportunities remains low, overwhelmingly restricted to women, and tends to affect promotion chances deleteriously.[127] Evidently, these three factors are interrelated. Just as legal causes of actions and remedies are shaped by the male standard, so, even when a male comparator is not explicitly required by law, so, too, are alternative patterns of employment. The association of flexible working and/or shorter hours with child care and, hence, with women, stigmatises these arrangements as deviant and non-professional, and ensures that take-up will continue to be restricted largely to women,[128] thereby reinforcing their stigmatisation. Consequently, optimistic accounts of successful part time working in the press can be misleading; rhetorical devices to appear equitable. For instance, one trade journal described a job share as a success story, quoting a partner at the employing firm as saying 'we have been impressed with just how effective job share arrangements can be. In the future major firms will need to offer this flexibility if they wish to retain and develop key personnel who have family commitments'.[129] The possibility that this positive approach might be cynical posturing for the press is raised by the accounts given by the women job sharers in confidential interview with the authors, in which they spoke of the hostility of the firm to their working arrangements, at all levels, the devaluation of their work and the fact that the arrangement had effectively curtailed all partnership hopes.[130]

The discursive construction of flexible working as deviant and intrinsically linked to women's (natural) role as child carers, and full time availability to a client as a natural or at least inevitable component of professionalism is revealed in a piece in *The Lawyer* which is otherwise favourable to alternative ways of working:

---

126 The claim against Goodman Derrick was settled ((1999) *Legal Week*, 15 April, p 2), and that against Manches in September 1999 ((1999) *Legal Week*, 9 September, p 1). The fact that such actions have, to date, all been settled out of court mean that even if (some) high profile women solicitors are now prepared to bring claims against their firms, the assistance these are likely to offer women as a class is diminished.

127 And see Epstein *et al*, 1999, pp 133–34.

128 Eg, a recent survey of parental leave commissioned by EJ *Legal* found that only 14% of male solicitors with young children would have taken parental leave had it been an option (Terndrup (2000) *Legal Week*, 15 June, p 22). This finding parallels the situation in countries such as Sweden, where parental leave has been available to both men and women for some time (Fredman, 1997).

129 Tyler, 1998, p 13.

130 Since juxtaposing these two conflicting accounts of dominant attitudes to job sharing could have unpleasant results for the women involved, we have not cited the journal in which a favourable depiction of their experiences was given.

Long hours and the legal profession go together like paracetamol and a hangover – one *naturally* follows the other ... but increasingly firms have to accommodate requests for *non-standard* hours or face the prospect of losing a star performer ... [but] flexibility has to come from the individual as well as the firm. When a transaction takes a week or more to complete, days away from the office may have to be built up and taken in one block. If a client wants advice on a solicitors 'day off' then the day off must be taken later ... almost all requests for non-standard hours come from female lawyers ... Hammond Suddards already has fears of opening a floodgate of staff asking for non-standard hours. 'Where do you draw the line?' asks Wright (the personnel manager). The bottom line is that the client must not suffer ... managing partner at Osborne Clarke speaks for many when he says 'if the client is going to notice then it can't be done' ... and the firm gets a lot of requests for non-standard hours which it turns down ... we're not suckers for it.[131]

These comments resonate with the conclusions of a study of part time arrangements in the US legal profession, which are worth quoting at length:

Reluctance to ask for part time schedules and the resistance of employers to grant it, have to do not only with the practical problems of coordination and economics but go to the heart of what it means to be a true professional. In law, as in other professions, commitment and excellence are often measured by the seemingly unlimited number of hours practitioners work, indicating that their first priority is their vocation. Practitioners who work circumscribed hours are considered to be 'time deviants'.[132]

These comments indicate both the very great difficulties in developing an alternative vision of professionalism and, therefore, the limitations inherent in discrimination law. Not only are different ways of working clearly marked out as abnormal, and threatening to the dominant paradigm and therefore only to be accommodated on sufferance, but the attempt to forge it is being made in a time of accelerating pressure to work long hours and meet increased bills.[133] Thus, at the very same time that the legal press carries reports on solicitors' desire for 'quality of life' and the need to adopt 'family friendly' policies, it also regularly features articles on the growing pressure to work even longer hours, especially in the corporate sector. For instance, an account of a day in the life of one corporate lawyer in 1997 concluded with the following paragraph: 'Ultimately, there is no choice. Apart from the most acute domestic emergency, organisational imperatives dictate the lives of partners and assistants alike ...'[134] The macho flourishing which accompanies the emphasis on long hours is evident in the following account of a corporate deal:

131 Tyler, 1998 (emphasis added).
132 Epstein *et al*, 1999, p 133.
133 Bedlow, 2000, pp 10–11.
134 Drummond, 1997, p 1855.

> There is a quaint notion still peddled at law schools that the best training for a corporate lawyer is a good degree. In fact, the ideal training is a misspent youth attending the wilder, more disorganised student parties which last all night and involve sobering up with a lot of black coffee over breakfast ... it is difficult to remember when it became axiomatic that no worthwhile deal is ever signed up in daylight hours ...[135]

It is, therefore, unsurprising that reports of stress also feature regularly; thus *Legal Week* reported a survey which showed that female solicitors particularly were reluctant to admit to stress for 'fear of jeopardising career prospects ...' and cited Hannah Wiskin, national committee member of the Young Solicitors Group, as saying that she felt that:

> ... women lawyers would be reluctant to approach males, who were likely to hold the senior positions within the firm and reveal any weakness in what is still often a macho culture ... (and) that it would also be useful for women lawyers to have successful role models who managed to lead a more balanced life which was not dominated by work and the need to work 12 hour days.[136]

Another account discussed both the problems of long hours and client demand and intolerable stress levels and attrition rates, especially amongst women. However, whilst noting that increased availability of flexi-time could be one solution, it stated that a 'more radical solution is the creation of support lawyers ...'.[137] The 'radicalism' of the solution is not revealed in the following account by one support lawyer in a multinational commercial firm, in which she compared a support role with being a 'mum':

> You feel you are packing their bags and helping them with their homework that they have left to the last minute, wishing them luck and waving them off ... Every now and again you have to remind them that you are in fact a qualified lawyer of many years and not a secretary or paralegal ... the men who do it are regarded as failures and a little 'wet' ...

In this example, we return to the starting point of this section. Like actions for indirect discrimination, the creation of posts designed to meet the 'special needs' of women serve not only to emphasise their difference, but also their subordination. The 'special' character of the post renders it simultaneously more difficult to find a male comparator, and more likely that the inferior status and reward will be seen as the product of the woman's choice.[138] The complexity and indeterminacy of the key concepts, the underpinning assumptions concerning women's domestic role and its relationship to the public sphere of employment, and the enmeshing of the law in a market which is greedy for the time of its employees, all render it very unlikely that more than a very few women solicitors will ever take their employers to a

---

135 (1999) *Legal Week*, 30 September, p 6.
136 Boxell, 1999, p 6.
137 Gillies, 1999, p 12.
138 Lacey, 1998, p 22.

tribunal. At the same time, however, actions for direct discrimination also serve to reinforce normative professionalism. Legal redress does not, therefore, appear to be an appropriate instrument for the kind of widespread change in corporate culture which would be necessary to advance women's position inside the profession. In the next section, we briefly review some alternative approaches which have been suggested.

(4) Alternative strategies

This section examines two alternative strategies to discrimination law for addressing gendered inequalities, namely, gender mainstreaming and corporate self-regulation. We will look at the strengths and weaknesses of each approach, and explore their relationship to governmental and juridical institutions, before evaluating their potential for supporting equity strategies in the legal profession.

'Gender mainstreaming' has, as a range of commentators have noted, become the fashionable means of addressing issues of gendered inequality, both in the UK and in Europe.[139] Mainstreaming seeks to overcome the problems arising from discrimination law's failure to address the reciprocity between the public and private spheres by 'shifting attention from equality of treatment to equality of impact.[140] Mainstreaming is designed to transform the situation of women by addressing the way in which government policies have a 'gender impact', and/or by transcending traditional, individual rights-based, models of political citizenship to provide women with enhanced access to decision making processes. In their review of mainstreaming in the UK, Beveridge *et al* compare the institutions and processes which have characterised the varied approaches in England, Wales, Scotland and Northern Ireland, and identify two principal approaches, respectively the 'expert-bureaucratic' and the 'participatory-democratic' models.[141] This latter approach may require that the numbers of women in positions in political institutions is increased, or that new political institutions, either governmental or quasi-governmental, are created specifically to examine or promote gender equality policies. Alternatively, it may mean that existing governmental institutions institutionalise channels of communication with extra-governmental organisations representing women. The scope of mainstreaming initiatives is very wide and embraces all significant areas of public policy: for example, education and training, employment, economic development and the environment. In addition, the trend of contemporary initiatives is to mainstream disadvantage and disadvantaged groups in general.

---

139 Liff, 1997; Lewis and Lewis, 1996; Vince, 1996; Beveridge *et al*, 2000; Shaw, 2000.
140 Beveridge *et al*, 2000, p 386. Cf Lacey's (1998) argument for collective remedial rights.
141 *Ibid*, p 390.

In her discussion of mainstreaming in the European Commission, Shaw points to some of the dangers of this approach: softer and more generalist legal frameworks may water down equality concepts, specifically as they relate to women, or, alternatively, may strengthen the concepts, but weaken the structures of enforcement.[142] Even where mainstreaming initiatives such as the national action plans promoted by the Commission are effective in inducing policy changes at a national level, the major impact is likely to be in areas where public policy affects the most disadvantaged, for example, in addressing the relationship between education and training and the high rates of unemployment among young women.[143] Their effect is not likely to be felt inside the walls of law firms in the private sector.

Mainstreaming clearly has the potential, however, to feed back into the framing of cultural assumptions of judicial decisions in discrimination law. Shaw has explored what would happen if fact situations were constructed not in terms of the disciplinary categories of EC law 'where symmetrical concepts of equal treatment and non-discrimination are dominant, but in terms, for example, of the policy approaches of "mainstreaming" or positive action'.[144] She provides an example in the judgment of the European Court of Justice in *Marschall* (Case C-409/95 *Marschall v Land Nordrhein-Westfalen* (1997) ECR I-6363, pp 29–30), where the opportunity was taken to signal the significance of women's experience in the private domain for the conception of equal opportunity, even though the judgment itself did not further the law in this regard.

Parker has examined corporate compliance policies in Australian law in the light of theories of the rise of a 'new regulatory State'.[145] She sees this approach as arising from a realisation, to be found in the work of a range of theorists, that neither the market nor the law is capable of exercising control over organisations from the outside, and that control can only be effectively achieved by offering incentives for the introduction of self-regulatory regimes.[146] These incentives take the form, in some instances, of a limitation on corporate liability for acts such as sexual harassment, dependent on the employer demonstrating that they took all reasonable steps to prevent any agent vicariously committing harassment. This appears to have encouraged the growth of in-house equal opportunities workers who can then exercise leverage for a kind and level of change which external legal regulatory frameworks cannot achieve. Parker's study of equal employment opportunity (EEO) workers suggests that, when they have become embedded within corporate structures, they can apply leverage to a wide range of areas, and

142 Shaw, 2000, p 21.
143 *Ibid*.
144 *Ibid*, p 5.
145 Parker, 1999.
146 *Ibid*, p 23.

through the mobilisation of management support, be the focus for transformative practice.[147] On the other hand, Goode and Bagihole have pointed to the way in which the conceptions of equal opportunities on which transformative struggles are based are ambiguous and the subject of power struggles and gender management strategies which may serve to subvert official policy and rhetoric.[148] One of the principal ambiguities which they found was exploited by opponents of equal opportunities was that of the equality/difference dilemma which we have discussed above.[149] Although Parker expresses the view that her research demonstrates that companies can be 'porous communities' amenable to drives for cultural change, she also notes that 'the general egalitarian principles of the law cannot be translated into the capillaries of everyday life without being transformed by the infra-law of everyday practices and dominations'.[150]

In addition, we need to pay attention to the circumstances under which the self-regulatory approach can be introduced. Paradoxically enough, it could be argued that it must be encapsulated within a framework of hard law, such as that cited by Parker, being s 106 of the Australian Federal Discrimination Act, or enforced by some external agency with regulatory authority or economic leverage, as is the case with the reform of the legal aid sector in England and Wales.[151] Compliance strategies in relation to the provision of legally aided services already encompass many aspects of what would once have been regarded as a firm's own internal organisational agenda, and raise the question of the extent to which they might be used by the State or the solicitors' own regulatory authority, the Law Society, to promote cultural change more actively than has been the case in the past. To date, the regulatory initiatives of the Society have been limited to a practice rule requiring all firms to have equal opportunities policies, and the production of a model policy.[152] However, the Society's relationship with its constituency, and the limited nature of its resources, render it difficult for more proactive policing to be undertaken.

McGlynn has noted how, in the last decade, the Law Society has depended on promoting the 'business case' for equality, but also notes how this strategy, which depends on persuading firms that they will derive economic benefit from equity-based policies, is flawed in several respects.[153] It is vulnerable to empirical disproof, and we have noted, both here and elsewhere, that women's utility as a second class factor of production may have been a key

---

147 Parker, 1999, p 23.
148 Goode and Bagihole, 1998.
149 See, also, West and Lyon, 1995.
150 *Ibid*, Parker, p 41.
151 Sommerlad, 1999.
152 The Law Society, 1995.
153 McGlynn, 2000.

element in the capacity of firms to expand in the past two decades. It would be naive to imagine that the benefits of having a labour force segmented along gender lines have escaped the predominantly male partners who preside over firms. The business case also runs counter to the ideology of liberal individualism which prevails in the profession, which sees human capital theory as 'natural' and right, and is hostile to any form of outside interference in a free labour market.

It may be argued, therefore, that some form of strong regulation which enables the possibility of audit to promote internal change is an essential element in addressing women's position within firms. Parker suggests that regulation may not need merely to focus on an obvious equality agenda, but may profitably address the way in which internal constituencies in firms may be given a voice, and she recommends that 'compliance scholars should therefore connect with progressive corporate law scholarship on the democratic reform of corporate structures beyond the shareholders'.[154] Alternatively, forms of external intervention, such as the Working Time Directive, which address issues which affect all employees, but which, because of the division of domestic responsibilities, have undue disparate impact on women, such as the long hours culture, may provide a focus for internal change without highlighting the gender agenda.

The tenor of this section, and the preceding one, might appear to be that the changes in the profession which would give women unrestricted access to all segments of its labour market will be, at the very least, difficult to bring about. However, we feel that the message to be taken from the review of the law and of alternative strategies is that change of the kind and order that is required is a political process, involving a reciprocal relationship between external regulation, with all its contradictions, and internal cultural change. It is, therefore, likely to be uneven, to occur in some professional sectors more than others, and be prone to reversals of fortune.

CONCLUSION

This book is about access to the legal profession, and women's right of access is now secure. For many years, they have constituted over 50% of entrants, and they appear to be welcomed as employees. However, the question of access must include consideration of what sort of access, to what level, and of retention, and here the record is less good. In this chapter, we have undertaken a discursive review of women's current position of the profession and explored the theoretical models which seek to explain the fact that this position appears to be one of differentiation and subordination. Despite over

---

154 Parker, 1999, p 42.

two decades of women's participation on a large scale, so that women have ceased to be a token presence,[155] there has been little disruption of the dominant model of professionalism which continues to be characterised by excessively long hours, generating an 'ideal worker' who is not only free of caring responsibilities, but will have domestic support.[156] This model is, therefore, predicated on the continuing divorce of the labour market from the costs of social reproduction, and indeed stands in a 'diachronic interrelationship' with existing gender relations.[157]

We have also explored the potential of both legal and corporate strategies to provide women solicitors with remedy or redress for their subordinated position. The dominant theme of this exploration has been the difficulties that arise from the contradiction between strategies which seek to achieve for women 'equal treatment' with men, and those which attempt to adapt the workplace to meet what are claimed to be women's particular needs. Both of these models tend to 'take the labour market as they find it', that is, as circumscribed by existing assumptions about gender roles, and are both, therefore, essentially assimilationist models which leave intact both the labour market and the domestic sphere.

Furthermore, unless the law can accommodate sophisticated sociological reasoning, empirical data gathering and causal modelling, it will be difficult for it to address structural disadvantage and the power relations embedded in existing arrangements. Despite, therefore, evidence of some such change in a range of the judicial decisions which we have reviewed, we have identified the following difficulties with legal redress as strategy: the conception of discrimination as being represented by an abnormal act rather than by systematic subordination as part of the workplace culture; the uneven introduction of indices of structural disadvantage within the concept of indirect discrimination; the weaknesses of liberal legalism in its reliance on the notion of the autonomous individual; and the way in which the enhanced 'vagueness' of the tribunal system in UK law's approach to equal opportunity law makes it difficult to entrench conceptual advances (mirroring the history of common law's approach to gender inequality). Enhancing women's capacity to make genuine choices in the solicitor's profession, and in all other areas of public and private life, is ultimately dependent on cultural change, for which we should regard the support of law and regulation as a necessary, but not a sufficient, condition.

---

155 See Kanter, 1977.
156 Seron and Ferris, 1995.
157 Witz, 1992, p 12.

CHAPTER 8

'UP OR OUT' – MEANS OR ENDS?
STAFF RETENTION IN LARGE FIRMS

Robert G Lee

The City of London seems to have almost a magnetic quality in attracting new recruits to the solicitors' profession. In the 1999 intake of trainee solicitors, the top 10 firms by size sought to recruit 930 trainees – over 20% of the training contracts registered for that year.[1] It seems improbable that such a large proportion of new entrants would choose to relocate to the City of London, but as with the Bar, the better opportunities for employment are in London and the best quality commercial work finds its way there. The work is unquestionably well paid. Recent advertisements for newly qualified solicitors in the London firms suggest salaries of between £40,000 and £45,000 are now common in the City firms,[2] and competition from the US firms based in London is driving this figure upwards.[3] This escalating wage level is a curious phenomenon. Recent surveys of large law firms indicate that there are now serious 'quality of life' issues facing such firms, and that staff retention is a major headache.[4] If, as the firms say, solicitors leave because of concern at the quality of their lives within law, then more money is hardly likely to address this problem. Indeed, a higher wage bill implies more or higher quality work must be sold to the client unless profitability is to reduce. And, in partnerships, falling profitability has a direct effect on the income of the owners of the business and is never welcome.

As with any other business sector, there are winners and losers amongst the largest firms. But, in general terms, these firms seem to go from strength to strength, outstripping the growth in other areas of the profession,[5] to the point that the top 10 firms may account not only for 20% of trainees recruited, but also the same percentage of turnover of fee income for all firms in England and Wales.[6] A study of published figures over the past five years shows that there has been steady growth in the size of each of the top 10 UK law firms.

---

1   Calculated from (2000) *The Lawyer* (Student Special) February.

2   'Solicitors' salaries war hotting up in the city' (2000) *The Times*, 9 May.

3   'City firms raid coffers to protect assistants from US salary hikes' (2000) *The Lawyer*, 28 February; 'Fried Frank entices first years with $100k salary' (1999) *Legal Week*, 19 June; within a year this had become £100,000 according to recruitment consultants Taylor Root; see Mizzi, 2000, and an earlier news item in (2000) *Law Society Gazette*, 18 May, p 11.

4   Lee, 1999; Cole, 1997; Gillies, 1999.

5   Galanter, 1992; Flood, 1989.

6   See *ibid*, Lee; but cf Glasser, 1990.

Together, the 'top 10' employ more than 3,800 solicitors, an increase of approximately 66% over that of five years ago. Interestingly, in terms of numbers of solicitors (though not necessarily in terms of profitability), the firms in the lower reaches of the top 10 seem to be making considerable strides to narrow the gap in size.

For example, using Chambers as a reference point, the range of figures for the number of solicitors (only as opposed to fee-earners) working either as partners or assistants in England and Wales during 1995 varies from 715 at the top firm to 262 at the 10th firm. By 2000, there are 975 solicitors at the number one firm and 404 at number 10. The table shows total fee-earners globally over the same period, eight[7] of the top firms which have not merged in the UK. The trend to growth is obvious. With an increase in worldwide mergers and competition from overseas firms within the UK, it is highly likely that the 'Big 10' will grow even more rapidly in their bid to stay at the top.

Global figures:	1995			2000		
	Partners	Assistants	Trainees	Partners	Assistants	Other fee-earners
Clifford Chance	239	886	223	362	2,207	423
Eversheds	268	415	140	337	638	507
Linklaters	162	451	222	235	+/− 844	202
Allen and Overy	130	347	124	245	944	289
Freshfields	153	426	133	308	1492	220
Lovells	146	317	130	247	449	253
Herbert Smith	119	227	112	147	398	236
Simmons and Simmons	136	269	99	147	436	207

Nelson has argued that with growth comes a tension between professionalism and bureaucracy, and a marked shift to greater specialisation.[8] This, in turn, produces increasing stratification within the profession. The solicitor within the large law firm leads a life very different from the solicitor on the high street, and, as time goes by, movement between such offices becomes rarer,

7   This table offers examples of firms and their growth. It simply chooses some firms to illustrate growth. Because it is compiled from a number of different sources and because categories such as 'fee-earners' are recorded differently across the firms, these figures represent estimates only. Note that some of these forms may have been subject to international mergers.
8   Nelson, 1988.

less likely, and perhaps even impossible. It follows that a choice for the large law firm may constitute a pragmatic approach on the part of the student in favour of the sector in which most opportunity is available. However, increasingly this is a route that leads in one direction with relatively few opportunities to make a U-turn or find an exit route.

The degree of specialisation now pursued must be appreciated. It is not simply that the largest law firms have forgone legal practice and moved into corporate and commercial law. Within that specialism itself, there is a bewildering array of options.[9] If one looks at an entry for 'Banking' in Chambers[10] it appears, but to understand the available legal services in this area one would have to check under other headings such as Asset Finance, Ship Finance, Capital Markets, Project Finance, Banking Litigation, Corporate Finance, etc. Even then, this would not immediately capture the solicitor specialising in securitisation of debt. Increasingly, groups within firms are organised according to the sector of the market that they serve rather than any legal discipline. A solicitor may work in the Energy Group, but only on gas projects (and then only off-shore gas). Add to this that the practices are global, and that a solicitor may be acquiring experience not within the UK, but within (say) emerging markets. Finally, bear in mind that a multinational client may have sufficient work to provide a continual stream that occupies particular solicitors. The work experience and contacts of the large firm solicitor may be limited even after five to 10 years of qualification.[11]

So career choices within law firms are fraught with difficulty as options narrow in the face of specialisation. Of course, if the solicitor remains with the firm that works within a particular specialism, and services a strong client base in that sector, then this may not matter. But, there is a problem here, caused by the curious shape of the corporate structures of the large law firm. The only available long term prospects within such firms are at partner level, and senior solicitors not making it to partnership will be asked to leave. So the solicitor may achieve the significant awards of partnership,[12] but, if she does not, then there is no option but to leave the firm and hope that there will be a chance to employ her talents elsewhere. This policy, often labelled 'up or out', is made more problematic because it is apparent that at best confusing and at worst misleading signals may be sent to solicitors concerning the prospects for partnership. The reasons for this are explained below, pp 192–95. This paper explores the working of the policy of 'up or out' and asks whether the adoption of this or similar policies might be described as unethical.

The survey findings which form the basis for the analysis contained below are part of an earlier study into the work of the largest law firms.[13] This study

9   Lewis and Keegan, 1997.
10 Chambers, 1999.
11 For some of the difficulties of specialisation, see Boon and Levin, 1999, p 80ff.
12 Malpas, 1999; Griffiths, 2000.
13 Lee, 1999.

examined the views of managing and supervising partners and of solicitors working on mainly large scale transactions, in 'top 10' law firms based in the City of London. The quotations that appear are answers given to questions asked in semi-structured interviews that followed a topic guide. These interviews were wide ranging and covered a range of material on globalisation, regulation, firm structures, etc. Part of the survey concerned the working lives of solicitors within these firms, and it is from these data that the present paper is compiled.[14]

AN ETHICAL APPROACH

There may be many ways in which one might reflect upon the employment practices of the law firm, and treating the issue as one of ethics might not seem the most obvious way in which to proceed. Yet, as Cranston has argued, legal ethics and professional responsibility are 'more than a set of rules', arguing that 'a commitment to honesty integrity and service in the practice of law' must also be included.[15] As he later writes: 'Issues of legal ethics do not come labelled as such, but arise in particular contexts of legal practice.' In a similar vein, Parker writes that the field of legal ethics is not exclusively rule-based, but that 'the customs and cultures of lawyers, to the extent that they have some effect on the delivery of legal services, should be included in an extended definition.'[16] But, this is not always apparent. Few writers have considered whether employment policies have an ethical dimension, although both the Bar Council and the Law Society have codes concerning discrimination in employment practices. One exception is Elizabeth Nosworthy who, in an essay on large law firms, states that she finds it: 'Very difficult to imagine how a firm can maintain high legal ethical standards unless its internal culture is also generally ethical both in the relationship between its people and in its governance.'[17]

Carrie Menkel-Meadow, in the same collection of essays, faces the question directly: 'Should a lawyer's "ethics" or morality be judged by how he treats others including his employees? Is the demand of brutally hard working hours in some legal employment itself an issue of ethical concern?'[18]

---

14 I am grateful to the Research, Planning and Policy Unit of the Law Society for supporting the initial study (Lee, 1999) and to Phil Thomas, Cheryl Jones and Allison Nyssens for assistance with the research. David Campbell and Derek Morgan kindly read through and commented on this chapter.

15 Cranston, 1995.

16 Parker, 1995.

17 Nosworthy, 1995.

18 Menkel-Meadow, 1995.

The writer answers her own question by saying that ethics as broadly defined includes making decisions about others, and that this process would be enhanced by taking account of the values of those others. However, accepting that law firms should act ethically towards their employees does little to settle the question of whether the practice of 'up or out' as described in this paper is, or is not, ethical. The fact that it may lead to disappointment for some, while proving advantageous for the firms, of itself tells us little about the ethical basis of the practice. If we are to decide whether the conduct is right and proper, one that ought to be employed by the firms, then it is to substantive ethics we must look for an answer. Drucker has argued that there is nothing particular or different about professional ethics that sets it apart from the discipline of ethics.[19] The large law firms operate more and more as businesses and face competition internationally[20] as well as nationally. Whatever professional obligations may remain in relation to qualification, training and supervision of staff, the firms are likely to argue that it is vital to remain free to shape their personnel to meet the needs of the client base.

From the employees' point of view, it is hard to argue that there is some 'right to promotion'. It may be easier to establish that any right to promotion should be based only on relevant criteria relating to the job. However, this chapter is not seeking to argue that the policy of 'up or out' is discriminatory as such, although it may be that more women are adversely affected by it, since fewer women still reach partner level.[21] Concern for people may be a prerequisite of good management, but this cannot mean that firms must continue to retain employees no longer required.[22] However, the argument may change if promotion is not offered when promised, or if evaluations of progress lead the employee to an expectation that is not fulfilled. This is what might trouble us about the policy of 'up or out'. Our worries concern how the policy operates in denying effective means of monitoring progress and prospects until a point at which, rather than gaining promotion to partner, the solicitor finds that his or her services are no longer required. Broadly, the issues, then, are whether the solicitors are accorded sufficient respect and the necessary autonomy to make appropriate career choices in the face of confused messages and misinformation about their progress and prospects.

DIGNITY AND AUTONOMY

There can be little doubt that the policy of 'up or out' is a major component of the employment structures of the law firms, but in assessing whether its

19 Drucker, 1981.
20 Flood, 1996.
21 Chambers, 1989; Sommerlad, 1994.
22 De George, 1999.

operation works ethically, it is necessary to look at how people are affected by it. This is because the ethical doubts concern the practice of 'up or out' rather than the policy itself. This paper does not intend to argue that a policy of retaining employees only to the point at which they are sufficiently experienced to become a partner is, of itself, unethical regardless of how persons are affected by it. There seems no reason in principle why firms should not hire and continue to employ on this basis. Indeed, it may be that some of those affected by the policy nonetheless benefit from a prolonged period of employment and experience with the firm in question, even though they are forced to move to work elsewhere. But the question asked here is whether the practices within the firms can be morally right, and whether, in a deontological sense,[23] the policies as operated conform with an ethical imperative? Kant, for example, located such a moral law in the nature of reason.[24] Acting morally is the same as acting rationally. And, for Kant, actions of a moral worth proceed from duty, so that an action undertaken by inclination has no moral worth unless, at least, there is also some concern to meet a duty.[25] Interestingly, in our context, this requires some self-regulation[26] to ensure that one acts in accordance with a rational maxim.

Reason can be seen to exhibit certain crucial characteristics, and particularly those of universality and consistency. It is in the nature of reason that it must lead to consistent results, so that actions that are moral should not conflict with each other. Moral rules are universal rules. Reason dictates that, if an action is moral, then it should be moral for everyone. It follows that any moral rule should be capable of universal and consistent application. In this way, the underpinning principle of an action can be tested in terms of its internal consistency if universally applied. This is not a question of consequences of the action if, for example, everyone was to pursue the action under consideration. Indeed, in the real world, such universality is unlikely. But it is possible on a conceptual level to ask whether a rule can be made consistently universal. In Kant's categorical imperative: 'Act only on that maxim whereby you can at the same time will that it should become a universal law.'

Kant claimed as a different formulation, a re-formulation, of the categorical imperative: 'Act so that you treat humanity, whether in your own

---

23 Boon and Levin, citing Bayles, 1981, state that the deontological approach is 'attractive to practising lawyers' and that it 'tends to accept the proposition that professionals are entitled to do whatever is permitted by the regulations promulgated by their profession' (1999, p 37). Without agreeing with this, I am happy to accept that the approach focuses on whether actions are right or wrong and that this is a more limited enterprise than some wider ranging teleological inquiry as to what good lawyers promote. But it suits this paper to engage with the profession on the ground upon which they feel most comfortable.

24 Kant, 1785.

25 Norman, 1998.

26 On self-rule and the legal profession, see Kronman, 1993.

person or in that of another, always as an end and never solely as a means.' This is to apply our own actions as a rational being in a universal and consistent manner by treating others as rational beings deserving of respect. That respect requires that another be treated with dignity as an end, another rational being, free to act, rather than being treated as a means only. There is much here which relates to Kant's view of persons with a will and able to decide what ought to be done as between duty and inclination. For Kant, doing as one ought to do as a rational being is the mark of acting in an autonomous manner.[27] In pursuing an action through reason, the actions must stem from duty rather than other extrinsic influences such as praise or blame, reward or punishment.

There is much in a Kantian approach that seems especially pertinent to the professional environment of a law firm. To a large extent and within a broad professional code, lawyers engage in a process of self-regulation. In the view of a number of commentators, this process of self-regulation is part of an historic attempt to exercise some control over the market for legal services by excluding possible competition.[28] However, Paterson has questioned whether lawyers have ever exercised any great deal of control over their markets, and that there is a process of bargaining, much of it of recent origin, between lawyers and the State as part of shifting and widespread re-evaluations of the market for legal services.[29] Paterson argues that ethical questions may form an important adjustment mechanism in this bargaining context because socially responsible conduct may assist in the preservation of professional boundaries.[30]

This (very brief) summary of the debate helps to illustrate that references to self-regulation connote an activity that from either perspective is market-led, and that there is an association between ethical behaviour and market position. Nonetheless, it is clear that, in the modern State, and in a manner consistent with either analysis above, lawyers enjoy fewer and fewer monopoly rights in relation to the supply of legal services.[31] It may become vital for them to establish trust with the client community.[32] But, this is not necessarily in conflict with Kantian notions of duty, since acting according to reason ought to produce a set of rules that can be consistently and universally applied, and on which the client may rely. In our case, the actions under review are directed at fellow professionals who would wish to act also in accordance with a moral code and to do so as autonomous individuals. For

27 Morgan, 1998.
28 Larson, 1972; Abel, 1988.
29 Paterson, 1996.
30 *Ibid*; Paterson, 1997.
31 *Ibid*, Abel.
32 Boon and Levin, 1999.

these reasons, this paper applies the ethical theory of Kant to the policy pursued in the firms in order to examine and evaluate its ethical basis.

EMPLOYMENT STRUCTURES

As large law firms continue to adopt the partnership as a corporate structure, internal hierarchies are clear and marked.[33] There is an obvious and inevitable division between employed solicitors and the partners who, in principle at least, own and manage the firm. More recently, as the firms have grown larger, the management of the firm as a whole has shifted to become concentrated in the hands of a few partners voted in by the partners as a whole.[34] Nonetheless, management of teams of lawyers within disciplinary, or sometimes sectoral, groups rests with partners. Distinctions between partners and solicitors, sometimes misleadingly labelled 'assistant solicitors', is there for all to see and is reflected in many aspects of the work of the firm – from dining facilities even through to entitlements to sabbatical leave. In part, any desire to become a partner will be driven not merely by hope of financial reward (though this may be considerable), but also to occupy this central position in the organisation.

Speaking of these structures, it is not uncommon to hear lawyers refer to a loss of 'collegiality' within the law inside and outside the work place. However, this is not inconsistent with Durkheim's notion[35] of collegia as a largely social grouping based on shared interest and the pursuit of 'the same moral aim'.[36] It may be that, looking at work within the largest firms, it is less easy to perceive the shared moral goal. Yet, the lawyers who speak of a lack of collegiality do so with regret, and would look to restore something of this quality to professional life. This endeavour may not prove easy in the face of increasing stratification, global legal practice, and intense competition in the legal services market.

For the firm, one immediate goal is profitability. Indeed, while we might like to feel that there are more pressing 'internal goals', such as the pursuit of justice, it is idle to pretend that lawyers are not, and should not be, free to work on behalf of those who have already acquired the resources to pay them most handsomely.[37] In pursuing profit, the employment of solicitors in an effective employment structure can be crucial. There is wide acceptance that 'gearing', the ratio of partners to other assistants, is a significant indicator of

---

33 Nelson, 1988; Stewart, 1983.
34 Lee, 1999.
35 Durkheim, 1957.
36 Boon and Levin, 1999.
37 See the debate between Williams, 1962 and Nozick, 1974.

the likely financial health of the firm.[38] The better the ratio, the greater the number of assistants to the partners, the more likely it is that the drawings of the partners from the profits of the firm will rise.[39] Indeed, recent investments in staff development and training programmes in the largest law firms may reflect a drive towards well geared and economically productive systems.[40] Referring to this 'pyramid staffing', Stewart, in his work on US partnerships, has written: 'More than any other factor, it is the capacity of the firms to staff matters in such a fashion – and to bill clients for associates' work at rates that exceed associate salaries – which produces the firms' immense profitability.'[41]

Strangely, in view of the numbers seeking to qualify into law, there is a difficulty in obtaining experienced and well qualified staff. Significant sums are paid to 'recruitment consultants' to locate qualified staff[42] and the cost of a departure of an assistant solicitor in terms of lost time and replacement costs has been estimated at £125,000.[43] Moreover, there is a particular difficulty in finding senior assistants. As a managing partner reported: 'Most law firms are hour-glass shaped, and at the middle level of senior assistants, there are always more required, but it (hiring) is never achievable.'

There are a number of factors which may explain this recurrent shortage. It seems unlikely that sufficient numbers of recruits are taken through training to serve the rates of expansion in the large law firms. Having said that, trainees may not be easy to find. In 1999, the number of training contracts registered exceeded the number of passes on the Legal Practice Course. When analysing this figure, it is worth remembering that over 20% of students fail, and are required to re-sit some element of this course at the first attempt. Training is expensive, and doubtless some firms under-recruit in the hope of hiring qualified solicitors trained elsewhere. Firms coming into London from the USA and elsewhere may seek to hire laterally. In addition, firms make offers of training contracts two, or even three years in advance, and some firms are acutely conscious still of having been caught in the recession of the early 1990s having made offers of training contracts that greatly exceeded human resources needs in the depressed market. Finally, the increased use of paralegals has diminished the available work for trainees, and, as one managing partner stated: 'There is much less trainee work around ... there is a natural cap on the number of trainees which we can take.'

Staff shortages also occur because of attrition rates. In Lee, one three year qualified solicitor had kept track of those trainees starting alongside her.[44]

---

38   Stewart, 1983.
39   Lee, 1992.
40   Greenebaum, 1996.
41   *Ibid*, Stewart.
42   Galanter and Palay, 1991, p 54.
43   (1999) *Legal Week*, 12 August.
44   Lee, 1999.

From an intake of 60, 18 remained with the firm. Some of the firms surveyed in this had rates of turnover in excess of 25% per annum for established, qualified staff. Some of this was to competitor firms ('retention is a problem ... and recruitment consultants do not help the situation'), described as a 'key moment in a lawyer's career'. This reflects the care that must be taken in surrendering the credit built up in one firm and beginning again elsewhere if the aim is to make partnership in a large law firm. Perhaps for this reason, the shift was greater for 'lifestyle' reasons, moving to smaller firms, or out of the City, or even out of law.

PROMOTION PROSPECTS

Those remaining with the firm are immensely valuable commodities. Increasing specialisation allows them to undertake work with relatively little supervision, or, more commonly, as a member of a team and, eventually, even the team leader reporting to the partner. They become the very people that the firm can least afford to lose other than certain partners with significant human capital. And yet, there is a curiosity that, if these members of staff do not become partners, then they quickly pass their 'sell-by date'. This is because all of the large firms pursue a policy of 'up or out'. In addition to this label, respondents also described the policy of one of 'all or nothing', meaning that either the big prize of partnership is won, or nothing else is on offer. On the rare occasions that one did find long term senior non-partner solicitors, this was described as 'not intended or planned'. The general reason for the policy was that anyone occupying such a position would become 'demotivated'. It was said that training in a law firm is towards partnership,[45] making it difficult to accommodate those not reaching this goal. The significance of partnership is highlighted in the explanation that these people would see their own trainees become partners, and that this would make them 'resentful'.

Indeed, the entrenched notion of 'up or out' is indicated by the mechanisms by which the departure of the failed partners is organised. Little active effort was needed to secure the departure. As reported, the people themselves 'take a view that they should go'. Although it was said that persons in this position 'are not encouraged to stay', neither was there any 'hurry' to cause these people to leave and no 'fixed time' for delivering messages about departure. Nor was there a fixed message, but what was suggested was along the lines of 'you should have had it (partnership) by now and if you haven't got it you should be looking somewhere else'. This lack of clarity in delivering messages in the run-up to consideration of partnership should be noted, as it is crucial to what follows.

---

45   And see Greenebaum, 1996.

The senior solicitor is in a precarious position. Great rewards, both in terms of money and status, are on offer in the partnership stakes, but the price for failure is high. The solicitor will be left trading in the market at a position of great disadvantage. The long investment in the particular firm is lost. It will be apparent in looking for a move to any new firm that the applicant has been 'passed over' for partnership. In the short life cycle of solicitors prior to partnership, it is already late for the candidate forced to move elsewhere. This problem is exacerbated by the 'hit and miss' process of making partnership, in which 'some luck is involved' and 'clubability is still there'. In addition 'sponsors are important; having an influential partner pushing is terribly important'. So starting again allows less time to develop the sponsors, the clubability and to ride one's luck.

Because of the shortages of senior solicitors, it would make every sense for the solicitor to move at an earlier stage if unsure about prospects of partnership. There is no question of the disadvantage of losing out if the solicitor stays until falling victim of an 'up or out' policy. But, can there be any cause for complaint if, having given good service to a law firm as a senior solicitor, the firm then decides that the solicitor fails to demonstrate the necessary qualities required of a partner in the firm? Given that different attributes, such as leadership skills, managerial capacity or the ability to generate work may be expected of partners, it is not necessarily surprising to find that perfectly competent solicitors do not make it to partner. It would be helpful to explore, however, the messages given to the solicitor concerning partnership possibilities and prospects.

PROBLEMS OF APPRAISAL

Given the problems of the recruitment and training of lawyers, virtually all the top 100 firms will employ personnel professionals. In the last 10–15 years, these personnel departments will have put into place structured approaches to human resources management.[46] This includes formal processes of appraisal. In interview, firms insisted on a reliance on such processes not simply in identifying staff development needs or problems with supervision, but in monitoring progression through the firm. However, it becomes apparent quickly, on interviewing staff within law firms, that the processes of appraisal are uneven both in terms of frequency and content. Whatever the expectations of appraisal, the involvement of partners as line managers is

---

46 The very label 'human resources' is of interest here, suggesting as it does the commodification of staff and the utilisation and, perhaps, exhaustion of these resources. It might be better to refer to staff development, allowing for the goal of enhancing the capacities of staff within the constraints of the organisation.

inevitable, and in the rueful words of one managing partner: 'You can't tell partners what to do.'

One does not need to look far to find that, in spite of formal processes of annual appraisal, this annual target is commonly not achieved. Solicitors make comments such as 'I missed my last yearly one completely', and managing partners admit that 'what we should be doing happens less so in some areas (of the firm) rather than others'. One firm had moved to six-monthly mini-appraisals, but staff interviews demonstrated that these, too, had been regularly ignored. Another firm had conducted a staff attitudes survey, which cited the infrequency of 'annual appraisal' as a 'significant complaint'. Indeed, alongside this evidence of a patchy system of appraisal was a desperate need for feedback on the part of solicitors, who admitted that they set great store by what was said to them in less formal settings such as the pub or in a taxi on the way back from a meeting.

In addition to the infrequency, doubts were raised also concerning the quality of appraisal. Human resources professionals described what went on as 'an initial system' and 'unsophisticated in terms of career management'. There were indications that the partners did not take it seriously, and it was referred to as the 'child care programme' in one firm. Solicitors described the processes as uneven between different departments and complained frequently at the poor training of the partners and disappointment with the process. There seemed, also, to be a lack of trust in the system. Managing partners doubted whether the solicitors themselves would admit to areas of weakness, and the solicitors reported clear patterns, discussed among themselves, for handling the appraisal process.

At an early stage, it seemed that appraisal had an overt link to partnership prospects, and according to some solicitors, from three years qualified onwards the 'partnership race starts'. Solicitors were aware of when formal consideration would begin ('I'm first due for partnership in a year and a half's time'), and it was expected that 'they [would] look at you a bit more closely' as this stage drew near. Yet, in terms of decisions about partnership, in a number of firms, only the latest appraisal would be examined. In the meantime, however, it seems clear that solicitors wanted to take messages from appraisal and that, overwhelmingly, they seemed to find these messages positive. Indeed, one of the curious features of the survey is that the solicitors interviewed, without exception, when asked, stated their belief that they would make partner at their current firm. This is at best improbable, and indeed, even in firms that have a strong history of appointing from within their own ranks of trainees, it was clear that a small minority of any group would eventually make it through to this level.

Looking at progress through the firms more carefully, it became clear that there were other cut-off points. For example, some firms operated a policy of looking carefully at staff at three or four years qualified. Sometimes this led to a formal advancement and a title such as 'associate', or increases in remuneration. Given the shortages of solicitors in this range of qualification, hurdles were not necessarily high, and most people did reach this level if they stayed. If they failed at this stage, then, in the words of one managing partner: 'if a solicitor stands no chance at this level, do you want them?' Once through this level, however, the firms hoped to retain these valuable staff. Indeed, a common reason given for some formal step-up in status at this stage was to aid retention of staff. So, at this stage, solicitors are being given positive messages, and these are unlikely to be followed soon thereafter by negative messages.

Indeed, there is some evidence that, for most solicitors, the messages stay positive until the final disappointment of not making partnership; though even this point is not clear since, according to one solicitor, only 50% of eventual partners make partnership on the first run through. One firm had no 'fixed time' and thought that it was for the solicitor to 'take a view that they should go'. Another firm cited 10 years of qualification as a point at which people couldn't be expected to stay, as 'there aren't that many jobs for persons of 10 years' call that carry that price and ... that can't be better done by a partner and two junior assistants'. At some ill defined point, therefore, the solicitor having received encouragement and endorsement from their supervisors for the last five years or more, reach the point at which 'it may be suggested to them that they may be better off somewhere else'.

On the whole, the policy of 'up or out' seems widespread across law firms. At one point, there seemed to be some suggestions in the USA that the policy was softening and that structures were emerging that allowed a wider variety of status through 'new staffing hierarchies'.[47] Certainly, in Smigel's early work on Wall Street lawyers,[48] the 'up or out' policy was shown as pursued with vigour, but by the early 1990s, Kronman could speak of the attenuation of the policy and even its 'demise'.[49] Yet, this seems to have been 'greatly exaggerated'. Writing at the end of the 1990s, Galanter speaks of a distinctive structure in large law firms that includes: ': highly qualified law graduates who compete over an extended period (five to 10 years) in a more or less meritocratic tournament in which only some are chosen to become partners; the others typically depart.'[50]

Making allowance for the period of the training contract and the common professional examination, this describes also the situation in England and Wales. In the following section I address the question of whether the operation of an 'up or out' policy constitutes an ethical employment policy.

---

47   Brill, 1989; Gilson and Mnookin, 1989.
48   Smigel, 1969.
49   Kronman, 1993.
50   Galanter, 1999.

TESTING THE POLICY

For Kant, it is a characteristic of reason that it is deductive, so that we can know that something is moral by reasoning alone, and not through experience. It is possible to apply the moral law to experience, but not simply to determine from experience that a particular action is or is not moral. Such consequentialist thinking plays no part in the equation. Thus, the moral rule is the *a priori* result of reason, and, as such, it can be tested in terms of both consistency and universality. When applied universally, could we still have a consistent rule? In trying to illustrate this idea, Kant offers various examples of duties that can be put to the test in this way. Interestingly, they include the 'perfect' duty to refrain from making false promises and the 'imperfect' duty to help others. An imperfect duty is one that can permit exceptions, so that there may be situations, other than through mere inclination, in which it may be permissible to refuse to help others. (Since another example is of the duty to refrain from suicide, it may be that such an exception would lie in endangering our own life by helping others.)

If actions cannot be universalised, or if they involve treating human beings as means only, then they will be morally impermissible. Thus, applying the examples in the manner suggested by Kant, we must produce negative tests to produce actions that might not accord with the categorical imperative. Thus, if the duty is not to make false promises, we can consider the application of the rule 'mislead others'. It seems unlikely that such a rule could be capable of being consistently universalised. If we all tried to mislead each other, then we should adopt continuing strategies of disbelieving what we were told and in the longer term the very action of misleading would become impossible as the defence strategies adopted would render misleading impossible. The universal and consistent application of the maxim cannot be achieved.[51]

In a similar manner, if we mislead people, then we deny their capacity as autonomous beings to act in the face of the truth. This may be because we do not wish to allow such autonomous action in the knowledge that it might damage our interests. Thus, we achieve our ends at their expense. They, in turn, become the means by which those ends are achieved. In other contexts, we might find this morally objectionable. Thus, suppose that an individual is suffering from an incurable health disorder, but we choose to mislead that individual by telling her that all is well. We might do so out of sympathy, feeling that the person would be better off without the burden of knowing of their impending death. But, given the denial of autonomy and the lack of

---

51 This formalism on the part of Kant has been criticised by Hegel, who would argue that there is nothing self-contradictory in the breakdown of promising unless we assume that promising ought to exist. So that, from the outset, according to Hegel, some form of moral content is assumed within the application of the former principle: Hegel, 1967.

respect for the individual, surely she has a right to be dealt with openly and honestly.[52]

This is no simple matter. Transferring the argument to the context of 'up or out', it seems that, in any situation in which people are employed, they are likely to be used as means. But, the Kantian injunction is not to use people *only* as means, but as ends in themselves. It is morally objectionable to have regard only to our own ends using others as the means to achieve this, without regard to the need to treat those others as rational beings who themselves have ends to pursue. In pursuing our own ends, according to Kant, we are precluded from adopting means that violate the sanctity of others. Concern for others, including concern for one's employees, is necessary to pursue the moral rule that we treat people as ends in themselves.[53]

If we look to defend a policy of 'up or out', the easiest route might be to argue that solicitors are not treated solely as means. We might argue that the ends of the individuals, within their professional lives, are served by the experience, training, seniority within the profession, etc, gained during employment as a senior solicitor. However, we are not examining consequences here, but asking whether the agent is wrong in pursuing an action that has the effect of denying people the opportunity to act autonomously, and whether they are provided with the means to pursue their own ends.

Looking at the practical workings of the 'up or out' policies in the largest firms, they would seem to be ethically doubtful. Appraisal schemes that represent the most formal process of feedback of future prospects are too frequently neglected, and seem to receive patchy support from supervising partners. In the absence of this, the solicitors set great store by less formal mechanisms of endorsement and encouragement. Yet, in large part, the task of a supervising partner will be to urge the team on to work harder, whatever the capacities or capabilities of the individual team members. It seems, in any case, that where no formal appraisal is given, then for some period of time, at least following some cut-off point at around three years of qualification, messages will tend to be positive. At this point, the senior solicitor is in short supply. If that solicitor should leave in the face of a clear message of limited prospects for partnership, the cost of re-hiring another such solicitor would be considerable. It does seem that messages given are, at best, confusing and, at worst, misleading. The effect is to deny the solicitors career choices based on honest and full appraisal of the available opportunities.

In this way, the autonomy of the individual is denied by conduct which offends the moral law that would seek to preserve autonomous action. By pursuing employment policies of the type described above there is fierce

---

52 Morgan, 1995.
53 De George, 1999.

competition for the profitable exploitation of qualified staff. But, in many senses, it is the adoption of these types of policy that exacerbates the cut-throat competition. Ethical constrains, according to Kant, would have the effect of producing a level of reasonable competition such that autonomy ought not to be threatened.[54] Freer movement of qualified solicitors based upon the honest appraisal of prospects and experience would benefit the system as a whole.

CONCLUSION

It is necessary to end with a word of caution. Many of the assumptions above involve not the policy, but the practice, of 'up or out'. It remains possible for more open and transparent dealings to emerge, as, indeed, this author hopes will happen. In so far as solicitors are misled by false messages and promises, this is objectionable. It is possible, however, that the practices are so ingrained within the law firm culture that they fool no one, and that solicitors are happy to remain as long as they can earn a high level salary until the day on which they are told they are no longer required. On this analysis, they already know that this will happen, but they themselves send out false messages in order to extend their earnings as long as possible. This seems unlikely, given the available option of trading in the market from a position of strength, prior to any rejection and in time to make partnership elsewhere. The trade may be downwards; the firm to which they transfer may not be so prestigious, but the partnership share ought to outstrip those of a senior solicitor. This leaves the possibility that some may stay on earning until the point at which they are rejected because it is at that point that they will leave law or make other lifestyle changes. But, at this stage, most will be aged not much more than 30 years old, and will have hardly earned a sum, however generous, sufficient to fund major downshifts.

All of this is speculation – sadly. It shows that we need to know much more about when, why and how solicitors make job moves. This research would not only support the type of analysis offered above, but it would be of considerable value to the firms themselves. Nonetheless, there seems to be evidence of less than open practice that misleads and misinforms the solicitor. In the course of the interviews on which this study is based, partners expressed some unease about the messages given to solicitors concerning partnership prospects. One respondent stated that: 'There are continual messages as one gets closer (to partnership). Also at this stage there is some outflow and therefore one is tempted to be less than frank. But if one is not careful, a reputation follows you, and trust is lost.'

---

54 Campbell, 1990.

In view of the discussion in the previous section, this demonstrates considerable awareness of what is at stake. However, it seems also, from some of the comments, that some partners succumb to temptation. For example, when asked what would happen to someone not making partnership, it was said that candidates could be told to 'go back and wait a year'. However, it became clear that this was no guarantee of success in the following year, but simply allowed the firm to keep its options open. Some partners defended this on the basis that the firm was owned by the partners, and they must retain absolute discretion as to admission to the partnership.

This must be the case, but the process was described also as one of 'risk management' – avoiding the wrong choice. Thus, negative factors could be given considerable weight. The solicitors seemed aware of this, stating that: 'the risk is that you get on the wrong side of someone you just can't afford to be on the wrong side of.' The partners admitted that 'some very good people don't come through'. Thus, from the solicitors' viewpoint, there is a process fraught with uncertainty in which they exercise little or no control. Bear in mind that these solicitors are conscious of the hours that they have recorded and of their billing rates. They can calculate that, through the long hours of their work as senior solicitors,[55] they have delivered income into the partnership at four or five times the level of their salary. This hard work and high pressure is accepted on the basis of (at least) the possibility of partnership opportunity. To fail at the latest possible stage, to be told that there is no place available under an 'up or out' policy, and to feel that one had not been dealt with fairly, must be an embittering experience.

Even if this does not happen to the senior solicitor, they can reflect upon the experience of others in their year group: 'People cannot make it for very odd reasons, and everyone at a relatively senior level knows people who they know perfectly well are extremely good lawyers, and who for one reason or another haven't made it.'

If one looks at the present state of employment in the largest law firms, there has been considerable change in a short period of time. Smigel reported lateral movement of partners as a rare occurrence.[56] Today, we read of new moves of this type each week, sometimes involving teams of lawyers.

Marc Galanter has sought to chart the decline of trust in lawyers, in the USA, through the emergence of jokes about lawyers.[57] Koehn argues also that the public appears 'highly ambivalent about attorneys' trustworthiness' and states that 'the large number of jokes made at attorneys' expense may be an attempt to puncture their illusion of invulnerability'.[58] It would seem also that

---

55   Bedlow, 2000, refers to 1,800 average billable hours for City firms.
56   Smigel, 1969.
57   Galanter, 1998.
58   Koehn, 1994, p 67.

considerable trust within the profession has been eroded. Ross has argued that the requirements of lawyers to act 'honestly and truthfully with other parties' – a duty that he labels 'candour' – can arise in many contexts of legal work.[59] This can surely include the employment relationship with the large law firm. Indeed, it may follow that, if internal employment procedures in the law firm are thought not to operate in accordance with such principles, then wider external trust may be lost also. Lawyers wishing to restore trust might do worse than beginning with their own law firms.

Indeed, it may be in the law firm's own interests to do so, for in Kantian terms there is strong evidence emerging that the practices are not sustainable in terms of their consistent and universal application. Staff retention is highly problematic, and many people, after years of training, seem to quit law in 'lifestyle' moves. The 'hour-glass' shape of the large law firm indicates the disappearance of middle ranking solicitors to the point that, at the moment, the large law firms seem to have human resources problems of almost crisis level. Disaffection with professional life leads to the departure of talented and trained personnel, leaving shortages of experienced and qualified lawyers. In a situation of short supply, the wage rates for solicitors in these firms are rising rapidly. But this is being paid for by ever-increasing billable hours, leading to yet more disaffection. In short, and in both senses of the word, the result is a vortex.[60]

---

59 Ross, 1995.

60 'Vortex, n, (i) A whirling motion of a liquid gas or fine forming a cavity in the centre, a whirlpool, an eddy a whirlwind, (ii) A pursuit, way of life, situation, etc, that engulfs one irresistibly or remorselessly, taking up all one's attention or energies ...' (*Chambers Dictionary*, 1993, Edinburgh: Chambers Harrap.)

CHAPTER 9

LITTLE JUSTICE – JUDICIAL REFORM AND THE MAGISTRATES

Luke Clements[1]

INTRODUCTION

It is, of course, inevitable, in this corner of the 21st century, that the public debate concerning judicial reform is dominated by argument over the imperfect system by which senior judges are appointed. We are living at a time of extraordinary constitutional change, not merely as result of the implementation of the Human Rights Act 1998, but also consequent upon the devolution legislation and the genesis of elected city mayors. In each case, the perceived democratic deficit is being addressed by measures that leave our senior judges with a greater constitutional role. The discharge of these new responsibilities will raise the public profile of these judges and, in turn, the system by which they achieve office is bound to become the subject of greater media scrutiny.

It is, however, arguable that this concentration of attention is misplaced and that the process by which magistrates are appointed is of equal or even greater importance. Indeed, it is likely that the High Court's role in 'day to day' justice will be diminished by this flood of constitutional measures and that they will curtail its supervisory jurisdiction over the lower courts. As a consequence, the High Court's role may become increasingly esoteric, such that there is an even greater requirement for it to comprise an elite, homogenous cadre of senior judges.

If the debate is refocused upon the functions and the appointment of the magistrates, a number of questions arise, not least as to whether justices (as presently constituted) have the necessary 'independence' required by Art 6(1) of the European Convention on Human Rights. However, the fundamental question concerns their legitimacy; how can they claim to be representative 'peers' of those upon whom they sit in judgment, when they lack experience of poverty? How can the magistrates administer justice for the poor, given that they make up the vast majority of the people with whom they have court contact?

---

1   I would like to express my particular thanks to Dennis Lee, Research Assistant at the Law School, for his great assistance in preparing this paper.

The title of this chapter echoes this point, deriving, as it does, from a familiar anecdote in which a wife explains that her husband takes all the big decisions; she just takes care of the little things. He decides, for instance who ought to be the next Prime Minister, if nuclear power is harmful and whether the euro is good thing. She takes the little decisions such as, whether they move house, where the children go to school and how to balance the family finances.

There is a resonance of this tale when the legal profession comes to debate judicial reform. We have tended to concentrate upon the appointment of judges to the Supreme Court and spent little time on the role of the magistrates court – where the vast bulk of cases are heard.

LOOSENING THE CHAINS

Precedent

Although judges hear less than 5% of all criminal cases and High Court judges less than 2% of all civil claims, these figures are not the measure by which their importance is assessed. Their decisions create new law, define the scope of permissible legal argument and have shaped the entire legal system. Through the operation of our rigid precedent system, the High Court exerts enormous control over the magistrates.

Thus (by way of example), a determination that an offence is 'absolute' removes all scope for discretion from the lower courts. Accordingly, when the Divisional Court held that a failure to send one's child to school[2] was an absolute offence (as it did in *Jarman v Mid-Glamorgan Education Authority*),[3] that was the end of the matter. It was irrelevant if the defendant had a cast iron defence under the European Convention on Human Rights (as did Mrs Jarman) or that there were truly extenuating factors: the justices' hands were tied. Likewise, a determination by the High Court that certain bodies have, in certain situations, public interest immunity[4] closes off significant tracts of potential litigation. A quick reference to *Stones Justices' Manual* frequently shows that the High Court has spoken on a particular point and that is effectively the end of the matter. Even in the face of monstrous injustice, the magistrates, like the younger Billy Goats Gruff, simply point to their bigger brother – further argument is impossible.

---

2 Contrary to what is now Education Act 1996, s 444.

3 (1985) *Law Society Gazette*, 1 May, p 1249.

4 Eg, the police in the investigation of crime, as in *Hill v Chief Constable of West Yorkshire* [1989] AC 53, and Social Services in relation to their public law duties under Children Act 1989 s 17, as in *X (Minors) v Bedfordshire CC and Others* [1995] 3 All ER 353 HL.

Precedent systems are, by their very nature, backward-looking and dependent upon a homogeneity of decision maker. Our senior appointments system achieves this consistency by what is, in effect, a cloning process. When the system matured several centuries ago, it was hardly surprising that the original 'Dolly clone' had all the white, well off, privately educated, male, Oxbridge scholar traits. Precedent produces predictability and is self-evidently conservative; its greatest threat coming from those 'hard cases' that might, in the hands of a liberal decision maker, make some bad law; good law is consistent; 'just' law is a secondary issue.

The Human Rights Act will, however, loosen the grip of precedent on the lower courts. Section 3 of the Act requires that all courts interpret legislation, not in accordance with precedent, but to ensure its compatibility with convention rights. Absolute offences and prohibitions on proceedings and processes will wane and justices will increasingly have to roll up their sleeves and decide the issue themselves, rather than sit on their hands as in former times. In each case, they will have to decide, in effect, whether they can adhere to a precedent decision without violating the defendant's convention rights. If this cannot be done, then s 3 requires that (in so far as it is possible) they distinguish or even disregard the unpalatable aspect of the precedent.

Proportionality

Section 3 and its curtailment of the principle of judicial precedent is not, however, the only aspect of the Act which will reduce the High Court's ability to restrict the exercise of magisterial discretion. The Act's extension of the principle of proportionality, into non-EC law disputes,[5] may result in an even greater loosening of this control.

Proportionality is inherent in almost every aspect of convention jurisprudence and has been described as the 'search for a fair balance between the demands of the general interest of the community and the requirements of the protection of the individual's fundamental rights'.[6]

Proportionality will significantly widen the latitude available to magistrates when reaching their decisions. It relies on the exercise of their judgment in deciding what weight should be given to conflicting convention rights. This, in turn, curtails the High Court's power to interfere with these decisions, since the justices had the benefit of hearing the evidence first hand before deciding where the balance of interests lay.

---

5   Whilst proportionality was acknowledged to be waiting on the substitutes bench, by Lord Templeman in *R v Secretary of State for the Home Department ex p Brind* [1991] 1 AC 696, it has made many appearances in European Community law reports, eg, *R v Secretary of State for Employment ex p Equal Opportunities Commission* [1995] 1 AC 1.

6   *Soering v UK* (1989) 11 EHRR 439.

In practice, this can be viewed as the magistrates' administrative margin of appreciation. However, the obligation to determine, in every case, what is a proportionate response, presupposes that the court has choice. Whilst most attention has focused on the justices' conviction decisions, this represents a very small fraction of their work, and of crucial relevance to the poor is their approach to sentencing and, in particular, to fines.

Fines cause poverty and can blight already difficult lives: they touch the whole household and their shadow chills the extended family, which often ends up having to pay them; fines spread misery to innocent parties. Fining poor people is central to criminal justice, just as discrimination against poor people is the unspoken basis of almost every other aspect of our civil society. Whilst to question this state of affairs attracts the censor of naïvety, it is increasingly difficult to see how fixed penalty schemes, which pay scant regard to wealth, can be sustained.[7] This is particularly so now, when the executive (through its control of Parliament) is engineering a situation whereby the justices are ceasing to have any discretion in relation to certain sentencing decisions. Recent examples of this trend include the prescribed minimum penalties in the Crime and Disorder Act 1998 and the Youth Justice and Criminal Evidence Act 1999.

Proportionality is the enemy of binding precedent and of absolute or predetermined rules that dictate when one interest or sentence must prevail. Proportionality requires of its decision makers an appreciation of justice; it requires judgment as to where a fair balance should be struck. Fairness and justice are, however, two words that have only rhetorical significance in our common law. The introduction of the proportionality argument into domestic disputes will change this. The Act will require of the magistrates, in particular, a sensitivity to fairness such that, when the law and justice collide, they will, in general, have to ensure that it is justice, not the (previously interpreted) law which prevails.

Costs orders

Historically, the High Court has had a further, significant power of control over the magistrates. If (for whatever reason) the justices were in defiant mood, then the Divisional Court could award costs against them personally. Over the last 50 years or so, the High Court has periodically had to resort to robust use of this power in order to curb some of the worst excesses of the justices: most notably, immediately after the war as a result of Lord Goddard's campaign on magisterial caprice and more recently, in relation to collective madness that afflicted the Bench over the poll tax.

---

7   See, eg, *Airey v UK* (1979) 2 EHRR 305, where the European Court of Human Rights came perilously close to suggesting that Art 14 might, in certain situations, prohibit discrimination against poor people.

Lord Goddard was clearly shocked at the relaxed approach of some Benches to the rule of law and attempted to convey his concerns by issuing practice directions[8] and by visiting and addressing local associations.[9] However, after almost 10 years of these patient attempts, exasperation eventually triumphed and he resorted to the making of costs orders using powers under the Review of Justices' Decisions Act 1872.[10] This show of force was such that no further such orders were required for almost 40 years.[11]

The extraordinary behaviour of justices during the poll tax debacle provided the occasion for the most recent use of these powers. I consider below, p 213, what this episode reveals about the extent to which justices identify with the executive arm (rather than the judicial arm) of the administration. Quite simply, however, when faced with a widespread failure by the poor to pay this tax, justices put aside the niceties of legal compliance in their determination to enforce collection. They imprisoned – without regard to the requirements of 'due process' – the mentally ill, the learning disabled, the elderly on their Zimmer frames, single mothers and, indeed, anyone who had the misfortune to come before them.[12] Faced with this astonishing disregard of basic principles of law, Collins J revived the use of the costs order, in *R v Doncaster Justices ex p Jack and Others*[13] It has been observed that: 'By occasionally imposing costs, the Divisional Court has achieved a dramatic reduction in the numbers of people committed to prison for failure to pay debts. The numbers committed have fallen from over 22,000 in 1994 to just over 6,000 last year.'[14]

In spite of substantial opposition and compelling argument to the contrary, the power to make such costs awards was repealed by s 98 of the inappropriately named Access to Justice Act 1999. Not surprisingly, local authorities (as tax collectors), have welcomed this repeal and have indicated that they will be encouraging Benches to return to their previously 'more robust decision making'[15] which Alan Murdie not unreasonably suggests is 'a euphemism for sending more impoverished people to prison'.[16] In his view:

---

8   *Practice Direction* [1953] 1 WLR 1416; *R v Camborne Justices ex p Pearce* [1954] 118 JP 488.

9   See his own comments in *R v Llanidloes Licensing Justices ex p Davies* [1957] 1 All ER 125.

10 See, eg, *Avery v Avery* (1954) *Times*, 27 July; *R v Highgate Justices ex p Petrou* [1954] 118 JP 151; *R v Llanidloes Licensing Justices ex p Davies* [1957] 1 All ER 125.

11 See *R v Newcastle-under-Lyme Justices ex p Massey* [1995] 1 All ER 125 and *R v Lincoln Justices ex p Count* (1995) *The Independent*, 31 July; (1995) ILR, 2 August.

12 See Verkaik, 1999.

13 [1999] RVR 308; (1999) *Times*, 26 May.

14 Murdie, 1999.

15 Russell, 1999, cited by *ibid*, Murdie.

16 *Ibid*, Murdie.

... giving justices and their clerks immunity from costs will effectively mean
that they are able to breach the law without fear of any personal consequences,
leading to more cases of wrongful imprisonment, and at a time when
magistrates are being granted even wider jurisdiction.

The decline of the Higher Court's supervisory powers in relation to the
justices is, as this commentator observes, mirrored by a corresponding
increase in the summary courts' jurisdiction. This dramatic shift of power calls
for a fundamental re-examination not only of the appointments procedure for
justices, but also of the qualities that are required of them.

In contrast, however, it appears possible that the High Court will become
increasingly marginalised in relation to 'day to day' justice. In turn, this
enhanced constitutional and high jurisprudential role will require of its judges
even greater displays of intellectual agility. Given these dynamics, Voltaire
(and his disciples in today's establishment) could advance a respectable
argument to the effect that our current senior judicial appointments system is
the best of all possible systems, in the best of all possible worlds.[17] Faced with
the unfathomable complexity of western society and the immense
sophistication of our constitutional, legal and commercial systems, it is at least
arguable that we need to retain a few select cloistered judges who (like
Hesse's glass bead game players) are so implausibly clever that they can
conceptualise the enormity of the system and yet, at the same time, are willing
to master its voluminous and frankly tedious rules. 'Those capable of
performing such a task belong to an exclusive club indeed.'[18]

Whether or not this is a respectable argument is, of course, the stuff of
many a moot. It is, however, a distraction for the vast bulk of 'customers' and
victims of the 'legal justice' system. This chapter, therefore, looks at the
judicial appointments process through the other end of the telescope, focusing
on the magistrates. It seeks to emphasise how important their role is in our
'justice' system and how dramatic is the need for reform.

The magistrates and their courts

We think in terms of apparatus when we, as lawyers, consider the 'law' and
the 'legal profession'. We do not think about its objects; our thought processes
are captivated by the grammar of subjects; of the Royal Courts of Justice, of
wigs and of those heavy serried legal volumes, measured out in yards, that
form the obligatory backdrop for every lawyer ever interviewed.

For the vast majority of its objects, however, the law and the legal
profession means either the magistrates' court or the bailiff's visit (of which

---

17 Without, of course, condoning the appalling social discrimination which so
    dramatically restricts the pool of potential candidates for these rarefied positions.
18 Hayes, 1997.

there are over two million each year). Go into any magistrates' or county court and you will see British justice at work. In the county court, you will see the bourgeoisie (by and large) enforcing payment against people to whom they should, by and large, never have been allowed to extend credit. In the magistrates' courts, you will see the justices, by and large decent, well meaning people administering a system that punishes people who, by and large, need help; poor people being fined by people who have no comprehension (or, at best, no recent memory) of the reality of poverty; of what it is like to exist on welfare benefits in a world of credit, of high rents, water rates, council taxes and the constant flaunting of consumer goods.

And it has ever been thus. The poor and the powerless have generally railed against the iniquitous behaviour of magistrates rather than the higher courts; from Winstanley and the Tolpuddle martyrs to the miners in the 1984 strike and the recent poll tax defaulters, it has been the justices who, when confronted by the objects of injustice, have meted out yet further injustice. The senior judges in their elevated courts may have condoned or even encouraged some of this action, but they have generally been far away.

What is apparent from any account of the struggles between the Diggers and the St George's Hill justices, the members of the Friendly Society and Mr Woolaston, the Tolpuddle magistrate, and today's accounts of these self-same courts, is their inability (and sometimes indifference) to see the injustice that confronts the defendants in their daily lives and their lack of life experience of what it is like to be socially excluded by poverty.

The issue, therefore, of primary importance in any analysis of the magistrates' court is that of poverty. Whilst the new 'social exclusion agenda' is prepared to admit the crucial role of poverty in other areas, it is still a taboo subject in relation to the activities of the magistrates' court. This is despite, for instance, 'Our Healthier Nation'[19] acknowledging not only that poverty is the major cause of ill health in the UK, but also that action to reverse this must concentrate attention on such areas as 'crime and disorder'. Regrettably, however, there is an almost total refusal by the executive to view the criminal justice system from this perspective.

Whilst the fundamental role of poverty in the magistrates' court is obvious to all who appear there, the simple truth is that policy is formulated by people who do not appear there. Senior judges and silks did not achieve their elevated status by tarrying in the magistrates', no more than did Home Secretaries or learned professors. In this context, Penny Darbyshire[20] has referred to the cursory (and at times ill informed)[21] coverage of the magistracy

---

19 Cm 3852, 1998, Department of Health.

20 Darbyshire, 1997b, p 861.

21 *Ibid*, p 873.

by: senior barristers (including Gifford, Mansfield and Robertson); academics (from Smith and Hogan to Zander);[22] the Home Affairs Committee;[23] the 1993 Royal Commission on Criminal Justice, as well as the Home Office and, indeed, both 'old and new Labour'.[24] Sadly, even JAG Griffith in *The Politics of the Judiciary* omits any critical analysis of the role of the magistracy.[25] And this failure to acknowledge and to bear witness to the injustice of a system which is responsible for all but about 3% of criminal cases, is perhaps the most eloquent expression of the two nations that continue to inhabit this island, and that, for one, poverty has become invisible.

It is not only the executive and judiciary that have failed to acknowledge poverty as the key determinant in our criminal justice system; there has also been a dearth of academic commentary on this issue. Nevertheless, the general principle has been emphasised in many analogous areas, particularly in relation to health policy, perhaps most ably by Gro Harlem Bruntland, who expressed the proposition with consummate simplicity: the 'challenge for us all is to look at the world through the eyes – and the spirit – of poor people'.[26]

THE GROWTH OF THE MAGISTRATES' JURISDICTION

The current and heated debate over the government's proposals to restrict further the right of defendants to seek trial by jury is but the latest chapter in a very long story. Sir William Holdsworth[27] refers to criticism[28] made in the reign of Elizabeth I by Lambard of Husey J (who was Chief Justice of the King's Bench in 1485) that he:

> ... did thinke that it was enough to loade all the justices of the peace of those days with the execution onely of the statutes of Winchester and Westminster for robberies and felonies; the statutes of forcible entries; the statutes of labourers, vagabonds, livery, maintenance, embracery and sheriffs ... How many justices thinke you now may suffice (without breaking their backs) to beare so many, not loads but stacks of statutes that have since that time been laid upon them.

Sir William Blackstone warned against the displacement of jury trial by 'new and arbitrary methods of trial which, under a variety of plausible pretences,

---

22 Darbyshire, 1997a, p 636.
23 *Ibid*, p 873, referring to the House of Commons Home Affairs Committee: Third Report 1995–1996 Vol 2, p 240, para 184.
24 *Ibid*.
25 5th edn, 1997.
26 Reith Lecture 2000; first broadcast on 3 May 2000.
27 Holdsworth, W, *The History of English Law*, Vol 1, p 288.
28 Made by Lambard in his *Treatise on the Justices of the Peace in Elizabeth I's Reign*.

may in time imperceptibly undermine this best preservative of English liberty'[29] and, in particular, against entrusting the jury's function to magistrates where 'partiality and injustice have an ample field to range in'.

Inexorably, however, the jury's influence has declined, albeit that on each occasion 'a variety of plausible' reasons have been advanced. The current proposals to erode its jurisdiction further have been justified on administrative grounds, rather than issues of legitimacy: essentially advocating the executivisation of the judicial process.[30] This approach suggests that the government has either not considered (or otherwise has an extremely relaxed approach to) the question of a 'separation of powers' in this arena; the implications of which are analysed below.

In practice, however, the crucial loss to the legitimacy of the criminal justice system, consequent upon the decline in jury trial, is the loss of any involvement in the judging process by poor people. In the alphabet of social class, judges and magistrates are overwhelmingly to be found in the As and Bs, whereas the defendants and the victims of crime are squeezed into the Ds and Es. In such a system, juries have been the crucial legitimisers.

THE MAGISTRATES: APPOINTMENT AND JURISDICTION

In 1997, Penny Darbyshire reviewed the available evidence on the extent of the magistrates' criminal jurisdiction. On the basis of reported decisions alone, she concluded that magistrates dealt with over 95% of all criminal business and that 'the true figure may be several percentage points higher'.[31] Extrapolating from the *Criminal Statistics* and *Judicial Statistics*,[32] she estimated that, in 1995, the magistrates' courts dealt with almost two million defendants, as opposed to about 89,000 in the Crown Court. In her view, less than 1% of defendants to criminal charges now have their guilt or innocence determined by a jury.[33]

Magistrates are the antithesis of the jury system. They are not chosen, but either nominate themselves or acquiesce in that nomination. They are not guided by a lawyer selected for his or her excellence, but by a clerk who will frequently be neither a barrister or solicitor. Justices of the Peace (JPs) are not representative of the majority who appear before them, indeed, from the dawning of the system they have been selected on social class, 'knights,

29 *Commentaries on the Laws of England*, 1st edn, 1769, Bk III, pp 380–81.
30 An executivisation that is also occurring in the civil arena, with the recent wholesale reform of civil procedures and child support payments as well as the imposition of ADR in family as well as commercial disputes.
31 Darbyshire, 1997a.
32 Cm 3421, 1996 and Cm 3290, 1996.
33 *Ibid*, Darbyshire, p 629.

esquires and gentlemen of the land' and (until 1906) subject to a minimum property ownership qualification.[34]

As with judges, the process by which they are appointed is secretive and the necessary qualities obscure. Dignan and Wynne[35] quote from 1988 guidance issued by the Lord Chancellor which refers to the need for 'integrity, good character and repute' as well as 'the ability to command the confidence of both public and colleagues, the capacity or potential to act judicially, and ... set aside personal prejudices ... and to think clearly and logically'. Candidates should appreciate the need for humanity, sensitivity and the rule of law. It is also desirable if they have some experience and understanding or knowledge of life outside the immediate circle of family and work.

There is little or no published material on how the selection process is actually conducted, and which of these 'wish list' qualities are, in practice, of greatest importance. It is, however, safe to assume that the foremost criterion is a willingness to stand and that a *sine qua non* is a firm belief in the basic fairness and decency of the present order. In contrast, the jury system panders to neither of these two traits. Unlike JPs, they contain the 'reluctant to judge' and contain poor people, unemployed people living on social security benefits, people who are daily upset by the *status quo* and who bear it no great affection or respect. People who are not overly sympathetic or protective when it claims to have been disturbed, particularly when the culprit, like them, shares a legitimate grievance of being socially excluded. As Stephen Wexler has put it, '[p]oor people do not lead settled lives into which the law seldom intrudes; they are constantly involved with the law in its most intrusive forms' and that '[p]overty creates an abrasive interface with society; poor people are always bumping into sharp legal things'.[36]

In 1997, Dignan and Wynne published their review of the recent studies on the composition of magistrates, together with the results of their own research into this issue.[37] The studies continued to portray the lay magistracy as a 'social elite that is still predominantly recruited from a narrow and privileged segment of the community[38] and that, in some areas, the Bench comprises a 'local self-selecting elite that is highly unrepresentative of the community from which it was drawn'.[39]

---

34 Holdsworth, *The History of English Law*, Vol 1, p 289.

35 Dignan and Wynne, 1997, p 185.

36 'Practising law for poor people' (1970) 79 Yale LJ 1049.

37 *Ibid*, Dignan and Wynne, pp 184–97.

38 Burney, 1979; Raine, 1989; and Baldwin, 1976, pp 171–74, cited in *ibid*, p 185.

39 *Ibid*, Dignan and Wynne, p 189, where they refer to research which had found that 59% of the Rochdale Bench were either Freemasons or members of the Rotary Club/Inner Wheel; Bartless and Walker, 1973, p 139.

Dignan and Wynne noted that very little attempt was made in official accounts of the magistracy to defend their selection and appointment on the basis of personal merit, but, instead, they were likely to portray 'lay magistrates either as representatives of the local community or even as being representative of the local community, at least in terms of its social composition'.[40] They accordingly sought to investigate the validity of this portrayal by undertaking a systematic analysis of the composition of a local Bench (selected on the ground that its catchment area was reasonably diverse in terms of its social profile, unemployment rate and types of economic activity).

Their study confirmed:

> ... other recent accounts of the magistracy in refuting claims that it represents a 'microcosm' of society, whether in terms of its social composition, political allegiances or social affiliations. Not only [was the] Bench far from representative of the local community from which it is drawn, the evidence ... suggests that large sectors of the population have no 'representation' whatever in the local Bench, while other localities are decidedly 'over-represented'. Although not as elitist as it once was, the uneven distribution of [the Bench], together with the findings on residential property values, confirm how far there still is to go in order to dispel once and for all the enduring image of a self-perpetuating social clique.[41]

In their conclusions, they focused on the key issue of the 'kind of local justice' that communities should be entitled to expect and analysed the argument that lay justices act as a 'judicial safeguard' by replicating the juries that they have come to displace. They concluded:

> Here, it would be the fact that magistrates are not professionally trained as lawyers, but are ordinary people coming from all walks of life that would be important, since they ought then to be better able to understand and show sensitivity towards the defendant's situation. In terms of recruitment and selection policy, this rationale would arguably require a much greater commitment to the goal of 'democratising' the Bench, to ensure that it is at least reasonably representative of the community from which it is drawn. However, it would still need to be acknowledged that, however closely Benches might reflect the composition of the local community, they would almost certainly be far from representative of the great majority of defendants appearing before them, and might still therefore be expected to lack legitimacy in their eyes.[42]

A strikingly similar, and no less authoritative, criticism of the magisterial appointments system has been voiced by Penny Darbyshire.[43] She also reviewed the research concerning the appointments process for justices, citing

---

40 Dignan and Wynne, 1997, p 185.
41 *Ibid*, Dignan and Wynne, p 195.
42 *Ibid*, Dignan and Wynne, p 196.
43 Darbyshire, 1997b.

with approval the complaint of the Magistrates' Association itself[44] that the process was 'shrouded in mystery' and was objectively a 'self-perpetuating oligarchy.[45] She singled out for particular criticism the lack of young people and people from ethnic minorities on the Bench. In relation to the former, she commented:[46]

> I invite any reader to walk into any lay magistrates' courtroom. They are virtually certain to find that the oldest group are on the Bench, possibly a generation older than the court clerk and those appearing before them.

She added that she knew of: 'no research which equates age with wisdom in the context of law-finding, judging character, understanding pre-sentence reports and sentencing.'

As to the issue of the racial imbalance, she suggested that attempts to appoint people from ethnic minorities are inadequate. She stressed the importance of redressing the imbalance, not merely because people from ethnic minorities are over-represented among defendants, but also amongst the victims of crime.[47]

Poor people, young people[48] and people who belong to a racial minority are, disproportionately, the victims of crime and often live in communities which consider themselves ill served by the law enforcement agencies. For example, in 1998–99, burglary rates in deprived areas were three times the national average, and 10 times the rate in the lowest-crime areas,[49] and the level of vandalism in such areas was also almost three times the national average.[50] Many live in poorly designed housing, on poorly lit, isolated and dangerous estates and have limited resources to take appropriate anti-theft/burglary precautions. Disadvantaged people are also likely to have less confidence in the police and are less likely to report crime.

This preponderance of crime is not restricted to property crime or neighbourhood intimidation, but also includes sexual and other violent assaults. The record of the police and the justices in dealing with such crime has, on occasions, defied belief. In relation to offences of the utmost gravity, such as rape, for instance, McConville[51] has shown how taped interviews have been rehearsed by police and detainees in order to avoid a charge having

---

44 House of Commons Home Affairs Committee, *Third Report 1995–96*, Vol 2, p 240, para 2.4.3.
45 Darbyshire, 1997b, p 866.
46 *Ibid*, p 865.
47 Fitzgerald and Hale, 1996, cited in *ibid*, Darbyshire.
48 See, eg, Harless *et al*, 1995.
49 Home Office, 2000.
50 Cabinet Office, 2000.
51 [1992] Crim LR 532, p 540, noting that 'just as bail was important to [the defendant], so the alleged rape/assault was unimportant to the police'.

to be made. Penny Darbyshire expresses similar concern about the way justices deal with serious offences and refers to an 'astonishing but not isolated example', namely:[52]

> The 1972 attack of Fred and Rosemary West on Caroline Owens, adduced as similar fact evidence in Rosemary West's 1995 trial. They abducted her, knocked her unconscious, then imprisoned her in 25 Cromwell Street, where she was raped, bound and gagged and sexually assaulted ... For this extravaganza of sexual torture, Rosemary and Fred pleaded guilty to assault occasioning actual bodily harm and indecent assault and were fined £25 on each charge by the Gloucester City magistrates, who were aware of all these admitted allegations except the rape, because that charge was dropped.[53]

The failure of the magistrates to reflect the concerns of poor people and to promote their interests should be at the top of any reform agenda: particularly of a government that has given such prominence to the issue of social exclusion. In stark contrast, however, this issue appears to have been overlooked or ignored and the proposals for magisterial reform have concentrated upon the issue of their perceived administrative inefficiency.

THE SEPARATION OF POWERS

The fallout from the widespread non-payment of the poll tax in 1990–91 is highly revealing of the way that justices and their clerks perceive their role. Whilst the High Court stood back and analysed the legality of local authority action, the magistrates' courts, by and large, identified themselves with the administration; with the system being attacked by the 'wilful refusers to pay'. For magistrates have never lost their perception of being the local authority; they issue liquor licences, hear all manner of local authority administrative appeals (from taxi to caravan site licences) and enforce local taxes. Just as their clerk was until recently also clerk to the council, so, too, within their collective unconsciousness, is the knowledge that, in former times, JPs were the local government.

The atmosphere within the magistrates' courts during the poll tax enforcement hearings was, at times, Soviet; the naked determination of the justices and their clerks to enforce the charge was, on occasions, intimidating. They stood shoulder to shoulder with the local authority, appearing to believe that they faced the dark power of anarchy – that the system itself was under threat. In reality, what was under threat was an absurd and unfair tax on the poor; however, when it came to the crunch, time and time again, the justices sided with the administration against the poor – whereas the senior judiciary,

---

52 See, eg, Gregory and Lees, 1996; and Rumgay, 1995.
53 Darbyshire, 1997a, pp 630–31.

at least, sided with the rule of law. The justices identified the status quo with the government: the judges identified the status quo with the rule of law. When the higher courts observed the magistrates (not the defaulters) upsetting the rule of law, they sought to re-assert this order by punishing the justices – wilful refusers to follow the law – by costs orders.

Whilst Montesquieu might be perturbed by the extent to which the magistrates discharge (or seek to discharge) both executive and judicial functions, what is of more interest is the extent to which this calls into question their independence for the purposes of the European Convention on Human Rights.

Historically, JPs were not 'independent' within the meaning of Art 6(1), in that they were the local authority. Even today, as noted above, they continue to discharge many of these functions, and indeed, many magistrates are also, quite anomalously, councillors, holding political office in the same locality as they sit in judgment.

Their independence from the police is also problematical. Here again there is (in part) an historical explanation, in that it was only 50 years ago that they dropped their official title of 'Police Court'. However, magistrates' continued membership of police authorities[54] means that they are, in effect, in an employer/employee relationship with the police. Objectively, this must compromise their ability to claim to be independent when a conflict of evidence between a defendant and the police is in issue. Magistrates must inevitably, in their capacity as members of the police authority, be caught up by the unceasing rhetoric and pressure from the executive on increasing detection, arrest and conviction rates. In consequence, it is questionable whether they can fulfil both functions and 'preserve their independence'.[55] This problem is exacerbated by the research evidence, which consistently reveals the justices' propensity to believe the investigating authorities (evidenced by their frequent utterances to this effect and their higher conviction rates).[56]

This identification with the administration embraces its officials as well as its structures. Charitably, one could characterise their approach as 'the police and other public officials must be believed in order to uphold confidence in the public administration'. More realistically, however, this tendency to believe such people is no more than a predisposition to give the benefit of the doubt to like-minded people (and people of a similar class). The advocate's perception that magistrates tend to doubt the integrity of poor and unemployed people would, of course, follow on from this reasoning.

---

54 Police and Magistrates' Courts Act 1994.
55 Faulkner, 1994.
56 See, eg, Vennard, *Contested Cases in Magistrates' Courts,* 1982.

For a Bench to find against a public official could undermine public confidence in the institution in which he or she serves: a qualm not generally shared by juries whose members may have good cause to question the integrity of some of these officers and institutions.

This class/office bias of the justices is a reality: it is the overwhelming view not only of defendants,[57] but also of the legal profession who regularly appear in such courts. In my experience as a solicitor, it was most clearly articulated by a chairman who told my client that the Bench had decided to take an exceptional step; something it had not done before and that he could not expect to be repeated: the exceptional step being that it had decided to give him the benefit of the doubt. Similar accounts abound. Penny Darbyshire, for instance, voices her surprise[58] at the number of magistrates who expressed their support for the chairperson's comments in *R v Bingham Justices ex p Jowitt* (1974),[59] namely that, where there was a direct conflict between a police officer and a member of the public: 'My principle in such cases has always been to believe the evidence of the police officer.'

The oligarchic nature of the appointments system for justices also calls into question their independence for the purposes of Art 6(1). There are no clear rules as to who can be elected and, by giving the justices responsibility for their own appointments, the system is geared towards the creation of cliques, secret clubs and unrepresentative groupings. In commenting upon this crucial failure to ensure adequate 'constitutional checks and balances', it has been observed that magistrates 'have no more business than circuit judges to be appointing and selecting their colleagues'.[60]

The role and qualifications of justices' clerks also calls into question the courts' independence. As Penny Darbyshire observes,[61] '[t]he other great secret of the magistracy is that lay benches are frequently dependent on court clerks who are not lawyers' and that 'clerking the court is normally left to one of 240 deputies or 1,550 court clerks of which "about 600 court clerks and 40 deputies are not legally qualified as barristers or solicitors"'.[62] These officials are either law graduates or holders of a diploma in magisterial law or have no qualification apart from being clerks for five years prior to 1980.

Clerks hold great power and, on occasion, act in a judicial capacity; it is, for instance, they who have authority to decide whether to hold certain hearings *ex parte* notwithstanding that an *inter partes* hearing is at the heart of

---

57 See, eg, Bottoms and McClean, 1976, p 89; and *The Distribution of Criminal Business between the Crown Court and Magistrates' Courts*, Cmnd 6323, para 36, cited in Darbyshire, 1997b, p 862.

58 *Ibid*, Darbyshire, p 869.

59 (1974) *The Times*, 3 July.

60 *Ibid*, Darbyshire, p 867.

61 *Ibid*, p 872.

62 Darbyshire, 1999.

the Art 6(1) right to a 'fair' hearing.[63] Their role as collection and enforcement officers for fines (and the way they have set about discharging these duties) has attracted considerable criticism[64] and, although some aspects of fine collection have now been transferred to justices' chief executives,[65] it is by no means certain that this transfer sufficiently separates the justices from this function to remove the question it raises concerning their independence.

The powers of clerks have recently been radically extended[66] and clerks are now being openly canvassed as potential replacements for justices. It has, for instance, been suggested that Auld LJ's inquiry into the criminal justice system will recommend that they have 'a more powerful role – akin to a judge' and that 'the magistrates may act like "mini-juries", guided by the clerk, whose advice could be binding'.[67] These are the self-same clerks who so ruthlessly pursued fines and who signally failed to restrain the justices when venting their fury on the poll tax defaulters.

THE 'EXECUTIVISATION' OF SUMMARY JUSTICE

The failure by magistrates to see themselves as part of the judiciary and not as an administrative arm of local government (the fine enforcement and council tax collection department) is a failure repeated by others, most notably the Home Office.

In articulating the need for reform in this area, the government speaks the same language as it uses in relation to local government reform – of best value, of cost per transaction and of efficiency savings. This 'increasing exposure of judicial administration to the budgetary and other disciplines of the 'new public management' raises concerns about the relationship between the executive and the judiciary being compromised.[68] Justice is but another commodity to be processed like passports or PAYE; and it is in this sterile area that the debate is conducted. Indeed, even legal aid is considered in this light. In order to process two million cases per annum, it is essential that the defendants' cases are marshalled and presented as briefly and as uniformly as

---

63 See, eg, Family Proceedings Court (Children Act 1989) Rules 1991, r 4 and Clements, 1999, where the clerk's exercise of this power is questioned from the perspective of Art 6(1).

64 See, eg, *R v Lincoln Justices ex p Count* (1995) *The Independent*, 31 July; (1995) ILR, 2 August, where Sedley J (as he then was), when making a costs order against the justices, described the clerks actions as 'incomprehensible'; and see, also, Darbyshire, 1999.

65 Access to Justice Act 1999, ss 90–91.

66 Crime and Disorder Act 1998, ss 49 and 50, and see *ibid*, Darbyshire, for a critique of these provisions.

67 Gibb, 2000, and see, also, Home Office, 1997, where a similar proposal was advanced.

68 Comment [1998] PL 1, pp 1–7.

possible. Without legal aid, the system would grind to a halt; legal aid oils the wheels, it is an administrative necessity,[69] not an Art 6(3) human right.

So far as I am aware, at no time has magisterial reform been approached from the perspective of prioritising the involvement and representation of poor people; the debate is dominated by accountants. Jury trials must be limited because they are (allegedly) expensive, and lay justices should be displaced by (allegedly) more efficient stipendiary magistrates. It depends upon what is being contrasted, 'a jury trial costs £13,500 compared to £2,500 for a case before the magistrates';[70] or jury trials are '10 times more expensive than those in the magistrates' court'[71] and the custodial sentences imposed by magistrates' courts 'cost on average 20 times more than non-custodial ones'.[72] That is the sum total of the contest between the pot and the kettle; between the unrepresentative, inefficient, unpaid, lay magistrate and the unrepresentative, efficient, case-hardened and well paid 'stipe'. Stipendiaries are good because they 'can get through the work of three Benches'[73] and so 'unfortunately justice can no longer afford amateurs, however gifted some may be'[74] and, in similar vein, lay magistrates should be replaced by stipendiaries, since magistrates are 'an unaccountable elite, enjoying lifestyles that inevitably leave them out of touch with those they are dealing with'.[75] On the other hand, the 30,000 magistrates are 'a democratic jewel beyond price',[76] who continue the 'strong tradition of involving ordinary people in the administration of justice',[77] and as for clerks and stipendiaries, they are 'people who have gone from school to law school, to pupillage or articles, to criminal law practice. In many ways, their natural growth has been – in the nicest possible way – stunted' and that 'justice is too important to be left to lawyers'.[78]

What none of these actors can do – be they lay justice, clerk or stipendiary – is argue from the perspective of the socially excluded, although this does not stop magistrates, in particular, from expressing an opinion on the subject. The journal *Justice of the Peace* in its editorials tells us that 'they' (which presumably encompasses poor people) are only interested in receiving a fair trial and that 'they rarely, if ever, give a thought to the political constitution of the Bench'[79]

---

69 See Editorial Comment (1992) *Legal Action* August, p 3.
70 Jacobs, 1999.
71 Verkaik, R, 'Jury trials' (1999) *The Independent*, 16 November.
72 *Ibid.*
73 Editorial, 'Gifted amateurs' (1991) 141 NLJ 6497.
74 *Ibid.*
75 McFarlane, 1999, p 5.
76 Mawdsley, 2000.
77 Editorial Comment (1991) 163(46) JP 901, pp 901–02.
78 Block, 1998, p 886.
79 Editorial Comment (1991) 163(46) JP 901, pp 901–02.

and 'they are far more interested in the quality and fairness of the proceedings' than the social or economic status of the Bench.[80]

Poor people deserve better, and better should have been expected of a government committed to challenging social exclusion and tackling 'the causes of crime'. Fines blight the lives of spouses and children and bring with them the terror of bailiff visits traumatising households, particularly young children. Fines lead to committal proceedings and, as has been observed:

> committal to prison works – in the sense that it extracts money – but all too often it is from someone other than the actual debtor. Typically it may be from a friend of a relative ... but in all too many cases there is no one available to 'buy out' the defendant, particularly in cases of single parents, the elderly and the mentally ill.[81]

To suggest to magistrates that they not use fines, or committal against poor people who fail to pay fines, would be met by disbelief. One might as well have suggested to a Victorian that a debt enforcement system could function without imprisonment for defaulters, or to the NYPD that law and order could be maintained by an unarmed police force.

If magistrates were truly independent and steeled with that conviction by significant representation of poor people, they could decline to use fines in such cases. Indeed, far from undermining the fabric of our society, such a course could save the Treasury vast sums. The poll tax, for instance, would never have been born if the government had been obliged to rely upon juries to enforce its payment, and the waste of several billions of pounds would have been avoided.

If the magistrates adopted such a course, the executive would have to re-order our divided society to address these issues. Justices could use their 'independence' to challenge the executive's crass policies. Just as civil society reorganised itself when imprisonment for debt was abolished (by restricting credit), so too could it in relation to fines and some of the more absurd administrative crimes. Television licence enforcement is a prime example. The consequent fines constitute one of the most significant causes of female imprisonment – as if the whole edifice of the UK's order would come tumbling down if the BBC, with its generally dreadful programmes, were forced to collect its revenue some other way. In similar vein, one can point to businesses' over-reliance on criminal enforcement (particularly when lax trade practices are involved), for instance, the absurd ease of cheque card fraud, shoplifting in supermarkets or car theft. In each case a commercial decision has been taken, that it is cheaper to tolerate the fraud than introduce relatively simple anti-abuse measures; in essence, an economic choice to accept a level of pilferage rather than invest in equipment or staff. A person who chose to leave

---

80 Notes for the Week (1998) 162(45) JP 873, pp 873–74.
81 Murdie, 1999.

his wallet on the gate or used blank cheques as calling cards might receive little sympathy from a court; but the magistrates still hand down severe punishments for cheque card fraud, shoplifting and car theft; as if supermarket warehouses, plastic money and insecurely designed cars were fundamental to our civil society.

It may be that the jury's importance has been over-stressed in terms of the business it transacts. Nevertheless, its symbolic role still dominates; most people believe that juries are fair and most defendants would prefer to be tried by them;[82] juries are the embodiment of one of our earliest and most fundamental constitutional rights – the right to be tried by one's peers.[83]

If the time has come when we must acknowledge the reality: that their involvement in our criminal justice system has declined to less than 1% of all cases, then this acknowledgment should be accompanied by a determination to reform the system so that it delivers justice for the 99%. This requires radical reform, but not of the 'fast track, number crunching, administrative' kind. What it requires is that, having transferred the jury's functions to the magistrates' court, we must now take steps also to transfer the jury's legitimacy; its representative functions. We must create a system whereby all people who appear before the summary courts are judged and sentenced by their peers. Whatever they may claim to be, whatever their respective merits, lay magistrates, justices clerks and stipendiaries cannot claim to be the peers of the vast majority of people who daily gaze upon them, either as defendants from the dock or as victims in the witness box or gallery.

---

82 See Bottoms and McClean, 1976, p 89.
83 Magna Carta, para 3.

CHAPTER 10

PROMOTING DIVERSITY IN THE JUDICIARY– REFORMING THE JUDICIAL APPOINTMENTS PROCESS

Kate Malleson

Thirty years ago, the judiciary in England and Wales was largely an anonymous body made up almost exclusively of elderly white men who were appointed solely on their intellectual and legal skills and their ability to stay out of politics and avoid any taint of scandal. The idea that their values and beliefs had relevance to their decision making, or that they ought to be demographically reflective of society, was heretical to all but a few academics.[1] The growth of judicial review, European Community law and, more recently, devolution and the Human Rights Act 1998 have brought about a attitudinal shift in the way we view the judiciary.[2] The argument that judging, particularly in the higher courts, is a non-political activity is now acknowledged by commentators, lawyers and the judges themselves as a fairy tale. As a result, questions of judicial accountability and representativeness are now on the political agenda. Some of the issues raised, such as how to strike the right balance between accountability and judicial independence, are complex and problematic; they give rise to a range of legitimately held differences of opinion. One area, however, in which there is a clear consensus, is the desirability of greater diversity in the composition of the judiciary. This is supported for a variety of reasons: to increase public confidence in the judiciary; to improve the sensitivity of judicial decision making; to enhance the democratic legitimacy of the judges; or for simple reasons of equity. Whatever the rationale for promoting this change, there are few who would claim that the question of who are the judges is an irrelevant one. Nor are these trends unique to England and Wales. They are mirrored in many other countries, most particularly, but not exclusively, in common law jurisdictions. The awareness that increasing judicial power is held in the hands of strikingly homogeneous elites has attracted growing and widespread public comment and criticism.

Against the background of these changes, this chapter considers the prospects for reform of the judicial appointments process in England and Wales. It draws on recent empirical research on the appointments processes for silk (Queen's Counsel) and judicial office. Based on questionnaires and

---

1 *The Politics of the Judiciary*, by John Griffith, was considered highly controversial when first published in 1977 for arguing that there was a link between the background of the judges and their decision making. See, also, Paterson, 1974, pp 118–35.

2 See Malleson, 1999; and Clements, Chapter 9, in this book.

interviews with senior lawyers, the findings identify factors which hinder or encourage applications from women and minority lawyers and highlight a range of reforms which might be implemented in order to increase the number of applicants from under-represented groups appointed to the Bench.[3]

POLITICAL AND STATISTICAL BACKGROUND

Throughout the 1990s, the number of women judges increased significantly, from 128 to 328. However, as a proportion of the judiciary, they remained low. In January 2000, 11% of judges were women, compared with 6% in 1992. Monitoring the equivalent figures for minority lawyers is hampered by the fact that statistics on the ethnic background of judges were only fully recorded for the first time in 1998, when the proportion stood at 1.7%. At the end of the decade, therefore, both women and minority lawyers remained significantly under-represented in the judiciary. In the light of the continuing slow pace of change, the debate on the composition of the judiciary intensified during the 1990s. In particular, there was concern about the continuing homogeneity in the make-up of the judges in the higher courts. Until 1999, Dame Butler Sloss remained the only woman in the Court of Appeal, having been appointed in 1989, and by 2000, no woman had yet been appointed a Law Lord. Minority judges were similarly absent in the higher ranks, with none having been appointed above the Circuit Bench.[4]

During a decade in which many other public and political institutions demonstrate significant increases in the proportion of their women and ethnic minority members, these figures have attracted increasing public attention as a result of which the judicial appointments process has been the subject of a number of official and unofficial inquiries and reports. In 1992, a committee of the legal reform group, JUSTICE, chaired by Professor Robert Stevens, scrutinised the judiciary, proposing the establishment of a judicial appointments commission and recommending the introduction of positive action to widen opportunities for the appointment of qualified women and minority lawyers.[5] In 1996, the Home Affairs Select Committee reviewed judicial appointments, hearing evidence from solicitors, women lawyers groups and minority lawyers groups who highlighted the presence of barriers

---

3   The findings are drawn from data from 136 questionnaires and 50 in-depth interviews with solicitors and barristers of between 15 and 22 years' call/qualification. The sample was drawn randomly, but designed to include lawyers from a range of backgrounds and practices. The respondents were asked about their experiences and opinions of the current system and their proposals for reform.

4   Lord Chancellor's Department, 1999, p 74.

5   JUSTICE, 1999.

to appointment in both the legal profession and the judicial appointments process.

In 1999, in response to this growing criticism of the silk and judicial appointments processes, the Lord Chancellor appointed Sir Leonard Peach to conduct an inquiry into the way in which the systems operate. Although the overall remit of the inquiry was criticised as being too narrow, since it specifically excluded from his review the question of who makes appointments, his report was detailed and far reaching. In general, it praised the professionalism, competence and thoroughness of the procedures, though it acknowledged that there was a polarisation of opinions about the consultations process which lies at the heart of the system.[6] The inquiry's terms of reference specifically included a review of 'the existence of safeguards in the procedures against discrimination on the grounds of race or gender' and the report proposed a number of changes specifically designed to encourage the appointment of more women and minority lawyers. Although the individual proposals themselves were well received, the report generally was dismissed as 'too little, too late' by critics of the system.[7] More radical proposals for change, which included abandoning the consultations process, were included in a report produced by a joint working party of the Law Society, the Bar Council and women and minority lawyers groups.[8] The publication of this report was preceded by the withdrawal of the Law Society from the consultation process. The decision that senior solicitors would no longer co-operate in the 'soundings' system by providing opinions on applicants was taken on the grounds that the system indirectly discriminated against solicitor applicants. Finally, in 1999, the Home Affairs Select Committee again looked into the question of the judicial appointments process and the composition of the judiciary in its review of the work of the Lord Chancellor's department and questioned the Lord Chancellor about the slow pace of change.[9]

Throughout these inquiries and reports, a recurring and key criticism concerned the difficulties faced by lawyers from non-traditional backgrounds in building up the type of practice and reputation necessary to take silk or be appointed to the Bench. The response of both Lord Mackay and Lord Irvine to this problem was threefold. First, they rejected any suggestion that there was direct discrimination within the appointments systems, stressing that all appointments are made on merit, regardless of gender, ethnic origin, marital status, political affiliation, religion or disability. To this list, Lord Irvine added sexual orientation in 1999 after giving a public commitment that gay

---

6   Peach, 1999, p 3.

7   'Judges' reform must go further' (1999) *The Guardian*, 3 December.

8   Joint Working Party, *Equal Opportunities in Judicial Appointments and Silk*, 2000.

9   Home Affairs Committee, Minutes of evidence, 2 November 1998, session 1998–99, paras 48–84.

applicants would receive equal treatment. Secondly, a number of changes to improve openness and objectivity were introduced by Lord Mackay and extended by Lord Irvine. These included the advertising of most posts, interviews for ranks below the High Court and the publication of selection criteria and job descriptions. The third official response was to stress that the continuing low numbers of women and minority judges was a result of the fact that the judiciary in England and Wales is appointed from amongst senior lawyers. The current judiciary could, therefore, be described as a reflection of those who entered the legal profession approximately 15–30 years ago, amongst whom women and minority ethnic groups were a small minority.

The figures for the proportion of women in the legal profession provide some support for this argument. In 1975, for example, women made up 10% of those called to the Bar, compared to 43% in 1998, with a comparable rise for women solicitors, who now form a majority of those joining the profession with 52% of new admissions being women.[10] The figures for minority lawyers are less reliable, for two reasons. First, it is relatively recently that statistics on ethnic origin have been collected by the Lord Chancellor's department and the professional bodies. The first survey of the ethnic origin of young barristers was carried out in 1989, when 12% of new pupils described themselves as being from a minority ethnic group. However, this figure should be treated with caution, and is probably an overestimate due to the fact that the completion rates of these self-report forms is generally low. Despite efforts to improve data gathering, more recent statistics are still incomplete and are not regarded by the Bar Council as reliable. Similar problems exist in relation to the figures for solicitors. Amongst those qualifying in 1999, 13% described themselves as being from a minority ethnic group. This compares with 10.1% in 1989, which is the first year that figures were collected by the Law Society. However, these figures are, likewise, considered by the Law Society to be overestimates because of low completion rates.

Despite the difficulties involved in obtaining detailed and accurate statistics, there is no doubt that the proportion of women and minority lawyers entering the legal profession has risen very considerably in the last 20 years. On the face of these figures, it is plausible to argue that it is a matter of time before women and minority lawyers 'trickle up' and are appointed QCs and judges in far greater numbers. Critics of this perspective, however, have questioned whether the process of change is a natural and automatic one and have identified barriers within the legal profession, the judiciary and the appointments process which limit the opportunity of qualified women and minority lawyers to take silk and be appointed to judicial office.[11] The starting point, therefore, for assessing the merits of these claims is to examine whether

---

10 The Law Society, 1999.
11 See, eg, JUSTICE, 1999; MacRae, 1996; McGlynn, 1988; TMS Consultants, 1992; Sommerlad and Sanderson, 1998.

or not women and minority lawyers are applying and being appointed in proportion to their numbers at the appropriate level of seniority in the legal profession.

APPLICATION RATES AND SUCCESS RATES

The average years post qualification/call of applicants for silk, assistant recorder and deputy district judge are 22, 19 and 16 respectively.[12] In 1999, the Lord Chancellor's department published the first detailed breakdown of the application and success rates of silk and judicial office.[13] Combining these figures with a breakdown of the proportion of different groups in the legal profession, there is evidence of some significant differences in the application and appointment rates of women and minority lawyers compared to white male applicants. The largest gap is found in applications for silk. In 1999, women made up 9% of applicants and 19% of the practising Bar of 22 years call. Men, in contrast, made up 91% of applicants and 81% of the practising Bar of 22 years call. These figures are significant in their own right, but also have an important knock-on effect on the judiciary, since taking silk is still, effectively, a prerequisite for higher judicial office. The under-application of women for silk can, therefore, be expected to impact on their numbers in the higher judiciary.

The gap in applications for assistant recorder is less marked. In 1999, women made up 17% of applicants and 21% of lawyers of 19 years call/qualification.[14] The figures for applicants for the post of deputy district judge show the proportion of applicants is similarly under-represented when measured against the proportion of women solicitors of 16 years post qualification (24% of applicants and 30% of lawyers), but almost equally matched when measured against the proportion of women barristers (24% of applicants and 25% of lawyers). While the application rates are generally lower, the success rates of women applicants are significantly higher than men in relation to silk and district judge, but almost the same rate in relation to assistant recorder. These figures are broadly consistent with those available for earlier years.

The figures for minority ethnic applicants suggest a difference between the application and success rates of barristers and solicitors. Minority ethnic barristers slightly over-apply in proportion to their numbers in relation to silk and assistant recorder and under-apply in relation to their numbers at the Bar

---

12 Figures provided by the Lord Chancellor's Department.
13 Lord Chancellor's Department, 1999.
14 Women make up 22% of barristers of 19 years' call and 21% of solicitors of 19 years' post-qualification.

in relation to the post of district judge. In contrast, solicitors from minority ethnic backgrounds overapply for assistant recorder and district judge in relation to their numbers.[15] Applicants from minority ethnic backgrounds are more successful in achieving silk in proportion to their numbers applying, but less successful in relation to assistant recorder and deputy district judge. However, the total number of applicants is so small that these figures should be treated with caution. Moreover, the fact that such statistics have only recently started to be collated with regard to ethnic origin limits the extent to which it is possible to say whether or not these patterns are continuing ones.

One response to the apparent under-representation in applications, particularly of women, has been to suggest that the problem lies partly with the attitudes of the lawyers themselves. In particular, it has been suggested that women lack confidence in their abilities, which inhibits them from applying for silk and judicial office. In evidence to the Home Affairs Select Committee hearing in 1996, the then Permanent Secretary of the Lord Chancellor's Department, Sir Thomas Legg, suggested that women might be 'diffident' in applying for judicial posts.[16] Lord Irvine has similarly attributed low application rates to women undervaluing their talents. In November 1998, he told the Association of Women barristers that the lack of confidence which women had in themselves was 'robbing' him of good candidates: 'There will never be more women judges unless more women lawyers put themselves forward for appointment.'[17] Women lawyers in turn responded that the 'unwelcoming' attitude in the upper ranks of the legal profession and the judiciary did not encourage women to have confidence that they were wanted and that their applications would be judged on equal terms with their male counterparts.

In order to assess the merits of these conflicting views on the causes of under-representation and prospects for change, research conducted by the author and Fareda Banda in 1999 sought to supplement the unreliable and incomplete statistics with qualitative data on the experience and attitudes of applicants and potential applicants. The following analysis of the findings sheds some light on the limitations of the current system and the possible reforms to the system needed to ensure that all well qualified lawyers have an equal opportunity of appointment to the Bench.

---

15 Figures for solicitor applicants for silk are too small to draw any statistical conclusions, being only eight applicants in total and one appointment in 1999.

16 *Op cit*, Home Affairs Select Committee, fn 9, para 83.

17 Speech to the Association of Women Barristers, 11 February 1998.

CONFIDENCE IN THE JUDICIAL APPOINTMENTS SYSTEM

A central issue for our research was the extent to which those who had applied, or considered doing so, felt confident that selection was based solely on merit. The answer to this question was not straightforward. On the one hand, the responses generally indicated approval of the quality of recent judicial appointments made, particularly at the higher levels, and there was no suggestion that incompetent candidates were being appointed for extraneous reasons. On the other hand, the research revealed a strong body of opinion critical of the indirectly discriminatory effects on those from groups who have not traditionally been included in the judicial recruitment pool. These different perspectives can be reconciled by the argument that, while the system ensures that those it appoints are chosen on merit, it does not necessarily guarantee that all those who are equally well qualified have the same prospects of selection. In other words, there is not a level playing field on which high quality applicants from different backgrounds can compete equally, so that applicants from certain groups were at an advantage. In the words of one female solicitor: 'It probably goes male members of the Bar top, women members of the Bar, male solicitors, women solicitors – that's probably the pecking order.'

Overall, dissatisfaction with the fairness of the system was greater amongst solicitors than barristers; female respondents than male respondents; respondents from minority ethnic backgrounds than white respondents and amongst those whose applications were unsuccessful than those who were successful. But despite these differences, a number of common concerns were expressed by respondents in all these categories: in particular, the lack of openness and objectivity and the continuing role of patronage through the consultation process, the dominance of an elite group of chambers from amongst which judicial appointments were disproportionately made and the need to be 'known' in order to be appointed. These factors were commonly identified by respondents as weaknesses in the processes and a deterrent to applications from under-represented groups.

THE CONSULTATION PROCESS

The heart of the current appointments process is the consultation process through which the views of senior lawyers and judges on the suitability of individual candidates are gathered. Each year, consultees are asked to provide their opinions on a list of applicants. Information on individual applicants is gathered over a period of years and kept on file in the Lord Chancellor's department. In order to be appointed, an applicant must have a body of supportive opinions from a significant number of judges. Thus, the key to appointment is to be known and well thought of by members of the senior judiciary. To become known, an applicant must have regularly appeared in the higher courts and/or have contact with judges and senior lawyers through informal social connections. Both of these routes were identified as indirectly discriminatory by many of the women, minority lawyer and solicitor respondents:

> They could start by dropping the secret soundings, which is really a licence to discriminate and perpetuate a judiciary which is perceived as being not only pro white and male, but which also has a built-in bias against minorities, women, solicitors and anybody who is perceived as not being a 'safe pair of hands'.

Because respondents did not know exactly who was being consulted, they were concerned that the process might fail to obtain the views of those who know the applicant's work:

> ... it still seems to be a bit of a mystery as to how they do the consulting. Although they tell you in the booklet that 'what we will do is circulate your name and presiding judges will be asked to comment'. But I don't know who has responded and so when they say there hasn't been much response you feel like saying 'well why don't you speak to so and so and so and so and they will tell you about that case'. But you can't do that.

In addition to the lack of openness, the role of social networking was criticised by many respondents for promoting a system in which those who lack the informal connections are disadvantaged:

> I think that, to a large extent, it still matters who you know and who you bother to spend time cultivating. If you are interested in your profession just as your profession and you don't want to spend lots of time socialising with people or running round in meetings for different associations, I think it is harder to advance ... the reality is that all of these judges come from certain chambers and to a greater or lesser extent maintain ties with people in chambers. And to that extent it's not simply about appearing before them – life is much easier if you also come across those judges socially.

Solicitors were particularly conscious of the fact that it was much harder for them to become known by judges, since few have higher rights of audience and most do not share the same opportunities as barristers for socialising with judges:

> To ask judges what they think of candidates, they're far more likely to have been dining with the members of the Bar on the list, had them in chambers, possibly had them as pupils, worked with them on cases when they were senior counsel before they were appointed. They're far less likely to know the solicitors on the list, and that's the way the system works.

Women and minority barristers also felt that they were often disadvantaged by being outside the social network: 'If I socialised and I went to the Bar mess and I went to the big dinners and I drank and I did all the other things they do, it might be different. But I don't.'

The effect of the importance of informal socialising was seen by many as placing at an unfair advantage those lawyers from chambers with a high proportion of QCs and judges. Because applicants from these chambers were personally known to judges, they could seek their advice and support and could expect the judges to 'speak' for them when consulted. The disproportionate number of QCs and judges appointed from a small group of select chambers was questioned:

> There are certain limited sets of chambers where Treasury counsel and silk come from. Now I cannot believe that all the talent is just there. There has got to be something else and maybe it's just connections and influence, which is quite wrong. It's wrong for the wider public because their talent is lost and it's wrong for the justice system because one should be making appointments on merits and on nothing else.

The natural consequence of a process which relies so heavily on the personal opinions of colleagues was criticised as encouraging a system of self-perpetuation:

> ... it just reinforces the current model of the judge because it is almost human nature to approve of people who resemble oneself. It is insufficiently objective and insufficiently open minded and prefers people of the same mould. PLU – people like us.

The result is that those whose face fits were seen to be at an advantage:

> ... it's not a problem with being a woman, it's more to do with being establishment – the fact that you can network and are the sort of person who fits the establishment picture.

In view of the strength and breadth of these critical opinions, it is unsurprising that, when asked what could be done to improve openness and objectivity in the system, respondents from under-represented groups tended to suggest the reduction or removal of the role of consultations and its replacement by more formal systems of assessment and placing greater reliance on the opinions of referees named by applicants.

These criticisms and suggestions for change mirror many of the arguments which have been put forward in recent years by the Law Society, women lawyers' groups and minority lawyers' groups. The common theme running through them is the effect of the consultations process in narrowing down the pool of candidates who stand a realistic chance of appointment to the higher Bench to a small group of barristers – an elite within an elite. Needing to be known by judges, through higher court advocacy or informal networking, inevitably has the most disadvantageous effect on the prospects of solicitors. However, even at the Bar, a number of factors will minimise the chances of many competent practitioners being able to demonstrate their skills to senior judges. First, many barristers have principally paper practices and do not appear regularly in court. Their chances of demonstrating their skills in court will be no better known than most solicitors. Equally, counsel who undertake contentious work, but have a good record in settling their cases early or using alternative dispute resolution methods, will rarely be seen by a high court judge. Thus, ironically, those lawyers demonstrating excellence in skills of non-adversarial style negotiation which the Woolf reforms have put at the heart of the court system are those who are less likely to be appointed to the Bench under the current arrangements.

In addition, as more cases are diverted to the lower courts, many of those members of the Bar with successful advocacy practices may now do most of their work in the county court. Moreover, even those who regularly undertake high court work are finding it increasingly difficult to become known to the judges. The expansion in the size of the Bar, the introduction of solicitors with higher rights of audience, albeit in relatively small numbers to date, and the increasing use of part time deputy High Court judges has reduced the opportunities to appear sufficiently often before a particular high court judge to become known by him or her.

The combined effect of these changes to the legal profession and the court system is to weaken the argument for retaining consultations, not just on grounds of equity, but also on the basis of efficiency. Many candidates for judicial office are now told that their application has failed, not because they are considered unqualified, but because 'no one out there is talking for you'. The consultations process is a huge exercise involving the collection of over 5,000 comments each year from a large number of consultees, but increasingly, many of those asked cannot provide any information about many of the applicants.

Despite these problems of practice and principle, the Lord Chancellor, Lord Irvine, remains committed to the use of soundings. In his evidence to the Home Affairs Select Committee in 1999, he argued that the beauty of the system was that it was very wide ranging, involving a large number of people and so reducing the risks of discrimination in any one case.[18] Sir Leonard Peach was also impressed by the scale and efficiency of the operation, which he described as surpassing other public appointments processes. He proposed retaining the system though, at the same time, he recognised its potential for discrimination and so supplemented this recommendation with the proposal that other methods of assessment should also be developed.

One related effect of these combined factors is to render the central role of advocacy in the process increasingly unsustainable. The suggestion that advocacy skills should no longer be a key factor has been argued for many years. The argument that good advocates do not necessarily make good judges has often been rehearsed. Moreover, the increasing importance of case management skills renders advocacy less important. Sir Leonard Peach supported this argument in his report and the Lord Chancellor appears to have accepted it. In practice, however, while the consultations process

---

18 *Op cit*, Home Affairs Select Committee, fn 9, para 76.

continues to occupy a central role, those with a strong advocacy practice will continue to enjoy an advantage since appearing in court will remain one of the main ways of becoming known to judge consultees.

WORKING PRACTICES IN THE LEGAL PROFESSION

The effect of the consultations process in prioritising an applicant's connections with senior barristers and judges means that decisions early in a barrister's career can be a determining factor in her or his chances of subsequent judicial appointment. Obtaining pupillage and then tenancy in a top-ranking chamber might be the determining factor in the chances of achieving judicial office in 20 years. In an interview, one successful QC and judge described the relationship between membership of a top-ranking chambers, silk and judicial office as a 'golden road'. In practice, many women and minority barristers are excluded from this elite group because of the difficulties which they face in obtaining pupillage and tenancy in prestigious chambers:

> Clearly there are first tier chambers, second tier chambers and third tier chambers and they have more minority ethnic members further down the scale … it's racial discrimination, it's part of the system … ethnic minorities have a difficult time getting into more established traditional sets. The one starting function is where they went to university, clearly the Bar is traditional, it helps to have a public school, Oxford background. So a limited number of minority ethnic people have a public school, Oxford background.

Outside the elite chambers, minority barristers are less likely to meet judges informally or be given the quality of work which would come to the attention of the senior judges:

> You know it's like an old fashioned class or caste system, it really is. I happen to be in a top class chambers and therefore the work that I get is fine. But if I were in one of the lower chambers which didn't have the sort of calibre or reputation that these chambers enjoy, I just wouldn't get some of the quality work.

For women respondents, a particularly pressing concern was the effect of balancing family responsibilities with the demands of their careers. Only one male respondent raised this issue as a problem, whereas women suggested a total of 27 proposals for changes within the legal profession and the judicial appointments process which would give greater weight to the particular demands which many women face in working the 'double shift'. These proposals included the introduction of permanent part time judicial posts, placing less weight on a practitioner's earning record and removing the requirement for High Court judges to be away from home travelling on circuit for lengthy periods. One highly qualified woman barrister with a young family specifically identified this last factor as a reason why she did not intend to apply for judicial office.

PROMOTION OF CANDIDATES FROM UNDER-REPRESENTED GROUPS

Despite the identification of structural barriers to appointment, a strong consensus was evident in the responses that judicial appointment should be made exclusively on the grounds of merit. Women respondents, in particular, were critical of any suggestion of 'tokenism' which might cast doubt on the merit of those women who were appointed and lead to stigmatisation. Some respondents whose applications had been successful argued that they already faced the suggestion, explicit or implicit, that their gender had been a significant factor in their appointment: 'The difficulty is there just because there are so many applicants for so few places as assistant recorder. There is inevitably going to be a degree of bitterness and blame – "so and so has got it, she's a woman, why didn't I get it?" I think it's schoolboy stuff.'

Nevertheless, while there was agreement on the primacy of appointment on merit alone through an open system of advertised applications, there was also support across the respondent groups for well qualified candidates from under-represented groups to be invited to apply:

> Under the old system not enough people from an ethnic background were appointed and under the new system not enough people from an ethnic background are appointed. It shows that neither system may be the right system. Maybe there should be a bit of mix and match, saying, 'well look, this person has not applied but I have seen him and she/he is good and let's get them to apply'.

Women respondents linked the need for giving active encouragement to apply with a tendency for women to have less confidence in their abilities: 'Men and women approach things differently. Men look down a list of criteria and say "yes, that's me". But women are more circumspect. Women need more encouragement than men do ... Women want to be sure before they apply whereas men will take a punt.'

The tension between selection on merit and the wish to promote positive action to improve diversity is, of course, one which is mirrored in many areas of public life. However, the idea that these two requirements are simple opposites has often distracted from a more productive debate about the definition of merit and whether the current selection criteria are, in fact, gender or race neutral. For example, the Joint Working Party on *Equal Opportunities in Judicial Office and Silk* has argued that the term 'authority' which is included in the judicial selection criteria is a highly subjective concept which is interpreted by some consultees as meaning to have a commanding presence in court; a quality which may have as much to do with social background as merit. It is also an implicitly masculine characteristic which, stereotypically, women are thought to lack.[19] Including 'authority' in the definition of merit, therefore, may leave non-traditional applicants at a disadvantage. Similarly, the criterion 'commitment' was highlighted as capable of being understood not as diligence and conscientiousness, but as being willing to subscribe to the 'long hours culture' and to work regularly in the evenings and at weekends. For applicants with family commitments, such an interpretation would, inevitably, be indirectly discriminatory.

These examples highlight the need for careful and ongoing scrutiny of the definition of merit, not just on paper, but in terms of the practical interpretation of the selection criteria. This is an essential part of the process of ensuring that the appointments system gives equal value to the qualities of all lawyers, and not just those who have traditionally dominated the bench.

JUDICIAL APPOINTMENTS COMMISSION

Most of the changes proposed by the respondents were detailed reforms of the existing system. Some respondents, however, proposed more structurally radical change through the creation of a judicial appointments commission. Some suggestions were very general, others proposed specific arrangements in terms of the powers and membership of the commission. The common theme running through all the suggestions was the need for a diverse range of members and for the commission to be strongly independent: 'There should be a commission separate from the Lord Chancellor's department and it should have a lay element and it should be done on a proper selection basis like people get selected for employment elsewhere.'

The views expressed in the research reflect the growing support in public debate on judicial appointments for the creation of a commission. When the Labour government came to power in 1997 it was expected that a commission would be established. Although the reform was not included in the Party's manifesto, it was supported in a 1995 Labour Party paper on the justice system.[20] However, after a brief consultation process carried out by Lord Irvine in 1997, the question was put on the back burner while the Lord Chancellor's department undertook other reforms such as the introduction of the Human Rights Act 1998. In December 1999, Sir Leonard Peach recommended the creation of a commission with a limited scrutiny role, and this has been accepted in principle by the Lord Chancellor.

---

19 Joint Working Party, *Equal Opportunities in Judicial Appointments and Silk*, 2000, para 2.5.2.

20 Labour Party, 1995, p 13.

However, as support for the creation of a full appointing commission has grown outside government, it is unlikely that its implementation can be postponed indefinitely. Moreover, the global trend is towards the use of commissions as a way of balancing accountability and openness with judicial independence in the context of growing judicial power. They are used in many states in the USA, and at federal and provincial level in Canada. South Africa created a commission in 1995, and other common law countries such as New Zealand and Australia have a growing body of support for their introduction. Closer to home, the devolution process in Scotland and Northern Ireland is almost certain to lead to the establishment of commissions in those jurisdictions. The experiences of those countries where commissions have been used suggests that they can be effective vehicles for increasing openness, improving diversity and increasing public confidence.[21] The success of a commission depends on the make-up of the membership and the level of political will amongst the public, the legal profession and the judiciary to find ways of introducing meaningful reform whilst ensuring the competence and integrity of those appointed to the bench. The findings from this research suggest that lawyers, at least, are ready for this change. A number of judges have also now joined the chorus of support amongst politicians, academics and the media for the introduction of a commission.

CONCLUSION

Despite the introduction of a range of reforms in recent years designed to open up the judicial appointments process and improve its effectiveness, there remains a significant measure of dissatisfaction with the fairness of the present system amongst lawyers from widely different backgrounds. The key to addressing these concerns is to open up the recruitment pool to include all lawyers who are qualified and competent. In particular, the system must adapt to allow solicitors equal access to the appointments process. The continuing marginalisation of approximately 90,000 lawyers from all but the lowest ranks has serious implications for the prospects of significantly increasing diversity in the judiciary, since it results in the effective exclusion of large numbers of women and minority lawyers. This limitation also has longer term implications for the quality of the Bench. Traditionally, it was assumed that the brightest and the best law students would gravitate to the Bar and so, in time, to the Bench. However, in recent years, the very great increases in the earning power of solicitors in commercial work and the increasing insecurity of practice at the Bar has changed the relative status of the two branches of the profession. Many talented and able young lawyers

---

21 See Malleson, 1997.

who might once have gone to the Bar are now choosing the solicitor route. If, in 15 years' time, when that cohort would naturally be applying for judicial office, the appointments process has not reorientated itself to draw them in, the quality of the Bench will suffer.

Opening up the system to all solicitors and to those barristers outside the traditional chambers can only be achieved through the removal of the central role of judges in the process, since this automatically gives an advantage to a small group who regularly appear in the higher courts and have social connections with the higher judiciary. The current system evolved at a time when both the Bar and the Bench were very small and when senior practitioners and judges were well known to each other. As the legal profession and the judiciary have expanded in size, the consultation process has become increasingly inefficient and unfair. For those in the inner elite, the system works reasonably well, providing a wide range of comments over a number of years. The majority outside that magic circle, however, are left with no way to demonstrate their qualities or compete on a level playing field. In order to reorientate the system to take account of the broad range of skills and experiences of lawyers in practice, the traditional link between advocacy and judicial appointment must be abandoned and alternative systems of assessing merit, such as assessment centres, more extensive interviews and a fuller system of named referees must be introduced. These methods, and many others, are used successfully in the recruitment of senior posts in business, the professions, the civil service and academia.

With the introduction of judicial training and greater public scrutiny of judicial decision making, the bench has lost much of its former mystique. The professionalism with which many judges now carry out their duties is not, however, matched in the way they are chosen. The appointments process remains the last aspect of the system which preserves the inward-looking and backward-looking culture of the old judiciary. Public confidence and legitimacy are dependent as much on improving diversity as on competence. There are many highly talented and able lawyers in practice who would have much to contribute to the Bench, but are currently effectively excluded from the system or compete at a disadvantage. The challenge to the appointments system, as to the legal profession as a whole, is fully and equally to include the previously excluded. The changes needed to achieve this are unlikely to be undertaken within the present system and for this reason, if no other, a judicial appointments commission should now be established.

BIBLIOGRAPHY

A

Abel, RL, 'Between market and State: the legal profession in turmoil' (1989) 52 MLR 285

Abel, RL, *The Legal Profession in England and Wales*, 1988, Oxford: Basil Blackwell

Aisenberg, N and Harrington, M, *Women of Academe: Outsiders in the Scared Grove*, 1988, Amherst: University of Massachusetts

Altman, D, *Practical Statistics for Medical Research*, 1991, London: Chapman and Hall

B

Bacchi, C, *The Politics of Affirmative Action: 'Women', Equality and Category Politics*, 1996, London: Sage

Bahl, K, 'The wages of professional inequality' (1996) *The Lawyer*, 5 November

Baldwin, J, 'The social composition of the magistracy' (1976) 16 Br J Crim 171

Bartless, D and Walker, J, 'Inner circle' (1973) *New Society*, 19 April

Bar Council Discussion Paper, 'Restructuring vocational training for the Bar', June 1999

Bargh, C, Scott, P and Smith, D, *Governing Universities: Changing the Culture?*, 1996, Buckingham: OU Press

Bartlett, K, 'Cross-dressing in the master's clothes' (2000) 109 Yale LJ 745

Bartlett, K, 'Feminist legal methods' (1990) 100 Harv L Rev 829

Bashi, V, 'Racial categories matter because racial hierarchies matter: a commentary' (1998) 21 Ethnic and Racial Studies 5

Basow, S, 'Student evaluations: the role of gender bias and teaching styles', in Collins, LH *et al* (eds), *Career Strategies for Women in Academe*, 1998, Thousand Oaks, CA: Sage

Bauman, Z, 'From pilgrim to tourist – a short history of identity', in Hall, S and du Gay, P (eds), *Questions of Cultural Identity*, 1996, London: Sage

Bayles, MD, *Professional Ethics*, 1981, Belmont, CA: Wadsworth

BDO Stoy Hayward, *Report on the 1999 Survey of Barristers' Chambers*, July 1999

Becher, T, *Academic Tribes and Territories: Intellectual Enquiry and the Culture of Disciplines*, 1989, Buckingham: OU Press

Becker, G, *A Treatise on the Family*, 1991, Cambridge, Mass: Harvard UP

Bedlow, D, 'Rich pickings – but at what cost?' (2000) Legal Week, 1 June

Bender, L, 'From gender difference to feminist solidarity: using Carol Gilligan and an ethic of care in law' (1990) 15 Vermont L Rev 48

Beveridge, F, Nott, S and Stephen, K, 'Mainstreaming and the engendering of policy-making: a means to an end?' (2000) 7 Journal of European Public Policy 385

Bhatti, H, 'Representation in criminal justice system still "unfair"' (1992) *Weekly Journal*, 30 May

Blackstone, W (Sir), *Commentaries on the Laws of England,* 1st edn, 1769, Book III

Block, BP, 'Endangered species' (1998) 162 JP 45

Boon, A and Levin, J, *The Ethics and Conduct of Lawyers in England and Wales*, 1999, Oxford: Hart

Bottero, W, 'The changing face of the professions? Gender and explanations of women's entry to pharmacy' (1992) 6 Work, Employment and Society 329

Bottoms, AE and McClean, JD, *Defendants in the Criminal Process*, 1976, London: Routledge and Kegan Paul

Bourdieu, P, 'The force of law: toward a sociology of the juridical field' (1987) 38 Hastings LJ 805

Bourdieu, P, *Language and Symbolic Power*, 1991, Cambridge: Polity

Bourner, T and Race, P, *How to Win as a Part-Time Student*, 1990, London: Kogan Page

Bourner, T with Reynolds, A, Hamed, M and Barnett, R, *Part Time Students and their Experience of Higher Education*, 1991, Buckingham: Society for Research into Higher Education and OU Press

Bowley, M, 'From each according to his means' (1999) 149 NLJ 1465

Bowley, M, 'Too old at thirty?'(1998) *Counsel*, April

Boxell, J, 'Stressed female lawyers fear admitting condition' (1999) *Legal Week*, 17 June

Boyd, S, 'Can law challenge the public/private divide? Women, work and family' (1996) 15 Windsor Yearbook of Access to Justice 161

Bradney, A, 'Law as a parasitic discipline' (1998) 25 JLS 71

Bradney, A and Cownie, F, 'Transformative visions of legal education' (1998) 25 JLS 1

Brah, A, *Cartographies of Diaspora: Contesting Identities*, 1996, London: Routledge

Braidotti, R, *Nomadic Subjects: Embodiment and Sexual Difference in Contemporary Feminist Theory*, 1993, Columbia: Columbia UP

Bridges, L, 'The Lawrence inquiry' (1999) 26 JLS 298

Brill, S, 'The law business in the year 2000' (1989) *The American Lawyer*, June

Brooks, A, *Academic Women*, 1997, Buckingham: OU Press

Brown, W, *States of Injury: Power and Freedom in Late Modernity*, 1995, Princeton, NJ: Princeton UP

Brownsword, R, 'Law schools for lawyers, citizens and people', in Cownie, F (ed), *The Law School: Global Issues, Local Questions*, 1999, Aldershot: Aldgate

Bundock, M and Cooper, T, 'Sex discrimination and trainees' salaries' (1998) 148 NLJ 600

Burney, E, *JP: Magistrate, Court and Community*, 1979, London: Hutchinson

Burrage, M, 'From a gentleman's to a public profession: status and politics in the history of English solicitors' (1996) 3 IJLP 45

Butler, J, *Gender Trouble: Feminism and the Subversion of Identity*, 1990, London: Routledge

C

Cabinet Office, *A Framework for Consultation: A Report on the National Strategy for Neighbourhood Renewal*, Social Exclusion Unit, April 2000

Calamandrei, P, *Elogio dei giudici scritto da un avvocato*, 1989, quoted in Oberto, G, 'L'administration judiciaire de la preuve dans le procès civil italien' in *Juges et Jugements: l'Europe Plurielle*, 1998, Paris: Institut de Droit Comparé

Campbell, AD, 'Individualism, equality and the possibility of rights' (1990) 6 Connecticut Journal of International Law 507

Caplow, T, *The Sociology of Work*, 1954, New York: McGraw-Hill

Carlen, P (ed), *The Sociology of Law*, 1976, Keele: Keele UP

Carr, A, 'Fat cats, thin kittens: a portrait of life at the junior Bar' (1999) 39 Med Sci Law 2

Cashmore, E, *Dictionary of Race and Ethnic Relationships*, 1997, London: Routledge

Chambers, DL, 'Accommodation and satisfaction: woman and men lawyers and the balance of work and family' (1989) Law and Social Inquiry 14

Chambers, *Guide to the Legal Profession*, 1994, 1999, London: Chambers

Chambers, M, 'Part-time partners: the Linklaters initiative' (1997) 19 Commercial Lawyer 21

Cheffins, B, 'Using theory to study law: a company law perspective' [1999] CLJ 197

Cheng, Y and Heath, A (1993) 'Ethnic origins and class destination' (1993) 19 Oxford Review of Education 2, pp 151–65

Cheyne, P, 'Linklaters booms, but partners are overstretched' (2000) *Legal Week*, 29 June

Chrisler, J, 'Teacher versus scholar: role conflict for women?', in Collins, LH *et al* (eds), *Career Strategies for Women in Academe*, 1998, Thousand Oaks, CA: Sage

Clements, LJ, 'Representing children and the Human Rights Act 1998' (1999) 12 Representing Children 252

Cockburn, C, *In the Way of Women: Men's Resistance to Sex Equality in Organisations*, 1991, Basingstoke: Macmillan

Cockburn, C, *Machinery of Dominance: Women, Men and Technical Knowhow*, 1985, London: Pluto

Cockburn, C, *Brothers: Male Dominance and Technological Change*, 1983, London: Pluto

Cole, B, *Trends in the Solicitors' Profession: Annual Statistical Report 1999*, 2000, London: The Law Society

Cole, B, *Annual Statistical Report 1993*, 1998, London: The Law Society

Cole, B, *Solicitors in Private Practice – Their Work and Expectations*, 1997, Research Study No 26, Research and Policy Planning Unit, London: The Law Society.

Collier, R, 'Masculism, law and law teaching' (1991) 19 IJSL 427

Collier, R, '(Un)Sexy bodies: the making of professional legal masculinities', in McGlynn, C (ed), *Legal Feminisms: Theory and Practice*, 1998, London: Ashgate/Dartmouth

Collinson, M and Collinson, D, '"It's only Dick": the sexual harassment of women managers in insurance sales' (1996) 10(1) Work, Employment and Society 29

Cotterell, R, *Law's Community: Legal Theory in Sociological Perspective*, 1995, Oxford: Clarendon

Cownie, F, 'The importance of theory in law teaching', in Sugarman, D and Sherr, A, *Theory in Legal Education*, Aldershot: Ashgate (forthcoming)

Cownie, F, 'Women legal academics – a new research agenda?' (1998) 25 JLS 102

Cownie, F, 'Searching for theory in teaching law', in Cownie, F (ed), *The Law School: Global Issues, Local Problems*, 1999, Aldershot: Aldgate

Cownie, F and Bradney, A, *English Legal System in Context*, 1996, London: Butterworths

Cranston, R (ed), *Legal Ethics and Professional Responsibility*, 1995, Oxford: Clarendon

D

Darbyshire, P, 'A comment on the powers of magistrates' clerks' [1999] Crim LR 377

Darbyshire, P, 'An essay on the importance and neglect of the magistracy' [1997a] Crim LR 627

Darbyshire, P, 'For the new Lord Chancellor – some causes for concern about magistrates' [1997b] Crim LR 861

David, M and Woodward, D (eds), *Negotiating the Glass Ceiling: Careers of Senior Women in the Academic World*, 1998, London: Falmer

Davies, N, 'Education in crisis: special report' (1999) *The Guardian*, 14–16 September

De George, *Business Ethics*, 5th edn, 1999, New Jersey: Prentice Hall

de Vaus, D, *Surveys in Social Research*, 2nd edn, 1990, London: Unwin Hyman

Deavere Smith, A, 'Public lives, private selves', in Mosley, W, Diawara, M, Taylor, C and Austin, R (eds), *Black Genius: African-American Solutions to African-American Problems*, 1999, New York: Norton

Delamont, S, 'Gender and British postgraduate funding policy' (1989) 1(1) Gender and Education 51

Delamont, S, 'Just like the novels? Researching the occupational cultures(s) of higher education', in Cuthbert, R (ed), *Working in Higher Education*, 1996, Buckingham: OU Press

Dezalay, Y and Garth, B, 'Law, lawyers and social capital: "rule of law" versus relational capitalism' (1997) 6(1) Social and Legal Studies 109

Dezalay, Y and Sugarman, D (eds), *Professional Competition and Professional Power: Lawyers, Accountants and the Social Construction of Markets*, 1995, New York: Routledge

Dhavan, R, Kibble, N and Twining, W, *Access to Legal Education and the Legal Profession*, 1989, London: Butterworths

Dignan, J and Wynne, A, 'A microcosm of the local community?' (1997) 37 Br J Crim 184

Drucker, P, 'What is business ethics?' (1981) *Public Interest*, Spring, p 63

Dunkin, MJ, 'Determinants of academic career advancement at an Australian university' (1991) Higher Education Research and Development 115

Durkheim, E, *Professional Ethics and Civic Morals*, 1957, London: Routledge and Kegan Paul

Dyer, C, 'Solicitors' firms "biased against black students"' (1994) *The Guardian*, 20 April

E

Editorial, 'Gifted amateurs' (1991) 141 NLJ 409

Endicott, T, 'Vagueness and legal theory' (1997) 3 Legal Theory 37

Epstein, C, Seron, C, Oglensky, B and Saute, R, *The Part-Time Paradox: Time Norms, Professional Lives, Family and Gender*, 1999, New York: Routledge

Equal Opportunities Commission, *Men and Women in Britain: at the Millennium*, 2000, Manchester: EOC

Evans, J, *Feminist Theory Today: An Introduction to Second-Wave Feminism*, 1995, London: Sage.

Evetts, J, 'Professional identity, diversity and segmentation: the case of engineering', in Olgiati, V, Orzark, L and Saks, M (eds), *Professions, Identity, and Order in Comparative Perspective*, 1998, Onati IISL

F

Farrell, S, 'City firms raid coffers to protect assistants from US salary hikes' (2000) *The Lawyer*, 28 February

Faulkner, DER, 'The functioning of lay justice' (1994) 50(1) Magistrate 4

Fenton, S, *Ethnicity: Racism, Class and Culture*, 1999, London: Macmillan

Filby, M, 'The figures, the personality and the bums: service work and sexuality' (1992) 6(1) Work, Employment and Society 23

Fineman, M and Thomadsen, N (eds), *At the Boundaries of Law*, 1991, New York: Routledge

Fishman, J, 'Ethnicity as being, doing and knowing', in Hutchinson, J and Smith, A (eds), *Ethnicity*, 1996, Oxford: OUP

Fitzgerald, M and Hale, C, *Ethnic Minorities: Victimisation and Racial Harassment*, 1996, Home Office Research Study 154

Flood, J, 'Megalaw in the UK: professionalism or corporatism? A preliminary report' (1989) 64 Indiana LJ 569

Flood, J, 'Megalawyering in the global order: the cultural, social and economic transformation of global legal practice' (1996) 3 IJLP 169

Fontes, P, 'The danger of discrimination' (2000) *Legal Week*, 6 July

Fox, R, and Stein, M, 'Making room for flexi-time partners' (1999) *Legal Week*, 8 July

Fredman, S, *Women and the Law*, 1997, Oxford: Clarendon

Frug, MJ, *Postmodern Legal Feminism*, 1992, New York: Routledge

G

Galanter, M and Palay, T, *Tournament of Lawyers: Growth and Transformation of the Big Law Firm*, 1991, Chicago: Chicago UP

Galanter, M, 'Law abounding: legislation around the North Atlantic' (1992) 55 MLR 5

Galanter M, 'Old and in the way: the coming demographic transformation of the legal profession and its implications for the provision of legal services' (1999) Wisconsin LR 1081

Galanter, M, 'The faces of mistrust: the image of lawyers in public opinion and political discourse' (1998) 66 Cincinnati UL Rev 905

Genn, H, *Evaluation Report on the Central London County Court Pilot Mediation Scheme*, Lord Chancellor's Department, July 1998

Gibb, F, 'JPs could play second fiddle to a bench lawyer' (2000) *The Times*, 29 March

Gibb, F, 'Women solicitors "exploited"' (1996) *The Times*, 12 October

Gillies, N, 'Retaining the best' (1999) *Legal Week*, 18 March

Gilligan, C, *In A Different Voice: Psychological Theory and Women's Development*, 1982, Cambridge, Mass: Harvard UP

Gilroy, P, 'Race ends here' (1998) 21 Ethnic and Racial Studies 5

Gilroy, P, *Between Camps: Race, Identity and Nationalism at the End of the Colour Line*, 2000, London: Penguin

Gilson, R and Mnookin, R, 'Coming of age in a corporate law firm: the economics of associate career patterns' (1989) 41 Stanford L Rev 567

Gilvarry, E, 'New boy blues' (1994) *Law Society Gazette*, 14 September

Glasser, C, 'The legal profession in the 1990s – images of change' (1990) 10 LS 1

Glavanis, P '"Race", racism and the politics of identity', in Beynon, H and Glavanis, P (eds), *Patterns of Social Inequality: Essays for Richard Brown*, 1999, London: Longman

Goriely, T and Williams, T, *The Impact of the New Training Scheme – Report on a Qualitative Study*, 1996, London: The Law Society

Granovetter, M 'Economic action and social structure – the problem of embeddedness' (1985) 91 American Journal of Sociology 481

Graycar, R, 'The gender of judgments: an introduction', in Thornton, M (ed), *Public and Private: Feminist Legal Debates*, 1995, Melbourne: OUP

Greenebaum, EH, 'Development of law firm training programmes: coping with a turbulent environment' (1996) 3 IJLP 315

Gregory and Lees, 'Attrition in rape and sexual assault cases' (1996) 36 Br J Crim 1

Griffith, J, *The Politics of the Judiciary*, 5th edn, 1997, London: Fontana

Griffiths, C, 'Magic Circle partners net £1 m' (2000) *The Lawyer*, 26 June

The Guardian, 'Judges' reform must go further' (1999) *The Guardian*, 3 December

Gubbay, J, 'Changing the way we work' (1999) *Legal Week*, 25 February

Guiner, L *et al*, 'Becoming gentlemen: women's experiences at one Ivy-League law school' (1994) 143 Pennsylvania UL Rev 1

H

Hagan, J and Kay, F, *Gender in Practice: A Study of Lawyers' Lives*, 1995, New York: OUP

Hakim, C, *Key Issues in Women's Work: Female Heterogeneity and the Polarisation of Women's Employment*, 1996, London: Athlone

Hakim, C, 'Five feminist myths about women's employment' (1995) 45 British Journal of Sociology 429

Halpern, D, *Entry into the Legal Professions – The Law Student Cohort Study, Years 1 and 2*, 1994, London: The Law Society

Halsey, AH, *The Decline of Donnish Domination*, 1992, Oxford: Clarendon

Hanlon G, *Lawyers, the State and the Market: Professionalism Revisited*, 1999, London: Macmillan

Hanlon, G, 'A fragmenting profession – lawyers, the market and significant others' (1997) 60 MLR 798

Harless, JM, Ditton, J, Nair, G and Phillips, S, 'More sinned against than sinning: a study of young teenager experiences of crime' (1995) 35 Br J Crim 114

Harrington, M, *Women Lawyers: Rewriting the Rules*, 1992, New York: Alfred Knopf

Harris, P and Jones, M, 'A survey of law schools in the United Kingdom' (1996) 3 Law Teacher 91

Harris, R, 'Openings, absences and omissions', in Owusu, K (ed), *Black British Culture and Society: A Text Reader*, 1999, London: Routledge

Hartmann, H, 'Capitalism, patriarchy and job segregation by sex', in Eisenstein, Z (ed), *Capitalist Patriarchy and the Case for Socialist Feminism*, 1979, New York: Monthly Review

Hayes, J, 'Appointment by invitation' (1997) 147 NLJ 521

Heald, S, 'Pianos to pedagogy: pursuing the educational subject', in Bannerji, H *et al*, *Unsettling Relations: The University as a Site of Feminist Struggle*, 1991, Toronto: Women's Press

Hearn, J and Parkin, W, *'Sex' at 'Work': The Power and Paradox of Organisation Sexuality*, 1995, London: Sage

Hegel, GWF, *Philosophy of Right*, 1967, Oxford: OUP

Hepple, B, 'The renewal of the liberal law degree' [1996] CLJ 470

Hills, G, *From Beggars to Choosers: University Funding for the Future*, 1999, Forum for Social and Economic Thought

Holdsworth, W (Sir), *The History of English Law*, Vol 1, 3rd impression, 1977

Home Office, *Recorded Crime Statistics – England and Wales, April 1998–September 1999*, Issue 01/00, 2000, London: HMSO

Home Office, *Review of Delay in the Criminal Justice System*, February 1997 (Narey Report), London: HMSO

Hood, C, 'A public management for all seasons' (1991) 69 Public Administration 3

hooks, b, *Killing Rage, Ending Racism*, 1995, New York: Henry Holt

Hull, K and Nelson, R, 'Gender inequality in law: problems of structure and agency in recent studies of gender in Anglo-American legal professions' (1998) Law and Social Inquiry 681

Hull, K and Nelson, R, 'Divergent paths: gender differences in the careers of urban lawyers' (1999) 10 Researching Law 1

Hunter, R and McKelvie, H, *Equality of Opportunity for Women at the Victorian Bar*, 1998, Melbourne: Victorian Bar Council

Hunter, R, 'Women barristers and gender difference', paper delivered to The International Institute for the Sociology of Law Conference, 'A Challenge to Law and Lawyers', 1999, Onati, Spain

I

Irons, P and Guiton, S (eds), *May It Please the Court*, 1993, New York: New Press

Itzin, C, 'Gender, culture, power and change: a materialist analysis', in Itzin, C and Newman, J (eds), *Gender, Culture and Organisational Change*, 1995, London, Routledge

J

Jackson, E, 'Contradictions and coherence in feminist responses to law' (1993) 20 JLS 398

Jacobs, G, 'Rough justice for the innocent?' (1999) *The Times*, 12 October

Jaggi, M, 'Casting off the shackles of history' (1999) *The Guardian*, 3 November

Jenkins, J and Lewis, V, *Annual Statistical Report 1993*, 1995, London: The Law Society

Jenkins, J, *Annual Statistical Report 1993*, 1993, London: The Law Society

Jenkins, J, *Annual Statistical Report 1993*, 1994, London: The Law Society

JUSTICE, *The Judiciary in England and Wales*, 1999, London: JUSTICE

K

Kant, I, *Foundation of the Metaphysics of Morals*, 1785 (reprinted 1964) New York: Harper and Row

Kanter, R, 'Some effects on proportions on group life: skewed sex ratios and responses to token women' (1977) 82 American Journal of Sociology 965

Kay, F, 'Flight from law: a competing risks model of departures from law firms' (1997) 31(2) Law and Society Review 728

Keane, G, 'Women no longer prepared to be treated with contempt' (1999) *Legal Week*, 23 September

Kentridge, S (Sir), 'A quiet revolution?'(1998) *Counsel*, December

Kingdom, E, *What's Wrong with Rights? Problems for Feminist Politics of Law*, 1991, Edinburgh: Edinburgh UP

Koehn, D, *The Ground of Professional Ethics*, 1994, London: Routledge

Koontz, P, 'Gender bias in the legal profession: women "see" it, men don't' (1995) 15 Women and Politics 1

Krieger, L, 'The content of our categories: a cognitive bias approach to discrimination and equal employment opportunity' (1995) 47 Stanford L Rev 1161

Kronman, AT, *The Lost Lawyer*, 1993, Cambridge: Mass: Harvard UP

L

Labour Party, *Access to Justice*, 1995, London: Labour Party

Lacey, N, 'From individual to group? A feminist analysis of the limits of anti-discrimination legislation', in *Unspeakable Subjects: Feminist Essays in Legal and Social Theory*, 1998, Oxford: Hart

Larson, MS, *The Rise of Professionalism: A Sociological Analysis*, 1977, Berkeley, CA: California UP

Law Society Fact Sheet Number 2, 1999, *Women in the Profession*, London: The Law Society

Law Society, *New Anti-Discrimination Measures*, 1995, London: The Law Society

Law Society, *The Guide to Professional Conduct of Solicitors 1999*, 1999, London: The Law Society

Law Society, *Training Strategy: Working Documents for Discussion*, May 1999, London: The Law Society

Law Society, *Annual Statistical Report 1999: Trends in the Solicitors' Profession*, 2000, London: The Law Society

Learning to Succeed: A New Framework for Post-16 Learning, Cm 4392, June 1999, White Paper

Lee, RG, 'From profession to business: the rise and rise of the city law firm' (1992) 19 JLS 31

Lee, RG, *Firm Views: Work of and Work in the Largest Law Firms*, Research Study No 35, 1999, London: The Law Society

Legal Week, '"Atmosphere of poison" at Edward Lewis' (1999) *Legal Week*, 23 September

Legal Week, 'Posner settles discrimination claim pre-trial' (1999) *Legal Week*, 15 April

Legal Week, 'Solicitor sues Goodmans for failing to promote her' (1999) *Legal Week*, 21 January

Legal Week, 'Why didn't Camerons stop the rot?' (1999) *Legal Week*, 23 September

Leighton, P, 'New wine in old bottles or new wine in new bottles?' (1998) 25 JLS 85

Leighton, P, Mortimer, T and Whatley, N, *Today's Law Teachers: Lawyers or Academics?*, 1995, London: Cavendish Publishing

Levy, A, 'This is my England' (2000) *The Guardian*, 19 February

Lewis, J and Keegan, J, *Defining Legal Business: Understanding the Work of the Largest Law Firms*, 1997, London: The Law Society

Lewis, S and Lewis, J (eds), *The Work–Family Challenge: Rethinking Employment*, 1996, London: Sage

Lewis, V, *Annual Statistical Report 1993*, 1996, London: The Law Society

Lewis, V, *Trends in the Solicitors' Profession: Annual Statistical Report 1996*, 1996, Chancery Lane, London: The Law Society

Liao, TF, *Interpreting Probability Models: Logit, Probit and other Generalized Linear Models*, 1994, London: Sage

Liff, S, 'Tell me what you want …: opportunities and pitfalls on the road to gender equality' (1997) 11 Work, Employment and Society 555

Lord Chancellor's Advisory Committee on Legal Education and Conduct, *First Report on Legal Education and Training*, April 1996, London: HMSO

Lord Chancellor's Department, *Judicial Appointments Annual Report 1998–1999*, London: HMSO

Lyndhurst (Lord), *Hansard*, 17 June 1833

M

MacErlean, N, 'Long hours: a sign of poor practice' (1998) *The Lawyer*, 6 October

MacRae, S, 1996, *Women at the Top: Progress after Five Years*, London: The Hansard Society

Major, LE, 'Divided they stand in the posh stakes' (1999) *The Guardian*, Higher, 1 December

Malleson, K and Banda, F, *Factors Affecting the Decision to Apply for Silk and Judicial Office*, 2000, London: Lord Chancellor's Department

Malleson, K, *The New Judiciary*, 1999, Aldershot: Ashgate

Malleson, K, *The Use of Judicial Appointments Commissions: A Review of the US and Canadian Models*, 1997, Lord Chancellor's Department Research Series No 6

Malpas, J, 'Recession: what recession?' (2000) *Legal Week,* 21 January

Marsh, S, 'The CNAA law degree' (1983) 17 LT 73

Mason, D, *Race and Ethnicity in Modern Britain*, 1996, Oxford: OUP

Mawdsley, H, 'Why magistrates need to improve their image' (2000) *The Times*, 8 February

McCarthy, P and Humphrey, R, 'Debt: the reality of student life' (1995) 49 Higher Education Quarterly 78

McConville, M and Mirsky, C, 'The State, the legal profession and the defence of the poor' (1988) 15 JLS 342

McDonald, P, '"The class of '81": a glance at the social class composition of recruits to the legal profession' (1982) 9 JLS 267

McFarlane, R, 'Time to lay off lay magistrates?' (1999) *The Times*, 9 November

McGlynn, C, *The Woman Lawyer: Making the Difference*, 1988, London: Butterworths

McGlynn, C, 'Women, representation and the legal academy' (1999) LS 68.

McGlynn, C, 'The business of equality in the solicitors' profession' (2000) 63 MLR 442

McGlynn, C , 'Ideologies of motherhood in European community sex equality law' (2000) 6 European LJ 29

McGlynn, C and Graham, C, *Soliciting Equality: Equality and Opportunity in the Solicitors' Professions*, 1995, London: Young Women Lawyers

Mears, M, 'No bias' (1995) *Law Society Gazette*, Letters, 29 October

Menkel-Meadow, C, 'Portia in a different voice: speculation on women's lawyering process' (1985) 1 Berkeley Women's LJ 39

Menkel-Meadow, C, 'Portia redux: another look at gender, feminism and legal ethics', in Parker, S and Sampford, C (eds), *Legal Ethics and Legal Practice*, 1995, Oxford: Clarendon

Metcalf, H, *Class and Higher Education: The Participation of Young People from Lower Social Classes*, July 1997, London: CIHE

Mizzi, A, 'Newly qualified salary war hots up as US firms top £100,000' (2000) *Law Society Gazette*, 18 May

Modood, T and Shiner, M, *Ethnic Minorities and Higher Education: Why are There Differential Rates of Entry?*, 1994, London: Policy Studies Institute

Modood, T, 'The number of ethnic minority students in British higher education: some grounds for optimism' (1993) 19(2) Oxford Review of Education 167

Modood, T, Berthoud, R, Lakey, J, Nazroo, J, Smith, P, Virdee, S and Beishon, S, *Ethnic Minorities in Britain: Diversity and Disadvantage*, 1997, Policy Studies Institute

Montagu, A, 'Introduction', in the expanded edition of Montagu, A, *Race and IQ*, 1999, New York: OUP

Moorhead, R, *Protecting Whom? The Impact of the Minimum Salary: A Survey into Salary and Debt Levels of Trainees and LPC Students*, 1997, London: Institute of Advanced Legal Studies

Morgan, DM, 'Doctoring legal ethics: studies in irony', in Cranston, R (ed), *Legal Ethics and Professional Responsibility*, 1995, Oxford: Clarendon

Morgan, DM, 'Where do I own my body?', unpublished, 1998, University of Cardiff

Mossman, M, 'Achieving gender equality' (1998) 32 Kobe L Rev 21

Mossman, M, 'Women lawyers in the 20th century: rethinking the image of Portia', in Graycar, R (ed), *Dissenting Opinions: Feminist Explorations in Law and Society*, 1990, Australia: Allen and Unwin

Mullally, M, 'Berwin Leighton re-evaluates "quality of life" for employees' (1999) *Legal Week*, 22 April, p 7

Mungham, G and Thomas, PA, 'Studying lawyers: aspects of theory, method and the politics of social research' (1981) 8 JLS 79

Murdie, A, 'The costs of immunity for magistrates' (1999) 149 NLJ 17

Murray, G, 'Women lawyers in New Zealand: some questions about the politics of equality' (1987) 15 IJSL 439

N

Naffine, N and Owens, R (eds), *Sexing the Subject of Law*, 1997, Sydney: Sweet & Maxwell

Naffine, N, *Law and the Sexes: Explorations in Feminist Jurisprudence*, 1990, Sydney: Unwin Hyman

National Committee of Inquiry into Higher Education (chaired by Sir Ron Dearing), *Higher Education in the Learning Society: Report of the National Committee*, 1997, London: HMSO (Dearing Report)

Nelson, R and Bridges, W, *Legalizing Gender Inequality: Courts, Markets and Unequal Pay for Women in America*, 1999, Cambridge: CUP

Nelson, RL, *Partners with Power: The Social Transformation of the Large Law Firm*, 1988, Berkeley, CA: California UP

Norman, R, *The Moral Philosophers*, 2nd edn, 1998, Oxford: OUP

Nosworthy, E, 'Ethics and large law firms', in Parker, S and Sampford C (eds), *Legal Ethics and Legal Practice*, 1995, Oxford: Clarendon

Nozick, R, *Anarchy, State and Utopia*, 1974, Oxford: Basil Blackwell

O

O'Donovan, K, *Sexual Divisions in Law*, 1985, London: Weidenfeld and Nicolson

Oberweis, T and Musheno, M, 'Policing identities: cop decision making and the constitution of citizens' (1999) 24 Law and Social Inquiry 4

Odgers, BW, *A Century of Law Reform*, 1901, London: Sweet & Maxwell

Olsen, F, 'Feminism and critical legal theory: an American perspective' (1990) 18 IJSL 199

Owusu, K, 'Introduction', in Owusu, K (ed), *Black British Culture and Society: A Text Reader*, 1999, London: Routledge

P

Paine, T, *A Letter to the Honourable Thomas Erskine on the Prosecution of Thomas Williams for Publishing the Age of Reason*, 1797, Paris

Parker, C, 'How to win hearts and minds: corporate compliance policies for sexual harassment' (1999) 21 Law and Policy 21

Parker, S and Sampford C (eds), *Legal Ethics and Legal Practice*, 1995, Oxford: Clarendon

Parker, S, 'Introduction', in Parker, S and Sampford C (eds), *Legal Ethics and Legal Practice*, 1995, Oxford: Clarendon

Partington, M, 'Legal education in the 1990s' (1992) 19 JLS 174

Pateman, C, *The Sexual Contract*, 1985, Oxford: Polity

Paterson, AA, 'Judges: a political elite?' (1974) BJLS 1

Paterson, AA, 'Legal ethics in Scotland' (1997) 4 IJLP 25

Paterson, AA, 'Professionalism and the legal services market' (1996) 3 IJLP 139

Peach, L (Sir), *An Independent Scrutiny of the Appointment Process of Judges and Queen's Counsel in England and Wales*, December 1999, London: Lord Chancellor's Department

Pierce, J, *Gender Trials: Emotional Lives in Contemporary Law Firms*, 1996, Berkeley, CA: California UP

Podmore, D and Spencer, A, 'Gender in the labour process – the case of women and men lawyers', in Knights, D and Willmott, H (eds), *Gender and Labour Process*, 1986, Aldershot: Gower

Posner, R, 'An economic analysis of sex discrimination laws' (1989) 56 Chicago UL Rev 1311

Posner, R, 'The efficiency and efficacy of Title VII' (1987) 136 Pennsylvania UL Rev 513

Prescians, RP, 'Award winning teachers' beliefs about teaching versus research' (1994) 13(1) Higher Education Research and Development 85

R

Raine, JW, *Local Justice: Ideals and Reality*, 1989, Edinburgh: T & T Clarke

Rees, A, Thomas, P and Todd, P, *Law Students: Investing in the Future*, 2000, Cardiff: University of Cardiff

Reskin, B and Roos, P, *Women and Men at Work*, 1990, Thousand Oaks, CA: Pine Forge

Reynell Legal Recruitment Consultants, *The Law at Work: The View from Within the Legal Profession: Report on a Survey of Assistant Solicitors*, 1997, London: Reynell

Rhode, D, 'The woman's point of view' (1988) 15 JLS 39

Rhode, DL, 'Perspectives on professional women' (1988) 40 Stanford L Rev 1163

Robbins Report, Report of the Committee on Higher Education under the Chairmanship of Lord Robbins, Cmnd 2154, 1963, London: HMSO

Roberts, Y, 'Cock and bull story' (1999) *The Guardian*, 31 August

Roper, B, Ross, A and Thomson, D, 'Locked out' (2000) *The Guardian*, Education, 2 May

Ross, D, *Bridging the Gap – A Report on Women in the Law*, 1990, London: Quarry Dougall Consulting Group

Ross, S, *Ethics in Law: Lawyers' Responsibility and Accountability in Australia*, 1995, Sydney: Butterworths

Rumgay, J, 'Custodial decision making in a magistrates' court: court culture and immediate situational factors' (1995) 35 Br J Crim 210

Russell, P, 'New access to justice' (1999) IRRV Insight, April

S

Sachs, A and Wilson, J, *Sexism and the Law*, 1978, London: Martin Robertson

Schlag, P, *Laying Down the Law – Mysticism, Fetishism, and the American Legal Mind*, 1996, New York: New York UP

Schultz, V, 'Reconceptualising sexual harassment' (1998) 107 Yale LJ 1683

Schultz, V, 'Telling stories about women and work: judicial interpretations of sex segregation in the workplace in Title VII cases raising the lack of interest argument' (1990) 103 Harv L Rev 1749

Seron, C and Ferris, K, 'Negotiating professionalism' (1995) 22 Work and Occupations 22

Seron, C, *The Business of Practising Law: The Work Lives of Solo and Small Firm Attorneys*, 1996, Philadelphia: Temple UP

Shaw, J, 'Gender and the court of justice' (1999) *Academy of European Law*, July

Sherr, A and Webb, J, 'Law students, the external market, and socialisation: do we make them turn to the city?' (1989) 16 JLS 225

Shiner, M and Newburn, T, *Entry into the Legal Professions: The Law Student Cohort Study, Year 3*, 1995, London: The Law Society

Shiner, M, *Entry into the Legal Professions: The Law Student Cohort Study, Year 4*, 1997, London: The Law Society

Shiner, M, *Entry into the Legal Professions: The Law Student Cohort Study, Year 5*, 1999, London: The Law Society

Sidaway, J, 'Salary lottery' (1997) *Law Society Gazette*, 9 July

Sidaway, J, 'The panel study of solicitors' firms: first findings', unpublished internal report, Research and Policy Planning Unit, the Law Society

Silverman, D, *Interpreting Qualitative Data: Methods for Analysing Talk, Text and Interaction*, 1993, London: Sage

Skordaki, E, 'Glass slippers and glass ceilings: women in the legal profession' (1996) 3 IJLP 7

Smart, C, 'The woman of legal discourse' (1992) 1 Social and Legal Studies 29

Smigel, EO, *The Wall Street Lawyer: Professional Organisation Man?*, 1969, London: Indiana UP

Smith, P, *Making Rights Work*, 1998, Dartmouth: Aldershot

Smith, R, 'The future of the legal profession' (1996) LA, January, p 6

Sommerlad, H and Allaker, J, 'Retrieve or retain', 1991, unpublished report prepared for the Law Society

Sommerlad, H and Sanderson, P, *Gender, Choice and Commitment: Women Solicitors in England and Wales and the Struggle for Equal Status*, 1998, Aldershot: Ashgate

Sommerlad, H, 'Can women lawyer differently? A perspective from the UK', in Schultz, U and Shaw, G (eds), forthcoming, Oxford: Hart

Sommerlad, H, 'The implementation of quality initiatives and the New Public Management in the legal aid sector in England and Wales: bureaucratisation, stratification and surveillance' (1999) 6 IJLP 311

Squires, J, *Gender in Political Theory*, 1999, Cambridge: Polity

Stanko, B, 'Keeping women in and out of line: sexual harassment and occupational segregation', in Walby, S (ed), *Gender Segregation at Work*, 1988, Milton Keynes: OU Press

Stata, *Stata Reference Manual*, Release 5, 1997, Texas: Stata

Statham, A, Richardson, L and Cook, J, *Gender and University Teaching*, 1991, New York: SUNY

Stewart, JB, *The Partners: Inside America's Most Powerful Law Firms*, 1983, New York: Simon & Schuster

Steyn (Lord), 'The role of the Bar, the judge and the jury: winds of change' [1999] PL 51

Sugarman, D, 'Bourgeois collectivism, professional power and the boundaries of the State. The private and public life of the Law Society, 1825 to 1914' (1996) 3 IJLP 81

T

Terndrup, P, 'Will lawyers finally get a life?' (2000) *Legal Week,* 15 June

The Lawyer, 'City Lawyers in secret talks to set up Law Society breakaway' (2000) *The Lawyer,* 29 May

The Learning Age: A Renaissance for a New Britain, Cm 3790, February 1998, Green Paper

Thomas, PA, 'The poverty of students' (1993) 27 Law Teacher 152

Thomas, PA (ed), *Socio-Legal Studies,* 1997, Aldershot: Aldgate

Thompson, A, 'Finding new ways to measure success' (1999) *The Times,* Higher Education Supplement, 14 May

Thornton, A, 'The professional responsibility and ethics of the English Bar', in Cranston, R (ed), *Legal Ethics and Professional Responsibility,* 1995, Oxford: Clarendon

Thornton, M (ed), *Public and Private: Feminist Legal Debates,* 1995, Melbourne: Oxford UP

Thornton, M, *Dissonance and Distrust: Women in the Legal Profession,* 1996, Oxford: OUP

TMS Consultants, 1992, *Without Prejudice? Sex Equality at the Bar and in the Judiciary,* London: TMS

Treichler, P, 'Teaching feminist theory', in Nelson, C (ed), *Theory in the Classroom,* Chicago, IL: University of Illinois

Trow, M, 'More trouble than it's worth' (1997) *The Times,* Higher Education Supplement, 24 October

Trow, M, 'The public and private lives of higher education' (1975) 104 Daedalus 113

Turner, ES, *May It Please Your Lordship,* 1971, London: Michael Joseph

Twining, W, 'Thinking about law schools: Rutland reviewed' (1998) 25 JLS 1

Twining, W, *Blackstone's Tower: The English Law School,* 1994, London: Sweet & Maxwell

Tyler, R, 'Is flexible working a waste of time?' (1998) *The Lawyer,* 6 October

V

Verkaik, R, 'Jury trials' (1999) *The Independent*, 16 November

Verkaik, R, 'Should magistrates pay for their mistakes' (1999) *The Independent*, 29 June

Vince, R, *Managing Change: Reflections on Equality and Management Learning*, 1996, Bristol: Policy

W

Walby, S, *Patriarchy at Work: Patriarchal and Capitalist Relations in Employment*, 1986, Cambridge: Polity

Walby, S, *Theorising Patriarchy*, 1990, Oxford: Basil Blackwell

Walby, S, 'Is citizenship gendered?' (1994) 28(2) Sociology 379

Ward, C, 'On difference and equality' (1997) 3 Legal Theory 65

Warr, J, 'The corruption and deficiency of the laws of England' (1649), in Sedley, S and Kaplan, L (eds), *A Spark in the Ashes*, 1992, London: Verso

Watson, A, 'Training for the Bar: an important year' (1997) 28 Law Librarian 1

Watson, D and Bowden, R, 'After Dearing: a mid-term report', 2000, Brighton: University of Brighton

Weller, P and Purdam, K, *Religious Discrimination in England and Wales*, 2000, Derby: University of Derby

West, J and Lyon, K, 'The trouble with equal opportunities: the case of women academics' (1995) 7 Gender and Education 51

West, R, 'Jurisprudence and gender' (1988) 55 Chicago UL Rev 1

Wexler, S, 'Practising law for poor people' (1970) 79 Yale LJ 1049

Williams, B, 'The idea of equality', in Laslett, P and Runciman, WG (eds), *Philosophy, Politics and Society*, 2nd series, Oxford: Basil Blackwell

Williams, J, *Unbending Gender: Why Family and Work Conflict and What to Do About It*, 2000, New York: Oxford UP

Witz, A, *Professions and Patriarchy*, 1992, London: Routledge

Y

Young, R and Wall, D, *Access to Criminal Justice*, 1996, London: Blackstone

INDEX

S

Index

Index